E-type Jaguar DIY Restoration & Maintenance

– A Kind Of Loving

Chris Rooke

Design by Andrew Garman

Porter Press International

First published in May 2010
Revised & reprinted January 2012
Revised & reprinted February 2014
Revised & reprinted December 2015
Revised & reprinted February 2022

ISBN 978-1-907085-06-2

Published by
Porter Press International Ltd.

Hilltop Farm, Knighton-on-Teme,
Tenbury Wells, WR15 8LY, UK
Tel: +44 (0)1584 781588
sales@porterpress.co.uk
www.porterpress.co.uk

Designed by Grafx Resource
Printed by Gomer Press, UK

Acknowledgements

I would like to take this opportunity to thank all those involved in this publication: the Porter Press team of Abi (ace photographer), Annelise, Mary and Louise who have worked so hard and given their unstinting support; Mark Holman in NZ for proof-reading; Rob Schulp for his wonderful work with the advertisers and to those advertisers for their support; [former] Editor of *The E-type* Malcolm McKay for helping me with the original articles in the *E-type Club* magazine and last, but by no means least, designer Andrew Garman for somehow creating a quality publication from my words and photographs of dubious quality.

Above all, I would like to thank Philip Porter not only for all his help and encouragement with the book, and his clear and incisive editing of my rambling style and illogical sequencing, but also for his role in keeping the legend that is the E-type Jaguar alive. Without him, and others like him, striving to preserve all things E-type, much that we have today that we tend to take for granted – plentiful spares, complete histories and the restoration of landmark cars – would not now be in existence.

I would also like to thank all the specialists and spares suppliers who have helped me over the years, often not for profit but out of a genuine love of the E-type and without whom this restoration would not have been possible.

This book is dedicated to Christine who for so long put up with so much for so little.

Contents

Contents

Contents

Contents

Foreword

We all make mistakes but how many of us have the courage to admit it, especially in public. Yet we all learn by mistakes, either our own or those of others. In this book, Chris Rooke has had the guts to detail his experiences, including his many mistakes, for the good of the rest of us.

If there was a possible pitfall, it seems Chris suffered it! Never downcast though, and not to be beaten by the challenges of restoration, he doggedly fought back and ultimately triumphed.

Not that this book is dominated by disaster; it is most certainly not. But what makes it different is that it has been written by a real enthusiast for other enthusiasts. Chris has had hands-on experience of most aspects of the complicated restoration experience and, where he has involved others, he has passed on the benefit of their wisdom or highlighted their incompetence but, above all, reached positive conclusions.

Knowing how not to do things is just as important as knowing the correct way forward. Again, this is what makes this book different. It is restoration, warts and all, first-hand.

Originally serialised in 50+ parts in *The E-type*, the monthly magazine of the Jaguar E-type Club, Chris has thus shared his wisdom with fellow enthusiasts in over 50 countries. He is unquestionably a hero.

Rewritten where necessary, expanded and improved, these articles (and more) have been combined in this book to give those contemplating, and tackling, E-type restoration or specific jobs or maintenance, a comprehensive, no-punches-pulled, nut-and-bolt account.

I have owned my E-types since 1977 and been writing about E-types since 1985. They are, without question, absolutely stunning cars with fabulous good looks and superb performance. The great reputation is deserved. They have a unique heritage and are very sexy. However, they have to be restored and maintained correctly otherwise they are dogs. It is, therefore, worth getting them right so you can enjoy the real E-type experience to the full.

Philip Porter

Introduction

This book covers the complete DIY restoration of my 1969 Series II E-type Jaguar FHC, virtually all of which I completed at home in the basement of our house – an area that is rather euphemistically called a garage. The book is designed to help those who also intend to carry out work on their car at home, with a step-by-step guide of the entire nut-and-bolt restoration with photos and detailed (but hopefully very readable) explanations. As I had never rebuilt an E-type Jaguar before, there were many pitfalls awaiting me that I had not anticipated and gaps in my knowledge that needed to be filled.

By reading this book, you should be able to avoid these pitfalls (well, most of them!) and gain the specific knowledge necessary to restore, or work on, an E-type. I have always tried to be totally honest about my trials and tribulations and, as well as learning from my mistakes, I hope you will find the anecdotes and mishaps recounted herein both amusing and encouraging.

Although the book covers the restoration of a Series II, I hope it will also be directly relevant to owners of all six-cylinder E-types. Although there are some differences (e.g. the braking and cooling systems), most of the information is common to all models. The book may be less relevant to owners of Series III (V12) cars, especially regarding the engine, but I believe there is enough common ground between the models for it still to be of benefit.

The Purpose Of This Book

This book is not designed to replace the various workshop manuals that are available (e.g. the Haynes manual and the Jaguar workshop manual) but to augment them from the perspective of the home restorer with limited equipment, space, skilled help or subject-specific knowledge. I have tried, wherever possible, to fill in the gaps that the manuals don't cover and to simplify and further explain some of the work where I found the manuals lacking. **This book should therefore be read in conjunction with workshop manuals** (I actually used four manuals, all of which were useful at some time or other – see the information at the end of this book). Other publications that proved useful were the parts books produced by companies such as SNG Barratt and the E-type parts manual on CD-Rom which are all helpful in identifying and ordering different parts, etc.

How To Use This Book

I strongly recommend that any potential restorer, or purchaser, of an E-type reads the whole book before commencing work. This will give an insight into the work involved, the order that work should be tackled and any problems that only came to light when everything was finally reassembled towards the end of the project. It should help you to avoid the many unnecessary and very costly pitfalls that litter the path to a completed restoration.

About The Author

I am a drama teacher by profession and from that nugget you will glean that I have no professional training in engineering or car restoration. What I do have is a passion for classic cars, and especially E-types, that I've had since I was a child. My first ever motorised vehicle was a Raleigh Runabout that I somehow took possession of at the age of 12. This was followed by a Lambretta and a Vespa Scooter at the age of 13. At the glorious age of 16, I bought a Casals moped, a pale imitation of the legendary Yamaha FS1E. Subsequent vehicles have included the following: BSA Starfire, Suzuki 350, 850 Mini, Matchless G3LS 350, Vauxhall HA van, Renault 6, Morris Traveller, Triumph Vitesse Mk II Convertible, Triumph Herald Estate, Mini Metro Vanden Plas 500 (!), Triumph Bonneville, Golf GTi Mk I and a Triumph GT6 Mk III.

By the time I was 40, I thought I was mature enough, rich enough and knowledgeable enough to embark on this restoration in the basement of our house. Nine years later I was the proud owner of a truly stunning piece of machinery that is both practical and beautiful.

It's been a long road but completely worth every minute, and I hope my experiences will make your journey that little bit easier.

Chris Rooke
Barnsley, UK

1.1 How I Came To Buy An E-type

I honestly can't remember when I fell in love with the E-type, but I think it was relatively late: I believe I was about 13 or 14 at the time. Since then, my love of all things mechanical has developed and flourished. People often ask where my mechanical knowledge came from. It was simply inherited from my father who was a keen handyman/ early DIY type. He never taught me a thing, but I suppose I inherited a talent from him for all things mechanical, just as one might inherit a talent for music or art (neither of which he was any good at and if anything I'm worse!). His major contribution to my upbringing was that there were always tools and bits of engines lying about for me to practise on.

My infatuation with E-types flourished but my ambition to own one

had to be put on hold for many years as I knew they were completely out of my price range. In the meantime, I turned my love of machinery to lesser things.

My first ever attempt at major mechanical work was on a Raleigh Runabout at the age of 12 (it never went again), followed by a Vespa 125 and a Lambretta SX200 at the age of 14 (both suffered the same fate). I used these to ride around the waste ground to the rear of our house – now a housing estate. Eventually I made it to 16 when I was at last old enough to have a licence and I bought my very first proper machine: a second-hand Casals moped! I think they were Portuguese and were a poor imitation of the Yamaha FS1Es that all my slightly better-off friends had - the mould was set for later life. I went on my first ever holiday without

my parents on that moped, to the New Forest with Geoff, one of my FS1E-owning friends. My exhaust fell off five times (poor design) and I got a wasp down my shirt while riding along!

When I finally made it to 17, I bought my first proper motorbike: a BSA Starfire 250cc which was the first machine I ever properly rebuilt - and it went afterwards! With hindsight, it was a complete heap when I bought it with little thought and the rebuild was necessitated by catastrophic engine failure whilst Geoff and I were on our second teenage holiday to Land's End. The mould continues to be cast.

I then bought an 850cc Mini – one with the long gear stick - which immediately failed its MOT due to having virtually no sills left at all. I subsequently failed my 'A' levels due

1.1-1 *My first car, a Mini 850 with long gear lever and floor-mounted starter button, seen here on holiday with my friends during the long hot summer of 1976 – five teenage boys in a Mini: doesn't bear thinking about now!*

My beautiful Matchless arriving **1.1-2** *home from Portsmouth in the back of my brother's Morris 1000 van in 1978. Not quite the triumphal return I had planned!*

to spending most of my revision time trying to repair the sills – with plastic padding! I was still only 17. It needed two complete sills welding on by the garage as they weren't too impressed by my plastic padding. This cost me £140; I'd bought the car for £100. However, it took us on our third teenage holiday to the South coast. With hindsight, it was an absolute heap when I bought it with little knowledge or thought. Are you beginning to see a thread running through my purchases?

I then bought what became the love of my life for many years, a Matchless 350cc single G3LS which I completely rebuilt and turned into my dream bike – a Chopper! I really loved that bike and I loved having it customised (I was still only 19 at the time). It taught me the lesson that you should never trust anything that someone else has claimed to have fully rebuilt. The engine had been completely rebuilt by the previous owner who then abandoned the restoration. As part of the rebuild he'd had the cylinder re-bored. I took the engine apart to check everything (about a 10-minute job for a Matchless!) but missed the vital clues which would lead to disaster. Immediately after finishing the rebuild (I mean the very

next day), I set off for France where I had been promised work as an ice-cream seller on the beach. Half way across Brittany I suffered catastrophic engine failure – he had re-bored the cylinder, but then put the original piston back in! The piston rings didn't take kindly to this and broke-up, taking the piston

with it. The bike was unceremoniously repatriated in the back of my French friend's estate car as far as the ferry, and then in the back of my brother's Morris van from Portsmouth. Lesson fully learnt.

I rebuilt the engine properly and pretended to be a 'biker' for a while, but

The first real love of my life: my **1.1-3** *ex-army 1954 Matchless G3LS 350 Heavyweight single, now heavily customised and converted to 500cc. I named her 'Idiot Wind' as I was getting nowhere fast. Same still applies today!*

1.1-4 *The second real love of my life: my 1976 Triumph Vitesse 2 litre MKII Convertible pictured here on its way to Rome – and back. Note the rather large panel gaps!*

How are the mighty fallen! **1.1-5** *Before buying my Vitesse, my transport was this 1972 Bedford HA van, beautifully hand-painted in dark green. It is seen here at Greenham Common! Another lifetime... another lifetime*

I was far too nice and middle-class for that! This bike was my only transport for many years – until the forks bent (my poor design!) and I stored it with the intention of rebuilding it properly in future years, when finances allowed. Ironically, it was this plan that finally led to me realising my dream of owning an E-type!

I then briefly owned a Morris Minor Traveller before fulfilling my more realistic dreams and buying a Triumph Vitesse 2-litre MkII convertible. I loved that car and owned it for many years, even driving it to Rome (and back!) for one summer holiday. However, it was really a wreck when I bought it (with little knowledge of the marque and my heart ruling my head). My naive idea of a 'rolling restoration' on a rust

bucket that was my everyday driver meant that eventually I took the car off the road and bought a Triumph GT6 MkIII. This was great until the MOT came around which it spectacularly failed due to extensive hidden rust that had been covered by the previous owner with filler, paint and a vinyl roof – GT6s rust heavily on the roof above the windscreen due to condensation, as I now know. With hindsight it was a heap when I bought it and my heart ruled my head. I took it off the road. I literally patched up the Vitesse and put it back on the road.

I then bought a Triumph Herald 12/50 estate car to restore, with the idea that I'd practise on this before starting on the Vitesse and GT6 (careful, I'm showing signs of near logic here). I spent a year rebuilding the Triumph Estate, and it wasn't bad! The trouble was that I had a sudden revelation. I was in the process of

once again welding a patch onto the chassis of the Vitesse on the lawn in the garden (the only space I could find) when in a blinding flash I saw the light. I thought, 'There must be more to life than spending every waking minute welding one rusty bit of metal onto another rusty bit'. I sold all three cars and bought a VW Golf. My days of practical classic cars were over!

I bought a Triumph Bonneville 750cc (another dream fulfilled) and restored that completely. We (Christine and I) then took it on a touring holiday to Spain, through France. When we returned from the holiday I sold the bike in a moment of madness in order to pay for the restoration and the holiday – bad move.

Shortly after this I realised that at last I could rebuild the Matchless (which I had managed to keep all this time, through thick and thin) *properly*, as I had the money and the bike was

1.1-6 *A very happy looking author pictured here with his Triumph Vitesse in the mid 1980s. (The car must have been running well at the time!)*

no longer my daily transport – I could take my time!

I decided to rebuild the bike to the highest specification possible so I sent the frame off to a professional custom shop in Hull for a high quality finish. They immediately went out of business and my frame disappeared into the ether. I tried everything, including expensive lawyers, the police, trying to break into the building myself, but to no avail. I never traced it or the owners of the business. I suppose I could have bought a new frame, but I was completely crushed by this turn of events - and the loss of my £200 deposit. So, incredibly, I sold the remaining parts to a dealer. It was a low moment. I had owned that bike for about 20 years.

And then it happened - I inherited a little money! I had already promised myself that if I were to have a classic car again, the *only* car I would consider would be an E-type. The problem was that they were so much more expensive than any other 'normal' classic car around. I had about £15,000 to spend. I could have bought the best Triumph Stag or TR5 around – but I wanted an E-type, I *needed* an E-type, I *had to have an E-type!*

The problem (with hindsight) was

that, whilst being fairly mechanically knowledgeable, I really didn't know that much about E-types. I think that I'd never really studied them that closely as they were so far out of my price range. I knew that there were Roadsters and Fixed Head Coupés, and V12 and 2+2 versions, but not much more than that. I certainly didn't realise that, in all, there were in fact at least 13 different types of E-type. I also knew that I loved the shape of the Fixed Head Coupé and the lure of a roadster. (Is the E-type the only production car where the roadster was consistently cheaper when new than the Fixed Head, or is that a general feature of the period?)

The general price of Roadsters put them out of contention and I knew I didn't want a 2+2. Apart from that, I was ignorant of the different models

made. I duly joined a Jaguar club and waited for the magazine to arrive, packed with E-types for sale.

I waited three weeks and nothing happened. I was getting impatient and had a large pile of cash burning a hole in my pocket. I went to see a 2+2 advertised in the local paper just to see what was out there – and so I could put my mind at ease by claiming that I'd not bought the first one I'd seen. Then a friend of mine told me of an E-type for sale with a classic car dealer in Huddersfield. I was in the car and off to view it at the earliest opportunity.

I was about to dive into the murky waters of disreputable classic car dealers, difficult decisions and the odd court case and, somewhere along the line, end up with my very own E-type.

Lessons Learnt

- Even at 40 money still burns a hole in your pocket
- Sometimes 'professional' restorers aren't quite so professional
- Patience is a virtue

1.1-7 *I had always aspired to owning an E-type but, in the late 1980s, all I could stretch to was a Triumph GT6 MKIII. Note the vinyl roof which covered copious rust above the windscreen although it was the copious rust everywhere else that led to its rapid demise*

1.2 How (Not) To Buy An E-type Jaguar

I arrived at the classic car dealer's and there was a beautiful Series I 4.2 Fixed Head Coupé (FHC) in Opalescent Silver Grey with a red interior – my favourite colour combination. And polished up in the showroom, it looked fantastic. There was also a Series II FHC in Sable with a beige interior – one of my least favourite colour combinations, but it still looked beautiful. I test drove the Series I. Unfortunately it was raining and it misted-up immediately, the wipers smeared the windscreen and water dripped in from the top of the doors.

I also drove the Series II, just to make a comparison. Although Sable, the paintwork appeared excellent and the chrome was gleaming. (See photos from when the car was purchased –

can you spot the signs that the car had not been properly looked after? Only later did I find these for myself) It had stopped raining by then and the car seemed to drive well. I then checked the paperwork with both cars. The Series I had had considerable work done recently, which I thought was a bad sign. The Series II was advertised as only having done 46,000 miles from new, the Series I had unwarranted mileage. The Series I was £16,500 and the Series II £14,600. The Series II had matching numbers (engine, gearbox and chassis) but the engine of the Series I was non-original. The bodywork was not perfect on either car, but there were more visible signs of rust on the Series I, especially around the bottom edges of the bonnet.

I thought that buying a car of

known low mileage would be more sensible as I did not want a car that had been messed about by many owners – and I could always re-spray it, couldn't I? The bodywork appeared to be very sound. I was also aware of the mechanical shortcomings of the Series I, namely poor brakes, lights and overheating problems. So, considering all the factors of price, condition and provenance, I decided to spurn the Series I and buy the Series II.

This was possibly one of the worst decisions of my life. I've learnt to live with it.

I say it was a poor decision for the following reasons:

- The Series I had my favourite colour combination of Opalescent Silver Grey paint and red interior. The cost

1.2-1 *Left: My E-type as purchased in 1997 – looking really good with a brand new re-spray and nicely polished up. This beautiful exterior hid a myriad of faults that I failed to notice*

Initially I thought the interior was **1.2-2** *nice and clean and well looked after. I soon learnt that this was only because all the leather had been painted cream*

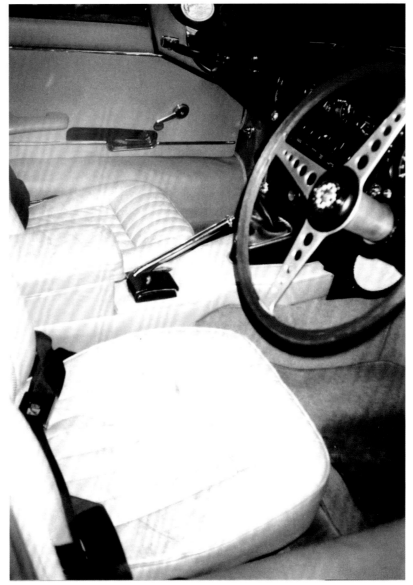

of changing either or both of these (as I am now) is extremely high.

- The Series I is generally more aesthetically pleasing (and this comes from a Series II owner).
- The mechanical shortcomings of the Series I can be relatively easily rectified by fitting modern upgrades (or so I am led to believe).
- Although the Series I did not have matching numbers, I think it was the correct type of engine, and this would have been acceptable for my requirements.
- Many of the advantages my car appeared to offer were later proved to be false.
- If I'd waited a few more days, I would have received my owners' club magazine containing many E-types for sale.
- I did not know the dealer and therefore didn't know whether or not they were reputable.

Anyway, who is to know what the Series I would have been turned out to be like?

I agreed the sale dependent on a full mechanical inspection that I would carry out myself the following week when I came to collect the car. Having left a sizeable deposit, the car was returned to the showroom. Where it had been standing was a large patch of oil.

The following week I returned. *My*

E-type was on the ramps as promised. The dealer had thoughtfully liberally sprayed the entire underside with Waxoyl – as a special surprise for me – how thoughtful! It was now impossible to distinguish any oil leaks from the Waxoyl. However, I was able to establish that the bodywork was sound which was my major interest. As far as I was concerned, mechanical problems were secondary; the condition of the body was paramount. (I had no idea of the cost of parts for an E-type compared to other classics) I had also had time to consider the "46,000 miles from new" claim. I realised I hadn't seen any supporting paperwork to this effect. I was informed that the mileage was "*believed*" genuine" on the simple

premise that there was no proof to the contrary. (The dealer subsequently offered a full refund within two months if I could prove the mileage was wrong. Without supporting paperwork, I discovered that it is as hard to prove that mileage is incorrect as it is to prove it is genuine. I tracked the history back to 1978, when log books disappeared and registration documents took their place. The earliest MOT I could trace was for 1982, the listed mileage was 43,835. I could find no history prior to this. I was therefore unable to prove that the mileage was inaccurate)

The garage owner and I had a serious argument and Christine had to intervene to break it up. I went ahead with the purchase. Why? I could give you several reasons, but if I were to be honest, it was simple pride. I had elected to buy the car and didn't want to admit that I'd made a poor decision. The car was supplied with a new MOT.

I drove home and my life with an E-type began. The car looked superb. However, the engine leaked oil like a sieve from the front of the cylinder head. Apart from that, everything seemed OK. I had the car checked over by one of my local specialist garages (Roger Brotton of 3.8) and he found the car was mechanically poor (and certainly not low mileage), particularly the brakes and the steering which he condemned as dangerous. However, he confirmed that the body was in generally good condition. Other problems highlighted were that the rear differential and the cylinder head were leaking oil badly and required immediate attention.

Not having the space or the equipment necessary to do the job myself, nor the funds required for a specialist like Roger to do the work, I entrusted the engine to my local garage for a rebuild. When they stripped the engine down, they found considerable damage to the block in the form of cracks between the waterways. The block and the head required extensive repairs (stitching) and machining. Roger suggested that I should claim on the warranty supplied by the dealer as he would have honoured such a claim himself. I asked the dealer to pay for repairing the head and block (but not the full engine rebuild) under the terms of the warranty that covered major mechanical problems. He refused. I then took the belated step of taking him to the Small Claims Court for this amount. I lost. The judge (probably quite rightly) decided that as the car hadn't actually broken down the warranty claim was ineligible. Caveat Emptor (Buyer Beware). The problem was that there was quite a lot wrong with the car but nothing specific that could be claimed against. I really only had myself to blame.

Whilst the engine was stripped, I took the opportunity to have the engine fully rebuilt: new valves, big-end and small-end bearings, main

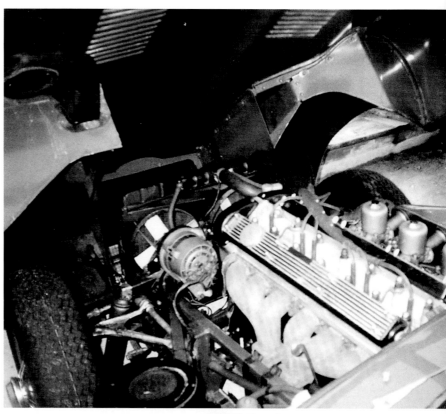

1.2-3 *Everything seemed OK under the bonnet – apart from a massive oil leak from the cylinder head, dangerous steering, brakes that didn't work, a dented bonnet and bodged wiring*

bearings, pistons, timing chains, etc. The total cost was £2085.49

I had the car re-MOT'd at an independent garage. It failed. As a result, the dealer fitted new steering rack mountings, a new universal joint in the steering column and rebuilt the front brake callipers. The car was marginally better. The dealer in question has subsequently gone out of business.

On the plus side, the car ran tolerably well and we were able to begin using it as a classic car for high days and holidays, as intended. However the car suffered from poor handling, water leaks inside the car, dodgy brakes and steering, and being generally tatty.

Looking back, I can honestly say that I hadn't really learnt from my previous experiences about purchasing a classic car. I did little

research and just rushed headlong into a purchase. Considering the amount of money riding on such a purchase you really need to be hard-headed about things and do as much research as possible. I thought that I was pretty savvy about cars and knew what I was looking for. In actual fact, I knew virtually nothing about E-types and when the time came to buy a car I was totally clueless. I didn't even know the difference between a Series I and Series II car. If you don't know that, you really shouldn't be in the market. It seems so easy and obvious to say all this now, but when you've made a decision to buy an E-type it's hard to be objective but you need to be. If I had been a bit more circumspect at the time then with the money at my disposal, I could probably have bought a decent car that didn't need rebuilding.

1.2-4 *The car looked even better from the rear, but note the protruding driver's door, an exhaust system from a 3.8 (central tail pipes) and a square yellow reflective number plate*

Lessons learnt so far in the purchase of an E-type

- Never let your emotions cloud your judgement.
- 'Believed Genuine' can mean anything.
- Always take someone with you who really knows about E-types and is not emotionally involved (Doing the inspection yourself is difficult as you have such a vested interest and it is hard to be objective).
- Get an inspection before you buy, not afterwards. Trying to get anyone to fix something *after* you've parted with your cash is much harder.
- Research as much as you can about E-types and consider which is the model for you.
- Read Philip Porter's excellent notes on buying an E-type on the *E-type Club* website (see information at the back of the book).
- Don't let your pride/good nature get in the way if things start to go wrong with the deal.
- Whilst the condition of the bodywork is paramount, the mechanical and trim parts of an E-type are very expensive to replace and so their condition is also important – virtually every part is available, but at a cost.
- Good, honest vendors sell good, honest cars. The opposite also applies.
- Buying from a reputable dealer means they will honour the warranty if things go wrong.
- The cost of inspections on cars you don't then buy is high, but not as high as the cost of buying a bad car.
- You need a nice garage to house your beautiful E-type. You need a very large garage with storage and working space if you are going to restore your less-than-beautiful E-type.
- Drive a few E-types (if at all possible!) so that you have an idea of how they should drive so when given the assurance "Oh, they're all like that," you will know if it's true.
- The E-type is the most beautiful car in the world – they all look fantastic regardless of condition.
- All of the above are simple common sense. I followed none of them.

There are many other lessons to be learnt in the purchase of an E-type – more of these later as the need for a complete rebuild of my car soon became apparent.

1.3 Why I Needed To Rebuild My Car From Scratch – And Why Yours May Also Need It

So, my life with an E-type had begun at last! The next few years were spent slowly improving the car and taking off on some lovely motoring holidays. However, trouble was never far behind and this would eventually lead to the start of a complete rebuild.

One of my first jobs was to build a garage to house the car. I had previously had a nice big garage, but after selling my previous classics, I'd converted it into a Summer House. So I feverishly set about the work as the local mechanics rebuilt the engine.

The problem was that the car came back from the engine rebuild before I'd finished the garage and with my finances completely depleted. As a result, the garage was more of a glorified car port, slowly taking shape as time and finances allowed. Unfortunately we were then hit by the massive storm of February 1999 during which the polycarbonate roof of the garage was completely ripped off (I never found it) and the glass from one window, only temporarily fitted, blew in and smashed onto the bonnet of the Jaguar. The paintwork suffered considerable damage. My then insurers, Footman James, were excellent, however, and arranged for repairs without fuss. The car came back looking better than before. However, the repair garage informed me that they had discovered, "a considerable thickness of filler on the top of the bonnet". I began to have suspicions.

As I drove the car more, the more I found its flaws. The handling was nothing short of dangerous with the car 'floating' at speed, which was extremely disconcerting, and the tyres wore very unevenly, especially the nearside rear which wore its outside edge very heavily. The brakes were poor and pulled hard to the left. The rear diff continued to leak oil excessively. Other incongruities you may have noticed in some of the old photos included:

- The exhaust system, although stainless steel, was for a Series I and an incorrect oblong rear reflective number plate had been fitted as a result.
- The HT leads were a horrible cheap modern red affair.
- The leather upholstery was painted.

The cabin leaked water quite badly and the door fit was very poor, including the rear hatch which didn't

Left: After having the sills replaced by my local garage, I now had a two-tone E-type in different shades of Sable and even worse panel gaps than before

With an MOT failure certificate *and very limited funds at my disposal, the local garage welded new sills on the car – big mistake*

All seemed to be going well with *the fitting of the replacement inner and outer sills – until it was finished and a two-tone car with big panel gaps emerged from the garage*

shut properly (on one occasion the rear hatch blew open on the motorway! – and I wasn't doing a 150mph road test for *Autocar* magazine at the time). The driver's door stood proud of the rear wing by quite some way. No amount of adjusting would solve either problem. The engine would sometimes idle at over 1500 rpm and only return to normal after blipping the throttle a few times. The radiator had a small leak. The beautiful paintwork was in fact a very recent re-spray which began to peel off in places (!) and suffered from

micro-blistering (very small bubbles under the paint which appeared in humid weather – apparently due to moisture in the painting process). The spare tyre would not sit in the wheel well properly. Despite these problems, I continued to slowly improve the car and tried to correct the many faults, but I soon realised I was only really scratching the surface of some fairly deep-rooted malaise.

Over the next year or so, I researched the car and found a little of its previous history which explained much. I

1.3-4 *To make matters worse, the roof was ripped off my part-built garage in the severe storms of 1999 and the glass from one of the windows fell onto the bonnet damaging the paintwork – sorted through my insurance*

discovered that the car had been in an accident in the early 1980s and had been 'restored' in the heady market of the late '80s. I checked the wheel well again to discover tell-tale signs of a rear-end shunt – the off-side rear wing and lower valance had been replaced but some of the brackets, etc., were bent and been partially straightened. I then found the passenger door shell was rather crumpled. It began to become clear that the car had been involved in a medium crash which had damaged the rear off-side, the near-side door and probably the bonnet centre section. (Hence the filler on the bonnet) This explained the ill-fitting doors and the rear hatch, and suggested that something, somewhere was very bent on the steering.

At this time the car failed its MOT as at least one new sill was required, and preferably two (the car wasn't too rusty, but there was some rot in the sills and the bottoms of the doors were beginning to bubble). I was very busy at work and didn't really have the facilities so again decided to get someone else to do the work for me. I received a couple of quotes from specialists: approx. £1250 per side dependent on

what they found underneath – worth every penny I'm sure, but at the time out of the question. So I entrusted the work to my little local garage – and they made a complete mess of it. The car came back with half of it a different colour to the rest and with massive gaps between the front section of the sills and the bonnet. See photos.

It was decision time. The car wasn't anything like as I wanted it – it was poor mechanically, it was the wrong colour (especially now), the brakes and handling were dangerous (despite passing the MOT), the rear differential continued to leak oil and the interior was painted. Above all, the car was generally tatty. The problem with 'generally tatty' is a big one – nothing is particularly wrong and everything kind-of works, but nothing is right. The carpets were stained and there was a crack in the dashboard covering; the near-side door trim was loose and the doors (and now the bonnet) didn't shut properly; the engine bay was OK but there was paint flaking off the bulkhead; there were little bits of rust and ingrained dirt everywhere and the bottom of the doors and the off-side rear wheel-arch had rust bubbling

through. The underside of the car was a complete mess. The bottom of the car and some of the bonnet was thick with underseal, **and I hate underseal!**

My initial thoughts were to go for a bare metal re-spray and re-dye the seats so I could get the car looking OK, and painted a nicer colour than Sable for not too much work. I had already spent some considerable time trying to sort out the car, but when the bulkhead needs re-spraying and when the doors, rear hatch and bonnet need fundamental adjustment you can't really do that with everything in situ. I rang a professional restorer to get a quote for such work. They quoted to remove the body shell, strip it and replace it. The quote was £10,000! (Please bear in mind that this was 1999 – that was a *lot* of money).

For the first time in my life I can honestly say that I was speechless on the phone for a few seconds. Not only that but it was made clear that this quote didn't include any remedial work that may be necessary to the bodywork when the paint was removed. I was told that if I were to re-dye the seats then the first thing to be done would be to strip them of the rather horrible paint that covered them. I therefore duly set about this with a tin of paint stripper and was left with the driest, roughest, most sorry looking seats that you have ever seen.

Having decided that the only way to get the interior to how I wanted it was to have a full re-trim I also decided to

+1 (203) 585-7326
jes@e-torque.com
www.e-torque.com

E-TORQUE, LLC
218 Millbank Avenue
Greenwich, Connecticut 06830
United States

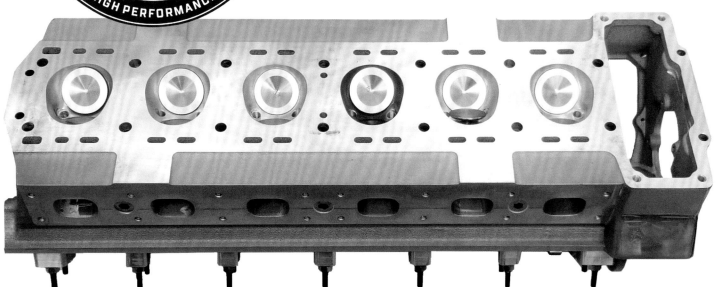

This assembly has the greatest bearing on the performance of your E-type

Designed to replace the original XK cylinder head, ours adds 100 horsepower and can produce as much as 400hp. Available in 3.8, 4.2 and 4.7 stroker displacements – single or Twin Spark™. We also offer vintage SU appearance EFI induction and pre-induction systems to further increase performance.

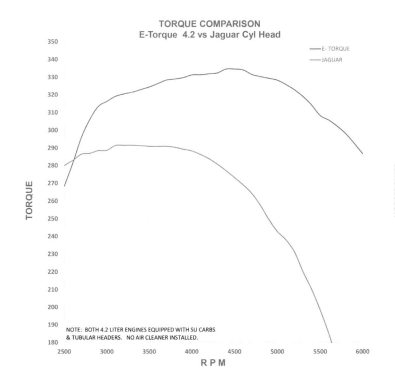

TORQUE COMPARISON
E-Torque 4.2 vs Jaguar Cyl Head

E-TORQUE
JAGUAR

TORQUE

NOTE: BOTH 4.2 LITER ENGINES EQUIPPED WITH SU CARBS
& TUBULAR HEADERS. NO AIR CLEANER INSTALLED.

R P M

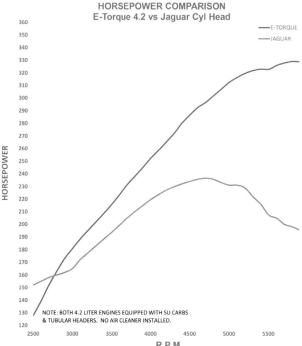

HORSEPOWER COMPARISON
E-Torque 4.2 vs Jaguar Cyl Head

E-TORQUE
JAGUAR

HORSEPOWER

NOTE: BOTH 4.2 LITER ENGINES EQUIPPED WITH SU CARBS
& TUBULAR HEADERS. NO AIR CLEANER INSTALLED.

R P M

strip the body down to a rolling chassis to see what was what in the bodywork department. I used a heat gun in the main and took off many layers of paint including a kind of plastic coating under the primer of the re-spray that

1.3-5 *The restoration begins. At this stage, I was still only contemplating simply a re-spray and interior re-trim. If only life were so simple!*

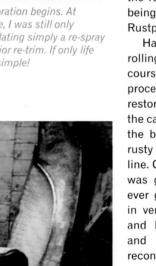

no-one ever seems to have heard of.

I began to discover more evidence of a very poor 'restoration' that had obviously not been done properly, but with an eye to making a quick profit. As I stripped the centre section of the bonnet, I found that it had a gash about a yard long in the nose that had been welded up and hammered out – hence the thick filler. I have to say that the bonnet looked perfect before and I would never have guessed what was underneath the paint. (I subsequently noted the large dent on the underside of the bonnet largely hidden by the wire mesh stone guard for the radiator.) The front wings were in good condition, but not perfect. The new rear wing became clearly visible. The main point of note here was that the new wing itself had later rusted and been repaired with a patch. The lesson being that the new wing had not been properly rust-proofed when fitted and was therefore ironically the rustiest panel on the car despite being the newest by some 20 years! Rustproof all new panels properly!

Having stripped the car down to a rolling chassis I decided that the only course of action was to continue the process and go for a full 'nut and bolt' restoration. The only way to go to get the car that I wanted was to start from the beginning. The body wasn't too rusty but was badly dented and out of line. Considerable remedial bodywork was going to be required if it was ever going to be right. The car was in very poor condition mechanically and I knew that all the electrical and mechanical parts required reconditioning. The only way forward regarding the interior was to get a

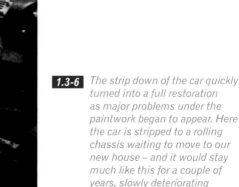

1.3-6 *The strip down of the car quickly turned into a full restoration as major problems under the paintwork began to appear. Here the car is stripped to a rolling chassis waiting to move to our new house – and it would stay much like this for a couple of years, slowly deteriorating*

new one. The decision was therefore a straightforward one: it was either a complete ground-up restoration or I sell the car as was. With the car now in a number of pieces and looking like a basket case, I knew its value was virtually nothing compared to what I'd paid for it. Therefore, a total rebuild it was.

I was just about to remove the rear axle assembly and front suspension when we decided to move house. Life is never straightforward. The 'restoration' process (still a destruction process at this time) was put on hold so that the car was in some way mobile to enable us to move it to our new house.

My next challenge was to move house, with a car in bits, to a carefully-selected Victorian town house in need of much restoration itself and with a garage the size of a shoe box.

1.3-7 *The rear of the shell showing a poorly fitted new rear wing necessitated by quite severe accident damage that had also buckled the boot floor and inner wing badly, dented the bonnet and crushed the passenger door*

Lessons learnt so far:

- If you want a car in excellent condition, by far the easiest way to go about it is to buy a car in excellent condition. Is this as satisfying as building the car yourself? Impossible to say, really. However, there's always something that needs to be done to any car and you can always fit upgrades, etc., to make the car your own. The best thing is you can drive the car from Day One!
- If you want an excellent car, it's probably not the best idea to buy a car in fair condition (as I did) as the only way to make it excellent is to go for a complete rebuild. This is a costly way to go. You may as well buy a restoration project for a lot less money. My car was in fair condition, but I'm now replacing or reconditioning all the components anyway so it makes little difference what condition they were in the first place. However, if you buy a complete, running car then at least you know it's all there and you can assess what's wrong with it before you begin the restoration.
- For most of us there are three main considerations when considering restoring an E-type: time, space and money.

1.4 The Main Considerations When Contemplating Embarking On A Restoration

Time

If, like me, you work full-time and have other commitments as well, you have to be sure that you really do have the time and dedication / determination / love of the E-type to carry the project through. Just look at how many unfinished restoration projects there are on e-Bay. You also need a fairly stable life. Such things as moving house, emigrating, having children, building an extension, changing jobs, etc., do not fit in well with a restoration project. If, like me, you can only work on the car for a very limited amount of time each week (and sometimes not for several weeks at a time), the restoration is going to take several years. Can you cope with this? Bear in mind that my restoration took nine years. Admittedly I wasn't working

on it for all that time – but why wasn't I? Because other things took precedence. Despite having a fairly stable life, there were still massive demands on my time that stopped me from being able to work on the car.

These were generally as follows:
- Work. Sadly this is something you just can't ignore and has to take precedence over everything else. The only alternative is to wait until you retire – but if you're like me you'll want an E-type **now**, not in 20 years' time.
- Moving house (in my case). Again, although I was fairly settled, the fact was that somewhere within the restoration time-frame moving house was very possible and indeed happened. In some ways I was lucky

as we moved before the car was totally dismantled so I still had a rolling chassis which was relatively easy to transport. Just imagine how hard it would be to move house with the car in pieces and the body shell, engine and rear axle, etc., all requiring transporting – a bit of a nightmare. The move itself was only half the issue in my case. The house we moved into was wonderful but required an awful lot of work to get it up to scratch. Not only that but we didn't really have a garage (see next Section) so a considerable amount of time (and money) was spent doing essential decorating/renovation work as well as turning the basement into a proper garage worthy of the name.
- Holidays and days out, etc. It may

1.4-1 *Left: Old Jaguars come in all shapes and sizes but have one thing in common - rust. The designs were brilliant, the execution less so*

surprise you somewhat to discover that your nearest and dearest doesn't quite share the same enthusiasm for the restoration of this rusty, oily heap you've purchased. For reasons best known to themselves they like things like holidays and days out, taking valuable time (and money) away from the restoration. It is essential that this time is given readily (well, fairly readily) if harmony within the matrimonial home is to be maintained.

So, don't underestimate the time required for a restoration. I decided at the outset that a conservative estimate was about two years. Nine years later I finally finished – and that was without restoring most of the body shell.

Money

If, also like me you don't have limitless reserves of cash, you need to realise the cost of a full restoration even if you're doing it yourself. One good thing about restoring an E-type is that virtually all the parts are readily available. One bad thing is that they cost an awful lot. It's difficult to make a direct comparison, and I'm sure some suppliers will shout me down, but I found E-type parts' prices particularly high compared to, say, Triumph or MG. I found that as soon as you uttered the word "Jaguar" the price doubled and if you then added the suffix "E-type" it trebled. A slight exaggeration maybe but just be aware that parts aren't cheap.

Not only this but before even starting to spend money on the car, there's massive expenditure required on the necessary tools and equipment for such major work, e.g. a MIG welder, an engine crane, an engine stand, a compressor, a variety of good quality spanners and socket sets, a whole heap of general mechanical tools, etc. Then there's the garage/workshop

itself which needs to be of a decent size to work in with proper heat, light and workbench, not to mention the fact that you can't put your everyday car in there so it has to live outside and therefore be subjected to the elements, both meteorological and criminal. My Ford Focus was broken into five times in three years as it was forced to live on the driveway (Ford Focus stereos were the most stolen in Britain for a while) and as a result I lost all my no-claims bonus – not funny when you've spent

A Series II restoration project **1.4-2** *from America. To reduce exhaust emissions these US cars were fitted with twin Stromberg carburettors and extra air ducts, etc. The engine can be converted back to UK spec. quite easily – but not cheaply!*

Assembling the body shell on a **1.4-3** *proper jig is essential if it's going to fit back together properly. This stripped tub with front sub-frames is mounted on a dolly to make it easier to move around in this state*

20 odd years building it up.

Finally, you have to consider what work you will need to contract out to the professionals. As an amateur restorer you're unlikely to be an expert in every aspect of restoration: mechanical, body work, painting, trimming or electrics. This means that several jobs will have to be entrusted to professional restorers who rightly charge a premium for their expertise. Neither will you probably have access to highly specialised equipment, e.g. chroming tanks, engine machine tools, camber and castor gauges, etc., which means you will have to pay someone else to do some of these jobs for you.

To give you an idea of how much it'll cost you, let me tell you that my restoration cost nearly £35,000 not taking into account the money spent on the garage, tools, equipment, etc., and doing as much of the work as possible myself. And just in case you were wondering, no that doesn't include the purchase price of the car (£14,600). Bearing in mind that the value of my car now is probably less than the purchase price and restoration costs combined, you don't have to be Carol Vorderman to work out that you don't restore an E-type to make money.

Space

One thing that many people don't think about is how much space is required to restore a classic car, and especially an E-type. You need roughly twice as much space again as the assembled car takes up to store all the parts when it's in pieces and as much space again to have room to work in. Remember you will have to store the body shell (including the doors and the rear hatch), the engine, the rear axle, the bonnet, the interior, all the bumpers and chrome work, the electrics, the gearbox, the windscreens and door glass, the

radiator and front suspension, steering, five very large wheels, the petrol tank, the braking system, etc., etc., and this takes up room, a lot of room. Not only this but you will then also require a space to work on these components and a space in which to store all your newly-acquired specialist tools and equipment (see above).

In the end I did indeed manage to restore my car in a pretty tiny basement, but I had to demolish three walls and store a lot of parts in the loft and in the outhouse which was unsuitable as it was damp. Not only this but I paid Nick who painted the body to store the bonnet at his workshop for the best part of a year and at various times left my old body shell on one neighbour's drive and stored my new body shell in another neighbour's garage. Without their help and understanding, I don't know what I'd have done.

Expertise/Skill

You need to know that you are fairly mechanically minded and preferably have some previous experience of classic car restoration or ownership. You can get the professionals to do more of the work for you but this is expensive so the more you can do yourself the better. Not only this but the motto, "If you want a job done properly, do it yourself" applies just as much to E-type restoration as anything else. Even with others doing the hard bits, you still need to know one end of a spanner from another if you're going to put the whole thing

together. But you also need to know your own capabilities/limitations and be prepared to hand things over when you've failed to do them yourself. In my case I didn't do the following myself but had them done for me: spraying the car, rebuilding the gearbox, rebuilding the rear differential, trimming the seats. You can't be a master at everything. It would be a real shame if there was a major problem with the car when you finished it because something hadn't been done properly.

Other Requirements:

- Determination. It's a long haul and at times you'll wish you'd never started. You've got to know that you can see the job through no matter what.
- Patience. Think you've had your patience tested to the limit? You ain't seen nothing yet.
- A sense of humour. When it all goes horribly wrong (and it will), you've just got to laugh.
- An understanding partner. Someone who'll give you a bit of time and space, and listen politely to your interminable mutterings about the restoration (and who preferably doesn't have access to your bank statements!).

But there is one simple requirement above all others:

- A love of E-types (preferably an obsession). If you have this, then everything else will somehow fall into place.

Since its foundation, **Pendine Historic Cars** has become one of the leading specialists in the sourcing and sales of Jaguar E-types. Our detailed knowledge of the early cars has helped us find new homes for numerous Outside Bonnet Lock examples, including the most original in existence. We always have a good selection of Series 1 cars available both on and off market. If you're looking to buy an E-type for either Road or Track, please call James Mitchell or Jonny Shears

PENDINE

Historic Cars for Road & Track

+44 (0) 1869 357126   www.pendine.com   cars@pendine.com   Located at BICESTER HERITAGE

2.1 How Not To Dismantle An E-type

At this point in the restoration process, I had stripped the car down to a rolling chassis. The engine was still in, together with the front and rear suspension and steering, and the handbrake remained operative. The bonnet was off the car and in separate pieces. I had stripped the paint from the whole car apart from the underneath.

In retrospect there are several points of note. I had stripped the car down thus far with a view to making a decision about how full a rebuild to carry out, and with some idea of possibly re-spraying the car in this semi-stripped condition. This simply made a lot of work for myself. Primarily, it meant that I stripped all the paint off by hand. (I used various methods but mainly either Nitromors or a heat

gun, depending on the panel) This was a particularly laborious job and I should really have simply stripped the car of its mechanical parts and taken the whole body to be grit-blasted, or similar, which would have saved a lot of time and effort.

There appear to be two main processes available to strip body shells properly: soda-blasting or chemical-stripping. Soda-blasting is more bodywork-friendly than the more common grit-blasting. One of the main advantages of this method is that it can be mobile so operators can come to you and treat either the whole shell or just parts, as you require. I have had various panels grit-blasted in the past and this has also been very effective, but is a very harsh procedure only suitable for very solid panels that can

withstand such treatment. The other method is chemical-stripping where the entire body shell is immersed in tanks of acid to remove paint, filler and underseal. This process costs around £1,500. Soda-blasting companies include Vapour Blast (www.vapourblast.co.uk) and Bedlam Autobody (www.bedlamautobody. co.uk). Chemical-stripping companies include SPL - Surface Processing Ltd (www.surfaceprocessing.co.uk) and Ribble Technology (www.paint-strip. co.uk).

I took the bonnet apart completely and stripped the horrendous gunge from underneath (underseal, oil, grease, etc). It was only at this point that I thought to get some of the panels blasted. I therefore took the remaining bonnet panels to be blasted

2.1-1 *Left: The newly widened garage ... and E-type rear axle assembly*

at a place in Doncaster that I found in the phone book – so much easier! However, they were not car bodywork blast-cleaning specialists and this meant that although they cleaned up the old panels well without making any holes, etc., they were unable to paint the blasted metal with any sort of protective paint so they were left as bare metal (as was the rest of the body shell that I'd already stripped). Needless to say, this was a big mistake. I should have painted the bare metal with something to stop it oxidising, but I didn't. Due to this, things were soon to get a lot worse.

As mentioned, I had hoped to only strip the car down to this level and get a bare metal re-spray. However, it became clear that if the car was to be right I needed to undertake a full nut and bolt restoration. I had therefore spent a lot of time and effort for nothing. I should have realised that I needed a full restoration from the outset, especially in view of the general condition of the mechanical parts of the car and that the front and rear suspension/steering were particularly poor.

Apart from failing to paint the bare shell, I had already made one fundamental mistake – not having taken any photos of the various parts before dismantling them. I cannot emphasise how important this is. Even with parts that I have taken apart only a week before, I forget how they go together. Simple things like where the brake pipes run and how the various sections of wiring loom fit into the car are impossible to remember without photos. When I came to begin the reassembly of my car, I was stuck.

Workshop manuals don't give sufficient detail and some parts are often completely missed, e.g. the handbrake operating mechanism on the rear cage. I am very lucky in that I live quite near to *Derek Watson Jaguar* in Derbyshire and they usually have several E-types

in pieces in their workshop at any one time. During the restoration of my car, they were kind enough to let me go out and take copious photos of every part of an E-type from the rear suspension mountings to the wiring inside the dash board. Not only this but I availed myself of every opportunity to photograph E-types: at club meetings, at classic car shows, at club technical seminars, at other restorers such as Ken Verity's in Rotherham. I also got to know a few local *E-type Club* members who were always willing to let me go and take a few more photos and then a few more as each new part of the restoration demanded – you can never have enough.

I got carried away with dismantling the car, without thinking too much about taking pictures, stripping half of it down without a thought of the rebuild – anyway, I'd remember it all, wouldn't I? No. Take as many photos as possible (especially as we are now blessed with digital cameras and you can snap away to your heart's content without worrying about the cost of film/devcloping) or else get friendly with your local specialist – you'll need them. Because of my lack of forethought and the fact that at the time I didn't know I was going to write a book on the restoration and as at that time digital cameras were virtually unheard of, I'm afraid I don't have many pictures of the strip down – my apologies.

Well, the car was stripped, with boxes of bits everywhere ... and we decided to move house. Thankfully, the car was still mobile (purely by luck) as a rolling chassis and so work on the E-type was suspended until we had moved, as there was little I could do in the meantime without rendering the car virtually un-transportable, and anyway all my spare time was taken with preparing our house for sale and then looking at houses to buy. My only criteria were that our new house should have a large garden and a large garage but other than that Christine could have the final say. We moved into a house with a small garden and a ridiculously small garage. I make no comment. The car was moved by a local transport company without too much fuss.

All I could do was put the half-stripped car into the exceedingly damp garage. (The garage was in fact the main part of the basement, which at some time previously had been dug out to form a 'garage' – 7' 6" [2.3m] wide) The house itself was much in need of restoration and upgrading and all my time for the next year was

Our newly excavated storage **2.1-2** *room*

spent getting it to a satisfactory (but nowhere near finished) state. This meant my body shell and bonnet sections, stripped of paint, were sitting in a damp garage with virtually no protection for over a year. The mistake of not painting/protecting the body shell was beginning to hit home.

As the house began to take some sort of shape, I was able to begin putting my master plan into operation. The basement was in fact three rooms side by side, with the main, central one being the garage. I realised that if we could demolish the two walls between the three rooms, I could end-up with a decent-width garage. At the same time I could damp-proof it, add proper power and light, and I'd be in business. Problem. As this was the basement of the house the two aforementioned walls did kind-of actually hold the rest of the house up. Also, if we were to have major structural work done on the basement and the driveway widened so we could park both our everyday cars, where was the E-type to go for the duration?

I was in luck in the form of my next-door neighbour – another Chris! By chance, he is also a classic car enthusiast, owning and having completely restored a Jaguar MkII and an Innocenti Mini Cooper. He volunteered to keep the E-type whilst the building work was completed, although it would have to sit outside, under a car cover.

Work duly began and for several months the front garden and basement were unspeakable. Finally, however, all was finished. I now had a suitable garage/workshop that was suddenly a wonderful 20' wide at its widest point. I also managed to excavate a previously sealed part of the basement to provide further storage space. However, the garage remains only 7' high and is not 20' wide for the whole length of the garage – we had to leave some of the walls up to support the rest of the house – shame.

The E-type once again took up residence, but the bare metal no longer looked shiny and silver. What had 15 months of languishing in a damp garage and three months outside done to the stripped bodywork? Not

knowing I was going to be writing this at the time, I did not take any pictures of it. If I had done, you would probably have cried too. I hadn't painted the bare shell as I simply didn't get round to it with the house move, etc., and I wasn't sure what paint to use. I had an idea that normal primer is porous and would actually attract moisture. I'm not sure if this is true but I'm sure that anything would have been better than nothing.

Anyway there was no time to dwell on these things – what was done was

2.1-3 *Our old Victorian wash-house made a good paint shop and general storage area. Can you spot the following: rear wishbones, a rear drive shaft in two pieces, a rear hub carrier, a radius arm securing strap and a long section of petrol pipe?*

2.1-4 *One very bent lower wishbone lever*

on this. Guess how I know that?

Then it was finally time to remove the engine and gearbox. I studied my various manuals to find out how to do this. There were two different methods: removal from above or below. Although the garage now lived up to its name, it still had a very low ceiling which meant that engine removal from above was impossible. The manuals' suggested alternative was to remove the engine from below, but in order to do this the car had to be a considerable height off the ground. I didn't have the necessary equipment to achieve this and my wonderful new garage was on a fairly steep slope so I spurned this method of engine removal too. After much head scratching, I came up with what seemed to me to be a very simple method.

I removed the engine by firstly removing the radiator then the steering and front suspension (the steering rack, the torsion bars and the upper and lower wishbones) and the front engine frame (the picture frame). With the picture frame removed, I undid the engine mountings, raised the engine slightly using my newly-acquired engine hoist, and eased the engine out forwards through the gap left by the picture frame, complete with gearbox, inlet manifold and exhaust manifold. I found this method of removal very successful in a very limited space like mine. The only snag with this procedure is that you can only carry it out as part of a complete rebuild: not if you only want to remove the engine. Once again let me apologise for the lack of photos. At this point I still didn't know I was going to write a book about the restoration – and I *still* didn't have a digital camera!

Once removed, the engine was then bolted to my other new acquisition, an engine stand, and put to one side. The main point of note during engine removal was that in the manual (page B.19 of the Service Manual) it tells you to relieve the pressure on the top torsion bar reaction tie plate bolts when removing the reaction tie plate, otherwise you'll strip the threads. I can personally vouch for the fact that this is true!

During the removal of the front

done and I needed to get on with the restoration (or rather get on with the dismantling prior to the restoration – I hadn't got very far in two years). Eventually, virtually two years after halting the restoration, I finally removed the back axle, the engine and the front suspension. Removing the rear axle assembly was fairly straightforward except that the whole thing is so heavy! You really have to be careful that it doesn't tip over as you lower it down, as the prop-shaft flange on the differential can be bent if it falls suspension, which was again fairly straightforward, I discovered what I hoped to be the main cause of the dangerous steering – one very bent lower wishbone lever. See photo 2.1-4. I assume that this damage was done in the bad accident that the car had obviously suffered before being 'restored' in the late 1980s, but never discovered/rectified. The discovery of so obviously bent a steering component helped to ease my mind with regard to the car's poor handling and floating at speed. If I had found no such damage, I would have continued to worry as to the cause of the problem. With the car now finished, I can happily report that this was indeed the main cause of the poor handling (undoubtedly exacerbated by exceedingly worn suspension bushes, etc) and the car handles like a dream.

I removed the doors with the glass in-situ (heavy) and discovered that the near-side door had new mounting holes drilled in the hinge to try and make it fit. Looking at it off the car from the inside it was clear what the problem was. The door had clearly been heavily damaged in the accident and was only about half the depth it should have been. The remaining depth of the door was made up of body filler. About 1½ inches thick! Drilling new mounting holes in the hinges was the only way the 'restorers' could get it to fit at all. No wonder it had been such a poor fit before. It was therefore clear that my car was the archetypal poor quality restoration from the late '80s when E-type prices were rocketing. Unscrupulous restorers could make easy money by slapping a bit of filler and paint on a car like mine and market it as a "fully restored". Needless to say, if I'd have had any kind of proper inspection on my car by someone who knew what they were looking for all this would have been easily spotted and I could have walked away. I thought I already knew enough, however, (never having looked at an E-type before) and trusted my own judgement. Poor decision. I had checked very carefully that the body shell wasn't too rusty, but I hadn't properly checked for

accident damage. I'd only myself to blame.

I unbolted the remaining engine frames from the bulkhead, which were inevitably rusted-in, but did eventually undo with heat, WD40 and a variety of metric sockets hammered onto the remains of the bolt heads. Nearly three years after beginning the dismantling, the car was now finally completely stripped to the last nut and bolt, and restoration work could finally begin by turning my attention to the now rather rusty (on the surface) bodywork – or was there to be yet another unexpected twist?

2.1-5 *With the engine successfully removed from the car by dismantling the engine frames around it, I bolted it to a sturdy engine stand and put it to one side while I began a thorough inspection of the bodywork*

Lessons learnt:

- Be fully aware of what you are about to take on before completely stripping your car down.
- Don't strip the paintwork by hand – use a soda-blasting or similar specialist.
- Having stripped the car down to bare metal, immediately cover it with some suitable form of paint to inhibit corrosion (a good soda-blasting shop that specialises in cleaning body shells should be able to do this for you – and they should know what type of paint to use).
- Restoring an E-type is expensive and time-consuming; building a suitable garage for it can be even more so.
- Take pictures at every step, then take some more. You can simply never have enough.
- Consult the manuals at every turn, but don't be afraid of trying something different if you think it'll work, e.g. engine removal.
- It's good to have understanding neighbours.

2.2 Assessin' The Body Shell

So, I finally had the complete bonnet and body shell stripped to the last nut and bolt. Time to assess the work required. As I had previously thought, the bodywork was not in bad shape. Rust had not taken firm hold of the major parts of the body shell and it was generally sound. There was rust in places that I had expected – the doors needed replacing, as did the footwells and the front wings had tiny pinholes near the bottom edge. Apart from that, the only rust was to the replacement rear wing and a small hole in the lower off-side bulkhead. Not too bad.

However, to offset this was the fact that the car was clearly accident damaged. The rear off-side had been hit, making a bit of a mess of the rear boot floor and possibly distorting the lower roof below the rear hatch. The centre

bonnet section was badly damaged and the near-side door had clearly suffered some impact. Both 'A' post pillars in front of the doors were badly dented, probably from the doors bursting open. Repairs had been carried out, but not to a very high standard - in fact to a particularly low standard. The only panels to have been replaced were the rear off-side wing and rear lower quarter (neither of which had been replaced properly). All other panels, including some very damaged ones, had simply been repaired. The car had been covered in filler, in places almost inches thick to mask this poor restoration.

My guess is that the car had been off the road for some time after the crash – hence the lack of rust – and then in the mid-80s, when the classic car boom really began, the car was hastily restored

and sold with a view to making as much money as possible, with little attention to the quality of the work being carried out. It is a sad reflection on society that such people exist to whom money is everything and honesty and integrity mean nothing. Caveat Emptor.

The good news was that the car did not appear to have suffered structurally from the accident – it appeared straight. However, as with the mechanical parts, I was once again faced with a dilemma. I wanted a pretty perfect car (if I was going to spend forever rebuilding it, it was going to be right!) and although there was little rust, there was some, and there was the accident damage to consider. For instance, the front wings were good, but not excellent. The bonnet centre section was badly dented and the whole rear end of the car was suspect due to

2.2-1 *My car, as bought, looking really nice and shiny – you could say that I was Rooked! Also note the car in the background – a Mini Metro Vanden Plas 500! What can I say - it belonged to my parents*

I visited the Design Museum **2.2-2** *in London where they had a stunning display of E-types in superb condition: righthand drive chassis number one FHC, a Series I Roadster, a competition Lightweight E and the last V12. Sights like these spur you on!*

the accident damage which meant that the rear hatch didn't shut properly. There was a new driver's side rear wing but it didn't fit properly and it was very rusty. The floors were sound, but not perfect and had gained many dents from poor jacking, etc., over the years.

How much of the bodywork needed to be replaced to make the car decent, how long would it take me and how much would it cost?

At this point I had two thought-provoking meetings. Firstly, I had an informal chat with Nick from the paint shop I intended to use for the re-spray. (Even at this point I knew that I wasn't going to spray the car myself) Nick is a classic car enthusiast himself, owning and having nearly finished restoring an Austin Healey 100 BN1, a Land Rover Defender 90 and a Mercedes SL. He basically said, "If you manage to restore your car, you'll be one of the few people I know who've managed a complete restoration without using a new body shell – everyone else gave up."

Secondly, I had a chance meeting with an acquaintance who didn't know I had the E-type, but was himself the proud owner of an absolutely pristine Alfa Romeo Spyder that he'd bought in

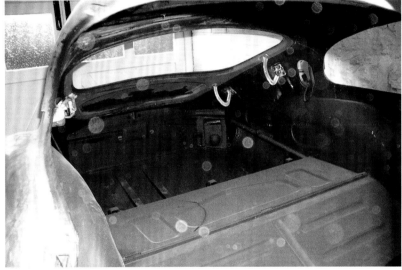

The interior of my new body shell **2.2-3** *complete with all new floors, bulkhead and wings. Nice*

Under the (brand new) bonnet **2.2-4** *of my new body shell showing seemingly good preparation of the bonnet and apparently immaculate engine frames. Unfortunately it later transpired that neither of these statements was quite correct*

2.2-5 *My brand new body shell safely in the garage – next door's garage that is (their basement was converted at the same time as ours). What price good neighbours? Note: the one real problem: the large hole in the roof*

concours condition. He was saying that he'd bought an immaculate car as he knew that he'd never have the time to restore his own, what with the pressures of modern day living, etc., etc.

These two conversations made an impact on me. Was I really up to all the work required? Would I ever have the time to finish such a project? I'd already had a two-year hiatus due to moving house and knew that I was facing an uphill task. And then it happened......

The very next month a completely restored Series II FHC body shell, rebuilt to concours standard, on a jig and boasting a brand new bonnet and doors was advertised in one of the Jaguar magazines. Was this fate? Despite the considerable price tag (£7500) I decided to take a look. It was indeed as advertised, having been built by a retired engineer to the highest standards and with a comprehensive folder of photos detailing the complete restoration process. It was now in the hands of an enthusiast/dealer as the chap who'd built it had given up on the restoration (sound familiar?) There was one problem (apart from the cost!) – it had a huge hole where the roof should have been to take a Webasto sunroof. I have nothing against Webasto sun roofs *per se* and I'm sure they're fantastic for summer cruising, but I just don't like them, especially on a coupé (as opposed to a 2+2) as they reduce headroom by a couple of inches and I think they slightly ruin the gorgeous lines of the E-type.

Anyway, to cut a long story short I bought the shell for £6000 with a view to fitting a new roof and sold my old shell, doors and bonnet for £1000 (which I think was a fair price for what it was). Unfortunately, my entire budget for the restoration was £8000 and so this made rather a large hole in it, but I thought it was worth it. All I had to do was buy a new roof from Martin Robey, weld it in, do a little sanding and send it off for a re-spray. Right? WRONG!

I discovered that Martin Robey makes every single body panel for an E-type ... apart from the roof!

I therefore spent the next three months looking for a second-hand roof section, which I finally bought at a Stoneleigh Jaguar spares day for £125. (I suppose we must be thankful that some coupés are now roadsters) I wasn't sure of the best way to weld the roof section in, but in the end I decided to cut out a section from the replacement roof and weld it into the hole left by the Webasto having used a joddler to step the edges. I didn't replace the entire roof by cutting through the roof pillars as I was worried about distortion (even though the body was on a good jig). In retrospect I think I made a bad decision. Probably the best way would have been to cut the roof out as near to the edge as possible, so minimising distortion. (I didn't do this as the strengthening lip on the under side of the roof is in the way) As it was, I took great care to prevent any distortion – clamping the sections tightly together and initially only spot welding at intervals. The result was ..... massive distortion of the roof panel. I think that when Colin Ford replaced the roof on the *Practical Classics* E-type he cut the spot welds out round the edges of the roof and did it that way. I think that that's a far more professional way of doing the job than mine.

As a result I spent many, many hours trying to correct the problem. Next time you get the chance to look at an E-type, really study the roof. You'll begin to appreciate, as I do now, the true beauty of the complex curves that go to make up the gorgeous lines of this panel. I had always intended to lead load any such work, but I took an early decision to use body filler. There was so much to do to the roof, and the lines were so difficult to recreate that I think I'd have struggled with lead (although the rest of the shell was lead loaded by the initial builder who appears to have done a really excellent job). Eventually, I think I managed to get it right, but it was a struggle. Fortunately I can report that now the car's been finished for a while the roof is still perfect and my rather amateur efforts seem to have worked OK.

I then proudly asked Nick to come and look at the shell with a view to re-spraying it. His verdict was not what I wanted to hear and heralded some of the darkest days of the restoration.

Lessons learnt:

- Hey, it's only money! What's that when weighed against one of the most historic and beautiful cars in the world?
- Check the availability of *any* part you think you may require – there's still the odd one that's unavailable.
- When in doubt, consult the experts – which I should have done over the question of the roof. I'm not really sure why I didn't, but I think it was probably that I didn't want to hear what they were going to say and took what I considered to be the easy route. Hence, I caused myself a large problem that proved very difficult to redress.
- Is it worth blowing £6000 on a new body shell and bonnet? Who knows? It is to me.

2.3 Restoring The Body Shell

One area of the restoration, therefore, that I didn't tackle myself was that of restoring the old body shell. The body shell I bought had been very well restored and virtually every panel below the waistline had been replaced with the car held securely in place on a jig. I also believed (erroneously) that new engine frames had been fitted (and the fact that they weren't new gave me quite a headache later when I discovered they were in fact the old ones that had been mended).

Unfortunately I never met the chap who had done the work as the shell was for sale through a dealer who was unable to provide much information about the restorer. All that I was given was a series of photos chronicling the rebuild of the body shell to some extent.

Points of Note

A Body Jig. Fixing the old body shell to a good jig is crucial to ensure proper alignment as various panels are removed and the shell weakens. Without a jig the body shell may flex as panels are removed and remain out of line as new panels are welded on. This is particularly true of roadsters (without the benefit of a roof to add strength) but is equally true of coupés, especially if all the floors and sills are to be replaced. This was the case with my car and will almost certainly be the case with any car. It would be a false economy in the extreme not to replace any suspect panels during the restoration process and, from my experience, this will mean the majority of panels if not all of them. Panels which appear sound at the outset will in fact

reveal themselves to be rotten on closer inspection as the shell is stripped. If any panels are left that may hide rust behind them, the rust will soon resume its merciless and relentless way through the 'new' body shell. Do the job once and do it properly.

Welding. E-types were originally welded together with powerful spot welders. These are very expensive and often out of the reach of many home restorers. The alternatives are therefore to either hire someone with a spot welder to come and help or to use a MIG welder or similar. In the latter case you then have to be very careful to make a strong enough weld. In most cases, this means more than simply welding the edges of panels. In the past I have drilled holes through mating flanges and then welded these up, thus ensuring a strong

2.3-1 *A fairly typical example of rot in the inner sill and floor panel of an E-type. This is almost certainly a sign of worse to come*

Using a MIG welder to repair the 2.3-2 *doors on an E-type*

joint. Whatever the case, if you're not sure about your welding skills, then think carefully before proceeding – the basis of any restoration is the body shell and if you get that wrong then you can forget the rest.

Lead or Filler? Another decision to make is whether to use lead to finish the panels as was originally used in the factory or use body filler. A few years ago, I attended a short course on lead-loading run by one of the car clubs and enjoyed it immensely. Furthermore most of my body shell had already been lead-loaded by the previous owner. It was, therefore, clear that I should also use lead – but I didn't. Why? I used filler because I thought I only had a little bit of finishing to do on the new shell (wrong!) and I didn't have the necessary tools, etc. Plus I had always used filler since I was a teenager and it was a medium I was used to.

With hindsight I wish I had used lead – not for reasons of originality but because sanding down copious amounts of body filler made a huge mess of the garage, covering everything in a thick layer of horrible grey dust. Whether using filler or lead, it is vitally important to ensure the metal is clean and dry in order to ensure good adhesion.

Lessons learnt:

• Do the body shell once and do it properly.

Lead loading a rear wing - the 2.3-3 *panel is first tinned before applying the lead*

It is amazing how much lead 2.3-4 *Jaguars had on them in the '50s and '60s*

2.4 Bodywork Blues

So, my new body shell had arrived, looking immaculate, and I thought I only had a few finishing touches to do to make it ready for painting. Hmmm ... the best laid plans of mice and men go oft awry: it was to be well over a year of horrendous work before the shell was finally finished and ready to be re-sprayed.

To start with I had had to weld in the new panel to fill the hole where the Webasto sunroof had been. I then had to finish off the bottom of the 'A' posts, which were the only areas left unfinished by the chap who'd actually rebuilt the shell in the first place. However, I then also realised that the panel gaps on the rear hatch were far from perfect, and that although the gaps on the two brand new doors on

the 'B' post and at the bottom were excellent, the gaps between the front edge of the doors and the 'A' posts were not. Wanting the car to be as perfect as possible, I decided to make all panel gaps 1/8 inch (3mm) wide.

I therefore duly began work on all the aforementioned areas. I had flirted with the idea of spraying the car myself but didn't for the following reasons:

- I had never sprayed a car before and didn't fancy learning on the E-type. I was aware that Nick knew all there was to know about spraying a car and all the pitfalls to do with incorrect paint mixture, damp in the atmosphere, poor preparation, etc., that could lead to trouble in the future.
- Being no artist I'm sure that even

with practice I'd make a mess of it.
- When finished, 90% of what people see of a restoration is the paintwork; it's essential to get it right. (The other 10% being the chrome wire wheels – it's true!)
- The cost of buying decent equipment was near the cost of a professional paint job, so I wouldn't have saved any money.
- Having bought my new equipment, I'd have to find somewhere to store it – space is always at a premium.
- A professional sprayer can use two-pack paint which is generally acknowledged to be far superior to the cellulose that I'd have had to use (Two-pack contains a poison – isocyanate – so only properly equipped paint shops are allowed

2.4-1 *Left: My new body shell as it arrived after purchasing and before I completed the final refinishing*

The new body shell now replete with solid roof **2.4-2**

to use it). Recently (2009) two-pack itself has been replaced with water-based paint. I've no idea if the home restorer can use this, whether any special equipment is required and how easy it is to spray, but this may be worth investigating further if you are considering spraying your own car.

Nick (who was to paint the car) loaned me several useful tools and pointed me in the direction of the local paint refinishing shop. He also advised that the dust from sanding down vast quantities of filler gets everywhere. What he failed to tell me was that the dust gets *EVERYWHERE!*

For the duration of the sanding process the garage was completely covered in a horrible thick grey coating that permeated every conceivable nook and cranny. The whole house was likewise covered in dust. Bear in mind that our garage is in the basement, trying to stop the rest of the house getting dusty was simply impossible - we even had dust coming up through the floorboards! Also, as the floor of the garage was always covered in thick dust, simply by walking through it you left a horrible grey trail of footprints wherever you went. Work clothes had to be washed on a daily basis and I'm sure that even my complexion became greyer – although whether through dust or stress is unclear!

I managed to achieve a uniform panel fit and appropriate panel gaps

More filler, more sanding ... more filler, more sanding ... more... **2.4-3**

by first fitting a set of seals to the 'B' post of the doors, the door sill, the rear hatch and bonnet. I then temporarily fitted the catch on the rear hatch (the others already being in place) and adjusted them all to give as good a shut as possible. Finally, I put a skim of filler right over the panel joins and ran a screwdriver with a 1/8th inch shank down the gaps to get a perfect fit. The hardest part of this was the door-to-'A' post gap as it is very difficult to get it right at the top, and you have to remove the doors to complete the job as you can't access the channel to the rear of the 'A' post to finish it properly with the doors in situ.

Having completed this process, I proudly asked Nick to come out and see if it was ready to spray. He delivered bad news. He ran experienced hands all over the shell and said that it was OK but nowhere near good enough. He

even said that the bonnet and doors still required work. "But, Nick, they're brand new, they look perfect - what could possibly need doing to them?" He showed me that you don't look at a panel to check if it's flat but feel it by running your hands over it. Sure enough, this method revealed slight imperfections, invisible to the naked eye, even in the brand new panels. The panels I'd actually completed were far worse and, to add insult to injury, he pronounced on my panel gaps. "These gaps are excellent – but they're far too small! You need a minimum panel gap of 3/16 inch (5mm) on any car as otherwise the doors can foul on the surrounding bodywork." So, I had spent much precious time achieving these small gaps, and now had the even harder job of opening them up again!

I set to work once more – more dust,

2.4-4 *Getting the rear hatch to fit properly was a nightmare, especially since the very low roof of my garage prevented me from actually opening it!*

more coughing and a little bit more expertise. Two months later I sent for Nick – the pronouncement was that the panel gaps were now spot on (thanks to another screwdriver, this time with a 3/16 [5mm] inch shank), but the rest of the bodywork was still not good enough! I had created beautifully smooth panels – mainly with the disc sander – but although lovely and smooth they weren't flat. Running your hand quickly over a panel revealed a smooth but wavy surface that was far from what was wanted. I had used the disc sander too much, rather than the long sanding plane that Nick had previously lent me and this had resulted in a smooth finish, but not a flat one.

Nick showed me how to use wet and dry sanding sheets, and the technique of covering the whole panel in a very thin skim of filler and then sanding it down to a uniform finish.

I therefore set to work *again* with more dust and mess, etc., and did the best I possibly could. Two months later I called in Nick again – this time it was surely ready? No! My best simply wasn't good enough. In the field of bodywork restoration, I had failed.

Thankfully, a full nine months after I began, Nick took pity on me and finally agreed to take the shell and complete the preparation himself. He hadn't wanted to do this as the job wasn't really financially viable. It was to take him a further six months (!) to finish the shell, and although he obviously didn't spend all his time on it, it was time he could have given over to the more lucrative side of his business – accident repairs.

N.B. It was only later, much later, that I realised I hadn't in fact done enough to ensure a proper fit on the doors. I should have trial-fitted the 'A' post seals as well as the 'B' post seals and trial-fitted the chrome window frames as well. Not doing this caused me no amount of problems when the car was finished and it was almost impossible to rectify.

Lessons learnt:

- Sanding down large quantities of body filler is the worst job I have ever experienced – and I've tried a few.
- My talent is definitely more on the mechanical side of things rather than the more artistic side: rebuild an engine? No problem. Create completely smooth and uniform surfaces on complex curved panels? Erm, no.
- Sanding down the body shell was one of the worst moments of the restoration.
- Seeing the body disappear off to the body shop so I could eventually clean the garage (it took a full week-end) was one of the best moments of the restoration.

The body shell nearing the **2.4-5** *end of months and months of preparation with near perfect panel gaps and (fairly) smooth bodywork*

Preparing The Body Shell

Nick's advice on preparing bodywork is as follows:

- First and foremost, Nick stresses the importance of having a really good clean surface to paint on to. He recommends blast cleaning the metal using an appropriate abrasive (e.g. soda or bead or grit, depending on the metal) and then etch-priming it as soon as possible as oxidisation occurs within 12 hours. The bodywork is then ready to work on. He also recommends acid-stripping the bodywork but emphasises that all traces of the stripping chemical have to be completely removed before etch-priming as otherwise this will interfere with the adhesion of the primer.

- He recommends using etch-primer on the bare metal as it has an acidic activator which ensures really good adhesion with the surface.

- With the metal satisfactorily primed, it is then time to begin preparing the bodywork for re-spraying. At this point any filler can be applied where necessary (as little as possible as if too thick it can crack or shrink or cause problems generally). One of Nick's golden rules is that there should be as little paint or filler as possible on the bodywork before re-spraying as too much of either can cause problems later on. He recommends using a flexible polyester filler such as Plastic Padding which, because it can flex slightly, reduces the chance of cracking.

- With the filler applied where necessary, it's time to begin sanding down (or blocking) and he recommends the use of a long sanding tool called a Bed Block (see Photo 2.4-6) on bigger surfaces to try and get a smooth AND flat surface – unlike the one I managed to achieve. He recommends starting with quite coarse Abranet abrasive sheets (as seen in Photo 2.4-6) which are more like a gauze. If the block is then attached to a vacuum cleaner, the filler dust is drawn through the gauze and into the vacuum, massively reducing the amount of dust in the

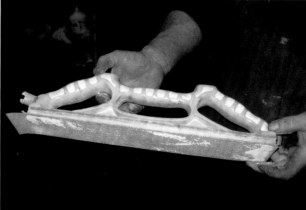

2.4-6 *Bed Block and Abranet sanding sheet*

2.4-7 *Moulded hard foam blocks for curved surfaces*

2.4-8 *Foam backed sanding sheet*

2.4-9 *The foam backing*

air. How I wish I'd done this when I did mine!

- There are different shapes and types of block available for the various curves, etc., on an E-type. These include hard foam ones as seen in Photo 2.4-7 and a selection of different shapes and sizes would be very useful.

- The grade of abrasive paper can slowly be reduced as the blocking progresses: up to 40 to begin, then up to 80, then up to 180 and finally up to 240 (all used dry).

- At this point the bodywork should be ready for priming if your blocking has been properly completed. Nick recommends either using etch-primer again or two-pack primer at this point. He does not recommend using primer filler as this puts on too much material and can cause shrinkage to occur - remember his mantra of only applying very thin coats of paint. Also remember that two-pack polyurethane paint can only be used in spray booths with proper filters as it is an isocyanate and very harmful to the environment if used outside.

- The primer should then be allowed to fully harden (not too long if a low bake oven is used, otherwise at least overnight).

- The second round of blocking then begins in an effort to achieve a really beautiful finish. Nick recommends starting with 400 grade foam-backed abrasive sheet used dry (see Photos 2.4-8 and 2.4-9). Nick emphasised that at this point you are not shaping the bodywork but removing any slight unevenness in the paint as a totally smooth surface is required to achieve a top coat with a really deep shine. Your objective is to remove as little paint as possible. See Photo 2.4-10 of the first coat having been sanded down.

- The car is then primed again and blocked again with 400 grade foam-backed abrasive used dry. See Photo 2.4-11.

- The above process is then repeated but this time the paint should be

2.4-10 *First primer coat which was then blocked*

2.4-11 *After the second coat of primer*

2.4-12 *In the spray booth awaiting first undercoat*

2.4-13 *Final sanding of undercoat using wet and dry*

Preparing The Body Shell

sanded down using 600/800 wet and dry sheets, used wet initially and then dry.

- The next step was for Nick to apply an undercoat to match the colour of the top coat and sand this down with 600/800 wet and dry used wet. See Photos 2.4-12 and 2.4-13.
- Now it's time to apply the top coat at last! Nick uses two-pack polyurethane paint and I can testify as to the results! See Photo 2.4-14.
- In my case the two-pack was then covered in a layer of lacquer (see next section) and polished with a good quality polish and proper polishing tool.
- Job done! See Photo 2.4-15 of Nick and me attempting to pose by the finished body shell (the car's definitely the star is this picture!).

2.4-14 *Top coat on!*

2.4-15 *Proud owner and painter*

2.5 Let Us Spray

So, the body shell was finally off at the paint shop where it was to undergo a long finishing process that was to take six months' hard labour, four coats of primer, two coats of undercoat, one coat of two-pack Opalescent Silver Grey and one coat of lacquer.

As soon as the shell arrived at the body shop, Nick gave it a coat of primer, to provide immediate protection for the many exposed panels (N.B. Never remove the black paint new panels arrive in, if at all possible, as this gives very good corrosion protection) That was to be the first of four coats of primer. Each time the shell was sprayed it was then comprehensively rubbed down. Nick estimated that approximately 80% of each coat was removed in this process, but that this

was OK, as too thick a coat of primer can apparently lead to problems in the future. He informed me that the best base for paint is a completely rust-free panel skimmed with filler. The filler adheres to the panel well and reduces the risk of a reaction between the paint and the panel. Poor preparation of what appears to be a perfectly painted panel starts to give trouble a few months or years after spraying. Again, beware the car that has had a very recent re-spray. It may look good now, but in a few months' time it could be a very different story.

After the second coat of primer had been applied, I realised that I hadn't trial-fitted the chrome bumpers. As this wasn't even the same body shell that they'd originally been fitted to, I feared the worst. I took all the

bumpers down and gingerly offered them to the shell. As it turned out, they all proved to be a pretty good fit and only a minimal amount of bodywork reshaping and bumper grinding was required. Luckily Series II and III cars have a greater tolerance for fitting the bumpers than Series I cars due to using a considerably larger rubber seal to the body.

After the third coat of primer, I had another belated but 'just-in-time' discovery. I had the rear suspension 'cups' (radius arm mounting points) grit-blasted, ready to paint and pop rivet to the floor of the car when I found a major problem. On my old body shell these nipples were only pop-riveted on and it was only when I requested new pop rivets that I was told that the rivets were only meant to hold the cup in

2.5-1 *Left: In the body shop with primer applied*

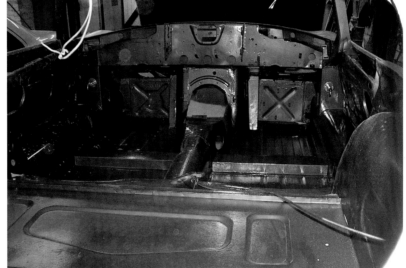

Trial-fitting the bumper blades **2.5-2** *should be done at an early stage of the body shaping because they are fitted flush to the body panels with only a rubber seal between and thus the contours of both must be the same. I left it rather late in the day!*

This shot of the painted interior **2.5-3** *gives a good idea of the E-type monocoque construction. Note: the bonnet catches were on the shell to enable us to properly fit and gap the bonnet*

These are the radius arm **2.5-4** *mounting cups being welded on at a rather late stage. They are sometimes known as the 'top hat' mountings*

place before they were welded to the floor of the car. As this was how I had found them, I'd assumed that was how they were supposed to be. I therefore quickly rushed down to the body shop and had the mountings welded to the new body shell, just in time ... WRONG! It transpires that the information I'd been given about the mountings being pop-riveted in place prior to welding was totally incorrect.

After the shell was painted, I came to learn the truth about how these mountings should be attached to the body. They should not be welded or brazed or bolted or riveted on but should be fastened to the body with special 'hook bolts'. These are apparently very special high tensile bolts that are very strong but are designed to snap at a certain pressure. This means that

2.5-5 *Jaguar's period colour options included Opalescent Gunmetal Grey which they used on the original prototype Fixed Head Coupé, 9600 HP*

As part of the difficult decision on colour, I considered Opalescent Silver seen here on this car **2.5-6**

they are strong enough to hold the rear suspension in place but will break under extreme duress (in the event of an accident) and ensure the integrity of the passenger compartment. These hook bolts look like rivets and are attached using a special machine like a rivet gun but are, in fact, bolts.

So now you know; and now I know that my mountings are incorrectly attached: those weird rivet-like things that I laughed at were, in fact, meant to be there all the time. Oh, well, you live and learn.

Eventually, after much laborious work, the time came for the first of two undercoats to be applied before the final topcoat. At this point, I started to have second thoughts about my chosen colour – Opalescent Silver Grey. The fact that it was not a colour that was offered on Series II cars was not a consideration. I simply wanted a colour that would look good and was preferably a genuine E-type one. However, was Opalescent Silver Grey the right colour? Was it even the colour I was thinking it was? Perhaps I'd seen the colour on another car *thinking* it was Opalescent Silver Grey when it was in fact a totally different colour.

To confuse matters further I also liked Opalescent Gunmetal, which is a shade darker than the Grey, and there's also Opalescent Silver, which is lighter. Which should I choose? This was one of the most fundamental decisions of the whole rebuild and I wanted to get it right. At this point Ken Jenkins rang to say that they had an Opalescent Silver Grey E-type in the workshop if I'd like to have a look as he was of the same mind that it was a beautiful colour. I duly went out to find an Opalescent *Silver* E-type. The car looked good, but was not the colour I had pictured. I therefore decided that the colour I had in mind had indeed been Silver Grey – but was it the best colour? Ken very kindly lent me the three colour swatches of the Jaguar colours: Gunmetal, Silver Grey and Silver and I carried on debating with myself, Christine, Nick, Ken and anyone who would listen as to the merits or demerits of the three. Ken also had a wonderful Opalescent Powder Blue car in the workshop that looked beautiful, but you can only have a black, grey or blue interior with that

colour and I desperately wanted a red interior.

Eventually, I made the difficult decision to stick with my original idea of Opalescent Silver Grey. The paint was duly ordered and there was no turning back. The day of the final painting came and I went to the paint shop immediately after work to find the body shell finished with its top coat, but without the final lacquer... It looked absolutely stunning! I can honestly say that I had a wave of childish joy sweep over me (not to mention sheer relief) when I saw it – simply breathtaking, especially after what it had looked like previously!

Everyone who saw it commented on how good it looked, and now it's finally finished it looks magnificent. After the final coat of lacquer had been applied, the car was left to bake in the oven overnight before extensive polishing the next day. At this stage the paint had not fully hardened and any minor imperfections could be buffed out and the lacquer polished to a deep shine. The final job was to remove the bonnet

2.5-7 *Nick gets to work sanding the first undercoat and one of his lads rubs down the under bonnet area*

as Nick had kindly agreed to store it at his workshop until required – a *big* help as otherwise it would have been so much in the way at home.

The remaining shell finally returned home courtesy of a breakdown truck whereupon I removed the doors and rear hatch as well as the engine frames (which were then refinished on the underside of the mountings to try and avoid corrosion) and stored them safely. I was now ready to begin the mechanical rebuild – at last!

Lessons learnt:

- Choosing the right colour for your car is one of the hardest but most satisfying parts of the entire rebuild.
- *All* chrome trim should be trial-fitted to the body shell before it goes off to the paint shop. I was to discover time and time again that when I went to re-fit a piece of re-chromed trim to my re-painted body shell it wouldn't fit properly. I was then faced with a difficult decision in order to get the trim to fit– risk damaging the re-chromed trim or the re-painted shell?
- Ensure the body is properly finished before taking it to the spray shop. Not only had I not fitted the trailing arm mountings but later on I discovered that the seal retainers around the doors and windows were missing too. I'd been in too much of a hurry to get the body painted and this led to small but fairly crucial mistakes being made.
- Radius arm mountings are secured to the body shell with special hook bolts, not by welding, riveting or brazing.
- If in doubt, always try and get the advice of two 'experts' in case the advice of one of them later proves to be incorrect (and in my case leading to mistakes that can't be rectified).
- Remember to keep smiling at all times.

2.5-8 *Nick spraying the engine bay*

2.5-9 *Oh, yes! The body shell sprayed Opalescent Silver Grey and finished with a coat of lacquer – simply stunning!*

3.1 Dismantling The Independent Rear Suspension

With the body now finally sent off to the paint shop, it was time to begin work on the mechanical side of things. There was no time to lose as I suddenly had the whole garage to work in whilst the body shell was absent. This was especially relevant for moving very heavy objects around like the rear suspension unit. First item on the agenda and top of the list therefore was the Independent Rear Suspension (IRS). I can't tell you how much I had been looking forward to rebuilding this as it's such a legendary piece of Jaguar history, but not one I was familiar with. I had heard all sorts of horror stories regarding the restoration of the rear axle and I saw it as something of a challenge. After the general nightmare of the bodywork, I was eager to get to grips

with something I was much more at home with – mechanical bits!

The first thing to note is that the unit is exceptionally heavy when assembled (and still pretty heavy in its component parts) and I was only able to move it around the garage with the aid of an engine hoist. Removal was fairly straightforward as per the manuals and, apart from all the grease, grime and oil (my differential had been leaking badly from the pinion oil seal for some time), it came off fairly easily. Raise the rear of the car quite high off the ground, support the rear axle with a trolley jack and undo the Vee mountings. But don't forget to put down some protection on the floor in case it falls over as you remove it.

When it came off the car, it was the most disgusting lump of metal with

thick oil and grease mixed with dirt all over it, flaking paint and the odd rusty bit. It certainly didn't look that legendary. As I'm sure you've heard before, the main problem with the rear suspension unit is ironically caused by the fact that it's so damned reliable! Unfortunately this reliability is combined with the fact that the unit as a whole is very hard to get at to work on. This combination of factors therefore means it usually gets ignored and left to its own devices, quietly wearing out and seizing up, hidden from prying eyes. This is one reason why the handbrake has such a poor reputation on Jaguars fitted with IRS – it's too much effort and expense to take the whole lot out and attend to it adequately so it tends to get worked on in situ where it can't be sorted out properly.

3.1-1 *Left: The rebuilt rear differential with reconditioned brake calipers, Greenstuff brake pads and my neighbour's brake discs*

Now for the admissions. The admissions of omissions: I just never got round to taking any photos of the dismantling of the rear suspension. All I can say in my defence is that it was the most horrible, dirty job and the thought of picking up my brand new digital camera in the midst of all this was too much. OK, OK, it's a poor excuse, but the dismantling process is well covered in the *Jaguar World* manual on rebuilding the IRS unit – see index at the back of this book. I

feel very stupid to have been so short-sighted in this matter but it's too late to start crying now as my father would say. Move on.

Anyway, having successfully moved the IRS across the garage – a feat in itself - I set to work. The first thing to do was to strip it down to its component parts, a really horrible job. Before tackling this, I consulted my four manuals as fully as possible (see index of titles at the end of this book). I recommend ensuring that you have such a wide variety of manuals to hand as one often contains information the others don't and none of them ever has the complete information required.

One of the first jobs was to pull the hub carriers from the half shafts. In this I was lucky that Chris next door had a proper Jaguar puller to fit hubs

with wire wheels. Without this tool I don't think I'd have ever been able to separate the two as they were both virtually welded to each other on my car and even with the hub puller it was a struggle.

I then removed the half shafts and the shims between the shafts and the rear discs, labelling the shims to ensure they were put back exactly as

The rear of the diff showing the **3.1-2** *filler plug and the breather pipe*

they came off – to ensure correct rear wheel camber, or so I thought at the time. It later transpired that as I had to use a new differential in a new body shell the original factory setting for the rear camber angles wouldn't be correct and I'd have to have them re-set when the car was finished.

Next, I turned my attention to the lower wishbones which have many washers and spacers and oil seals associated with them. One of my manuals, the *Jaguar World 6 Cylinder Engine and IRS Overhaul Manual,* specifically dedicated to rebuilding a Jaguar rear axle states: "Don't worry about the washers and seals that fall; these will be replaced later on." Don't believe everything you read! I followed this advice and allowed many of these items to be thrown away with all the dirt and grease, etc., that littered the garage floor. I was later to discover that this was to be a relatively expensive and totally unnecessary mistake.

When all was in pieces, I cleaned everything up as best I could and sent the myriad parts off for plating or powder-coating. My policy for this rebuild was simple: do it once and do it right. I was trying to do the best possible job at every stage and to replace/recondition every part no matter what the apparent condition. *All* nuts and bolts, etc., were either plated or stainless steel (where allowable – stainless fixings cannot be used in places of high stress, e.g. suspension, engine frames, etc.). The idea is that I won't have to strip it all down again because I didn't replace 'X'. Above all, I will not *worry* as to whether or not a part needs replacing as I'll know it's already been done.

I turned my attention to the rear differential. I knew my diff. was in poor condition and I'd previously bought a rebuilt one. However, was the new one properly rebuilt? (I had already had nasty experiences with items previously rebuilt by others and I now never trust them) I took the back off and had a nose about but wasn't sure. I therefore took it to a specialist (who had better remain nameless) who informed me that it wasn't an E-type diff. at all but from an XJ6 and that it had far too much backlash – both of

these statements later proved to be incorrect.

The good news was that I was told that differentials should only really be rebuilt by experts and that I shouldn't try it myself. I was very happy to hear this as I'd thought such a job was always a bit beyond me and to have such a decision taken out of my hands was somewhat of a relief.

I therefore duly took both differentials to Eric, the diff. man, and he did the job properly for me. It turned out that my original diff. was totally useless (a clue here being that it leaked oil badly. This meant that at some time it would almost certainly have run dry, causing irreparable damage) but the other diff. was indeed the correct one and had been rebuilt quite well – with the correct amount of backlash. However, he replaced the differential case as it was worn to excess. A point of note here is that the rear output bearings are apparently no longer available (being a strange size) so you have to use the best used ones you can find. My original diff. was scrapped.

I had wanted to convert the new differential to Limited Slip (I don't think that this is the same as a *PowrLok* unit which simply locks both wheels. A limited slip diff. does just that, providing limited power to each wheel depending on its amount of grip). Unfortunately the Limited Slip pack was an extra £300 and I just simply couldn't justify it – I wasn't planning on doing hill climbs in the rain. The cost of reconditioning the already reconditioned differential was about £400.

With the diff. back, it was painted red (rather garish, I admit) and I began reassembly. The first items to be bolted on were a pair of genuine rear

discs (with anti-squeal bands round the edges – also garishly painted with heat resistant paint). They came from another neighbour who had his Series 1½ E-type Roadster stolen many years ago and it was never recovered. He'd bought new rear discs for it and never got round to fitting them (having now rebuilt a rear axle I can fully understand why!) and they were all he had left. So, it was quite nice to include them on my car. The discs were fitted with any shims between the discs and differential being replaced as they were – there may be shims on either side of the discs. By the way, you can see just how heavy a differential unit is by the way in which it's bending my Black and Decker Workmate!

I then fitted my shiny new calipers which I'd also sprayed with a lacquer for added corrosion protection. I'm not sure how effective this will be, especially on items like the calipers which get very hot, but I thought it would be better than nothing. Next I centralised the calipers relative to the discs with shims, having first temporarily bolted the discs in place. I fitted new *Greenstuff* brake pads, the only upgrade I'd decided to make to the braking system. I hope they're OK, but I have heard stories of bad brake squeal. To this end, their new pads are covered in an anti-squeal compound – the brown gunge in the photo. (With the car now on the road, I am able to report that I'm really happy with the *Greenstuff* brake pads: they don't squeal, they work well and of course there's no brake dust – highly recommended) The final job was to wire the caliper mounting bolts together with stainless steel locking wire. Next was the notorious handbrake mechanism!

Lessons learnt:

- Sometimes even the experts get it wrong.
- Never throw anything away until you actually have the replacement in your hands. Too often I've thought, "This is totally useless" and thrown it away only to find that it is irreplaceable or I've needed it for reference, etc.
- Using the proper Jaguar tool can make life so much easier.
- Starting to bolt shiny new parts together is heaven after the trials and tribulations of the dismantling process and bodywork restoration.

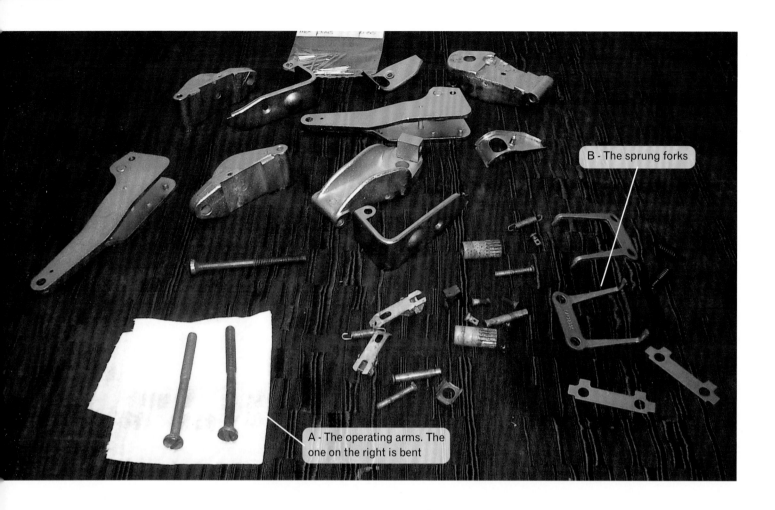

B - The sprung forks

A - The operating arms. The one on the right is bent

3.2 The Handbrake Operating Mechanism

With the new calipers in position I turned my attention to the handbrake assembly. Having had the outer parts nickel-plated and with the interior thoroughly cleaned, the first thing was to examine the various parts for damage and then to establish exactly how the self-adjusting mechanism worked. If you understand how something works, then you've a fair chance of mending it and making it work properly.

On first inspection the operating arm on one of the handbrakes was bent, which had allowed the handbrake pad to skew sideways and not make proper contact with the disc. (Apologies I should have a photo of this but I didn't get round to it and I can't go back now) Referring to Photo 3.2-1, I therefore replaced the bent operating arm (A)

with a new one. During trial-fitting I also broke the small sprung clip that holds the pawl in place - (C) in Photo 3.2-2 - and so replaced it and the one on the other mechanism as well as they seemed brittle and liable to break.

As a matter of course, I also replaced the sprung forks which help to free the handbrake when it's released, together with their locking plates - (B) in Photo 3.2-1.

With all parts replaced and cleaned, I trial-assembled the unit to establish how the thing actually worked. Referring to Photo 3.2-2, the lug (D) engages with the pawl (E) and when the operating lever (F) is operated by applying the handbrake the lug is lifted and, if there is sufficient free play, engages with the next spline on the pawl thus turning it. This action

adjusts the handbrake by screwing the pawl further down the operating arm, bringing the pads closer to the disc.

Having mastered the mechanics of the system, I reassembled the units, packing them with grease, and mounted them on the brake calipers. It was then that I realised what seems to me to be the basic flaw in the design of the handbrake. When the handbrake is applied, the pads are pulled onto the disc, but only at the top, not the bottom. The bottom of the arm holding the pads simply pivots to allow the tops to be drawn together.

This means that with normal square brake pads only the top edge of the pad comes into contact with the disc with the bottom edges nowhere near it. So, only about 10% of the pad area is in effect used. Referring to Photo

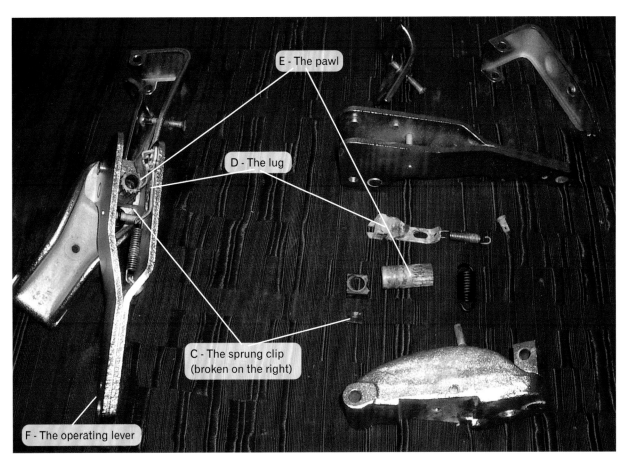

E - The pawl

D - The lug

C - The sprung clip (broken on the right)

F - The operating lever

3.2-1 *Left: The component parts of the handbrake mechanism*

Above: The handbrake self-adjusting mechanism **3.2-2**

The handbrake pads clamp at an angle to the disc **3.2-3**

3.2-3, the brake pads pivot around the mounting bolts (G) and are drawn together at the top by the operating arm (A) leaving the bottom edge of the pads (H) nowhere near the disc.

The only way I could see around this was to have chamfered brake pads. I have discussed this with a few people and they think that original pads may indeed have been chamfered but, if they were, they are no longer available. I therefore removed the units and

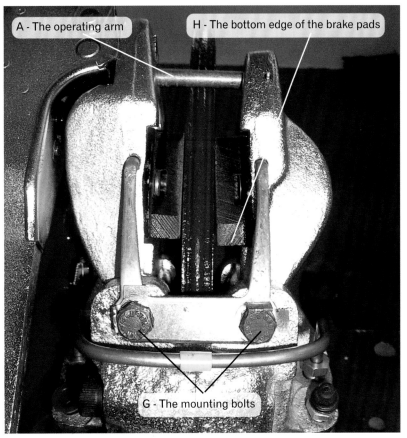

A - The operating arm

H - The bottom edge of the brake pads

G - The mounting bolts

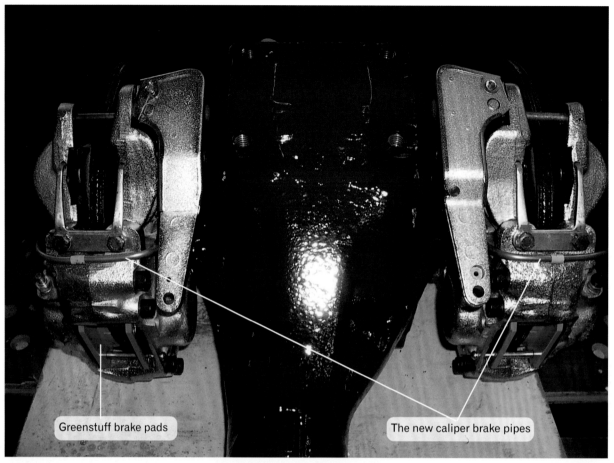

Greenstuff brake pads

The new caliper brake pipes

chamfered the pads myself with a file to try to have more surface in contact with the disc. Of course this will occur naturally as the brake pads wear, but it'd be nice to have a properly working handbrake from the beginning.

I also began to fit my replacement brake pipe kit. I decided to use a replacement *Kunifer* brake pipe set from SNG Barratt and this has so far fitted well. One or two people I spoke to previously said they recommended copper brake pipes, but I'm not sure why. The main problem I've encountered with the pipe set is using the special bending tool from *Machine Mart*. It bends up to 90 degrees no problem, but for bends beyond this and anything approaching a tight bend, it is useless. I have therefore resorted to the old method of forming the pipes around a wooden hammer shaft and this seems to be satisfactory, if not good. N.B. Fit the caliper brake pipes *before* bolting on the handbrake mechanisms as otherwise access to the pipe union is very restricted. My

other new tool from *Machine Mart*, my special pliers for plaiting locking wire, is great if rather expensive for what it is – a pair of pliers that lock shut, but it does enable you to make a really tidy job.

3.2-4 *Both calipers and handbrakes mounted after fitting the first of the new brake pipes*

Lessons learnt:

- I know how the handbrake is supposed to work.
- I know one reason why the handbrake doesn't always work too well.
- Special tools are sometimes wonderful; at other times, they leave a lot to be desired.
- They didn't make Greenstuff handbrake pads when I built my car, but they do now.
- Always take photos – you never know when they'll come in handy.
- Fit the brake pipe that links both sides of the calipers before fitting the handbrake mechanism.

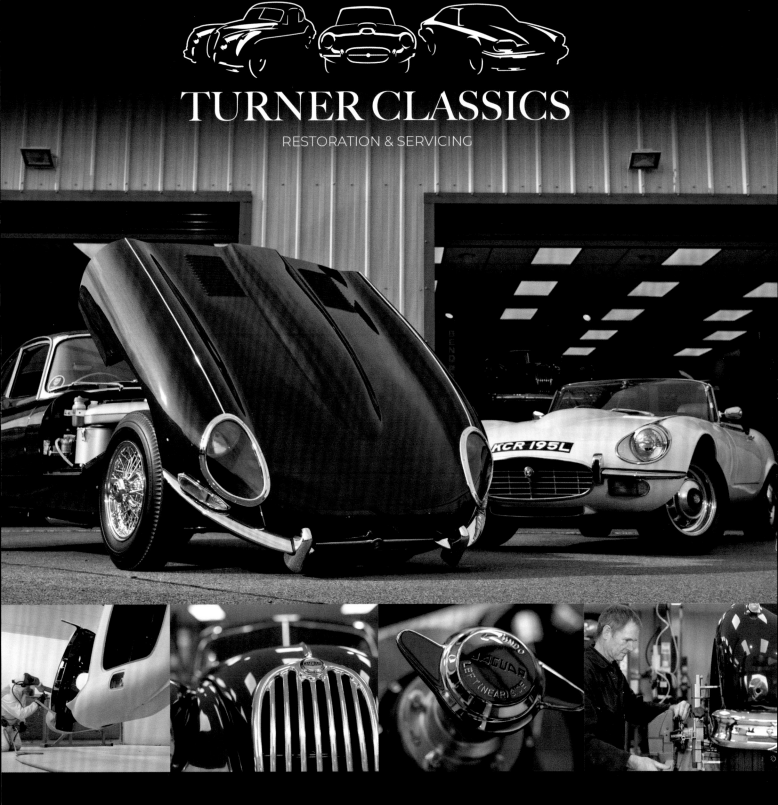

3.3 Rebuilding The Independent Rear Suspension

With the reconditioned calipers and rebuilt handbrake assembly in place, I was able to bolt the cage onto the differential. I'd had the cage, rear drive shafts and lower wishbones powder-coated previously and these were now ready to be refitted. Note that when having parts powder-coated ensure that bearing surfaces are blanked off prior to painting. My powder-coating company simply used kitchen foil glued onto the relevant surfaces.

I loosely bolted the cage to the top of the differential (see Photo 3.3-1) and then inverted the whole assembly and fitted the lower wishbone carriers. To do this I loosely fitted the inner fulcrum shafts through the cage and the inner fulcrum mounting brackets to line everything up and then, using shims

as appropriate, centralised the whole caboodle so that when the fulcrum bracket mounting bolts were tightened to the required torque, it all still lined-up (see Photo 3.3-2). The carrier bolts were then tied with locking wire, see Photo 3.3-4.

I decided to fit new Universal Joints (UJs) in the half shafts as part of my philosophy of, "Do it once and do it right" which basically meant either taking time to examine every item, reconditioning as appropriate, painting and plating everything in sight, or spending an awful lot of money for no good reason depending on your point of view.

Many years ago I'd tried to fit some new UJs to a half shaft and had made a complete mess because, as I tried to fit them, some of the little roller bearings

3.3-1 *The powder-coated cage loosely in place on the completed differential and brake assembly*

Right top: The fulcrum brackets **3.3-2** *are bolted in position by temporarily inserting the fulcrum shafts and then inserting bespoke shims as necessary*

The square shims between the **3.3-3** *drive shafts and brake discs were replaced in the order they had been removed. The drive shafts were then bolted-up using Klevelock nuts, which are immune to heat created by the brake discs*

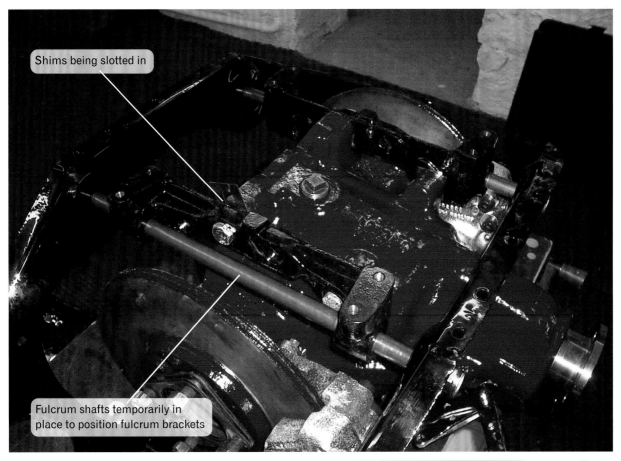

Shims being slotted in

Fulcrum shafts temporarily in place to position fulcrum brackets

Locking wire

3.3-4 *Left: The half shaft with new UJs fitted. The fulcrum brackets have been torqued up and fitted with locking wire*

inside became dislodged and got stuck under the bearing cap. It took me ages to undo it all again and sort it out.

This time I was determined not to let it happen again. So I greased the needle rollers heavily, to keep them in position, and set to work, carefully. Having successfully completed three of the four, I breezed into the final one and of course the needle rollers fell out and jammed under the bearing cap - again! Not only that, but this time the whole thing was well and truly stuck. I spent several happy hours attempting to get the joint apart which involved much use of heavy hammers and the

loss of the majority of my expensive powder-coating from around the shaft next to the UJ. It also led to two cracked floor tiles in the garage when I dropped the lump hammer on two occasions! My smallish vice also suffered as I managed to bend its operating arm whist trying to over-tighten it. The joint itself refused to budge. I therefore had to take it down to my local machine shop and had to pay about £60 for them to sort the whole thing out for me. Not good: a real bodge job in the true tradition of back street mechanics.

When the half shafts were finally ready to be attached to the differential - after patching up the chipped paint with Hammerite - I refitted the shims between the discs and the half shafts in the same order as they had been removed. In this case, there were a lot of shims - about six per side although I knew I'd probably have to adjust the shims when the car was finished due to the new differential and bodyshell.

One of my two most useful workshop tools came into play for this

– my freezer bags! I have three boxes of different size, re-sealable freezer bags on hand. These are great for keeping parts in. They are plastic and therefore don't rot and don't leak oil, etc. They are transparent so you can see what's in them, and they're re-sealable which is very handy and means that damp can't get in. Use a black marker to write the contents of the bags on the outside and you've got the perfect storage system! My other most useful tool is kitchen towel – use it once and throw it away – great! No more oily rags.

Having extricated my shims from their 'high tech' storage, I bolted the shaft to the disc using special dome-shaped locking nuts. These special nuts called *Klevelock* are locking nuts but without the normal plastic inside, as this may melt with the heat generated by the rear brakes. See Photo 3.3-3. The half shafts were now in position (see Photo 3.3-4) and it was time to turn my attention to the rear shock absorbers – surely an easy job!

Lessons learnt:

- Always, always, always label everything up as you remove it and put it into proper storage freezer bags!
- I may be older and wiser now, with more money and equipment than I had before, but I can still bodge it with the rest of them if I try hard enough.
- When replacing such items as UJs, etc., always use high quality parts, as cheaper parts can be a false economy – you only want to build the axle once.
- Use *Klevelock* nuts to attach the half shafts to the discs.

Examples of shims and heat-resistent locking nuts that must be used **3.3-5**

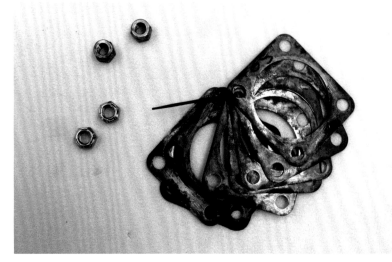

3.4 Refitting The Rear Shock Absorbers

My next job on the rebuild of my Series II FHC was a very simple one – on paper. All I had to do was fit the shock absorbers to the rear springs and then bolt these to the axle unit. The various manuals recommend using a special tool to fit the shocks to the springs – but surely I wouldn't need this? I'd fitted more shocks to springs than I'd had hot dinners, and all with a simple pair of spring compressors. Special tool my foot! How many times had I thought I'd need a special tool for some job or other only to be told that it wasn't really necessary and there were ways round it? Surely this was just such a case.

First of all, I had to choose which shocks to fit. There were four basic choices: standard, Konis, Gaz or Spax. I immediately decided against standard

as I wanted a superior quality ride. So the choice was between the last three. I then discounted the Spax shocks as I'd had them fitted to several vehicles in the past and I didn't think much of them. This left the choice between the Konis and the Gaz. The Konis were what I might describe as old technology, the Gaz new technology. The Konis look rather old-fashioned and uninspiring, whilst the Gaz are much more modern and hi-tech in appearance. However, in the end I plumped for the Koni Classics. Why? Because they were tried, tested and trusted technology. I'd heard of the odd problem with Gaz shocks and, although they might well be better than the Konis and the stories may be untrue, I stuck with the Konis as I knew what I was getting – not necessarily the best, but reliable. All I had to do now

was fit them to the coil springs.

I duly bought a new pair of sturdy looking spring compressors and set to work. I soon realised the problem with standard spring compressors on this application – they don't work. One problem is that you can't get the hooks of the compressor over the coils near the end of the springs as there's not enough clearance between the coils so the compressor clamps lower down the spring and then is only able to be tightened-up at a rather dangerous, twisted angle. When you do finally manage to compress the springs, the shocks won't slide down inside them as the clearance between the shocks and the springs is tight and, with the spring compressor attached to the springs, the shock absorbers foul on the hooks of the compressor.

3.4-1 *Left: Damaged shock during attempt at fitting*

New shock absorbers ready for fitting with powder-coated springs **3.4-2**

There were three ways round this that I could think of:

Grind the ends off the hooks on the spring compressor to allow the shocks to slide in.

Highly compress only the lower part of the spring as the bottom half of the shock is thinner than the top so you can just about fit the shocks in.

Hire a special tool and do the job properly.

I decided that the first option was too dangerous and the third option unnecessary; so I opted to compress only a small part of the spring (which was probably far more dangerous than option one) and off I went.

After several hours work, I did actually manage to fit one shock absorber and then managed to damage the second one quite badly – only

cosmetically, but this was not good (see Photo 3.4-1). I also didn't know if I needed to fit the adaptor ring supplied with the shocks or not as it is only used for some applications. I elected not to fit them and nearly caused myself serious injury when I discovered the whole tension of the spring was resting on a tiny ridge of metal and could have exploded apart at any time (see Photo 3.4-3).

After much angst and self-recrimination at my bungled efforts I finally rang Ken Jenkins to see if he could help. He couldn't have been more helpful and told me to bring the remaining shocks out to the workshop and they'd fit them for me – for free! I immediately went there and they pulled out their patent shock-fitting jig and, with the help of a compressed air socket drive, had the remaining three shocks fitted in less than five minutes (see Photo 3.4-4). It had taken me about two full days to fit one shock and damage another. No comment.

As I came to fit the shock absorber/spring assemblies to the axle unit, I was able to solve a long and infuriating

mystery. Some weeks before, I had taken various parts from the rear axle assembly to Brian Perkins at Prestige Electroplaters, near Barnsley (who happens to own a 1939 SS Jaguar 100, a 1949 MK IV Saloon, a 1953 XK 120 Roadster and an immaculate 1963 E-type Series I 3.8 roadster). When I got all the bits back, there were two circular spacers left over and I had absolutely no idea where they went. I studied the manuals and in particular the exploded diagram of the rear axle assembly for hours and hours – nothing. I knew they went somewhere – but where? WHERE? In the end I had to swallow my pride and took them with me to the workshop and was forced to ask the question I'd been dreading asking; "Erm, can anyone tell me what these are and where they go?" They were immediately identified as spacers on the wishbone shaft that the bottom of the shock absorbers bolt to. This spacer enables removal of the radius arm without the need to fully dismantle the wishbones (see Photo 3.4-5 from later in the assembly process).

Why couldn't I find these spacers

in the manuals? Because it's a modification made for Series II cars and so isn't *in* the manuals! I now realise that there is no such thing as a Series II manual. All the manuals are based around Series I cars (including the exploded diagrams) with updated sections on major alterations, e.g. the braking system, but with no references to minor alterations. There are infuriating gaps when the information simply isn't there at all for the later cars. If you have a later model, you need to be aware of this as there are quite a few anomalies that suddenly make sense.

Derek nonchalantly fits the new **3.4-4**
shocks in seconds using his
bespoke fitting jig

Lessons learnt:

- If it says you require a special tool for a job, then it means you require a special tool for that job.
- I now photograph all parts, clearly labelled, before sending them off to the platers (the wonders of digital photography!) so I have some idea when, several weeks later on their return, what on Earth they are and where they go. This is especially true when taking in whole bags of assorted nuts and bolts for instance, or lots of small parts from different bits of the car.
- There is no such thing as a Series II workshop manual.

Shocks and springs fitted – with **3.4-5**
mystery spacer!

It goes here!

3.5 Ordering Replacement Parts

You also need to be aware that there's no such thing as simply a Series I or a Series II or Series III car as alterations/improvements were made continually throughout production. An early Series II car is therefore very different from a late Series II. Knowing the date of manufacture and engine number, etc., is consequently important when ordering parts. Not being aware of this when I first owned the car caused problems as, when ordering parts, I couldn't understand why I sometimes received completely different parts than the ones fitted to my car, e.g. heater and choke decals, not realising that they changed during the production run. See the list of production changes in the back of the book *Jaguar E-type - The Definitive History* by Philip Porter for further details.

One virtually indispensable aid to ordering parts that I only discovered towards the end of my restoration is the E-type parts manual on CD-Rom. If you can use this or the parts books produced by some of the big parts suppliers to source part numbers before ordering, everything is so much simpler – less time spent on the phone to salesmen who are desperately trying to work out what part it is you actually want: "The thingamabob on the end of the thermostat whatsit" doesn't go down too well. Even when they have ascertained what part it is you want, they then have to find the part number so that by the end of the call you've doubled the cost of the part in phone charges alone. More time (and expense) can then be spent sending the wrong parts back, etc., etc., and much frustration as you can't do anything until the correct part arrives by which time the period you'd allocated for working on the car has gone.

Restoring an E-type is exceedingly expensive and frustrating without making it unnecessarily worse!

Lessons learnt:

- There is no such thing as *a* Series I or *a* Series II car, etc. – they're all different.
- Try and find the part number before ordering – you know it makes sense!

3.6 Fitting The Lower Wishbones

Time to fit the lower wishbone shafts. The main problem with this is the myriad of spacers, collets and seals that slot together around the inner fulcrum shaft. When I'd dismantled the whole assembly, the manual had said not to worry about all these as they'd be replaced anyway. As a result, I'd allowed myself to be lulled into a false sense of security and had merrily pulled the thing apart without too much attention to all the little bits. It's all too easy to read something like that in a manual and believe it because you want to believe it. Checking everything carefully as you dismantle it is so much harder and less fun.

In keeping with this orgy of destruction, I'd then thrown a few of these 'little bits' away together with the tons of crud and grease that was left on the garage floor after dismantling was complete. Not only that, but when I came to reassemble the wishbones I had little idea how it all went together as I'd expected clear, detailed notes in the manuals – but they were not there! Remember, take as many photos as possible of the dismantling procedure of any parts.

With the shafts nicely powder-coated, I began to try and make sense of all the spacers and shims, etc. There are a lot of them and it's very confusing! (see Photo 3.6-1 – the paper towels are there to stop any bits getting in to the new roller bearings - see Photo 3.6-5) I'd even had some of the spacers nickel plated as I wasn't sure what they were or where they went when I'd finished dismantling the whole thing and so had them plated with some other

parts in error. It was at this point that I realised I needed all of the bits that I'd thrown away and that there had been absolutely no need to replace them in the first place. The only parts to replace are the roller bearings inside the wishbone and the oil seals which fit inside some of the spacers. I therefore had to needlessly buy seven spacers at £3.00 each.

I eventually worked out how all the spacers and oil seals fitted together. Basically there's a big disc spacer and a spacer in two parts with an oil seal in the middle on each side of the bearings – four in all (the manuals aren't very helpful here – probably because they assume you've thrown them all away!) I assembled the two-part spacers and oil seals on the wishbone shafts, holding them in place with grease (see

3.6-1 *Left: All the shims and spacers for the inner wishbone shafts. The roller bearings have already been inserted in the wishbones*

Photo 3.6-2), offered the wishbones up to the cage and inserted the disc-shaped spacers which fit either side of the fulcrum bushes. In the middle, between the fulcrum bushes, go two long spacers (seen at the bottom of Photo 3.6-1) When the whole caboodle was lined-up in the cage, the fulcrum shafts were tapped through, so fitting the wishbone shafts in place. This all sounds so simple writing it down now, but actually fitting the fulcrum shafts took about five goes to get right as various spacers inevitably fell out during the assembly process and holes invariably didn't line-up, etc. But, with a little patience, it was finally all back together. See Photo 3.6-3.

One mistake I actually avoided which the manuals don't tell you about was not putting the wishbones on the wrong way round, facing backwards. The brackets for the radius arms should face the front of the car but there's nothing to stop you putting them on facing backwards and then having to take them all apart again and reassemble them correctly.

It's at this point that I feel compelled to share with you one of the books I've read that have had a profound effect on me for one reason or another. In this case it's *Zen and the Art of Motorcycle Maintenance* by Robert M. Pirzig. In this inspired novel he chronicles a journey (in more ways than one) by himself and his son across America on a motorcycle. If you're at all interested in mechanics and epic travels, then this is a must read. (However, be warned, the first half of the book is great, the second half of the book is incredibly complex philosophy that is pretty impenetrable stuff)

I mention it now because one of his mantras sticks in my mind and often helps in infuriating situations. It's quite simply this: if you put something together and it's wrong or you've missed a part out, or assembled it backwards, etc., don't worry. Take it

3.6-2 *The roller bearings inserted in the wishbone with the two-part spacers and oil seal covering them*

Wishbones now back in position on the fulcrum shafts with all spacers, etc., in position **3.6-3**

all apart and rebuild it again. As it's the second time you've done it, you'll complete the job in half the time and you'll understand the workings of that particular part so much more clearly. This simple axiom has often enabled me to remain calm when faced with an, "Oh, no. I'm going to have to take it all apart again!" situation.

Anyway, the final job was the radius arms and my newly-assembled rear shocks. The rear radius arms were fitted with new *metalastic* bushes to both ends. This was despite the fact that I'd had them replaced a few

months before taking the car off the road. The steering had been so out of line that, as a result, at least two of the bushes had begun to disintegrate with the added stresses put on them. The large bushes that go in the wider end of the radius arms that bolt to the body can be fitted in one of two ways.

There are small oval holes in the bush to enable it to have a little 'give'. If these holes are mounted along the line of the car (as recommended by Jaguar and as can be seen on my car in Photo 3.6-4), the ride is more compliant. Those wanting a sportier feel to their car can fit them across the line of the car which therefore provides a harsher but tauter ride. I wanted a more comfortable car for long distance European cruising – hopefully! – which is why I decided on the softer option. Note the spacer next to the bottom of the shock absorber on the right in Photo 3.6-4 – those are the little devils that had me flummoxed earlier when I had no idea what they were on their return from the electroplaters. This spacer means there is just enough room to get at the bolt that holds the radius arm on without dismantling half the rear suspension when the unit is on the car.

May your wishbones never be assembled backwards!

3.6-5 *The new needle roller bearings being inserted into the wishbone. Note: Ensure there is no old grease or dirt in the hole for the grease nipple as this will be injected into the bearing as soon as you grease the assembly later on*

Lessons learnt:

- Never throw **ANYTHING** away until you either have the replacement in your hand or are sure you don't need it.
- If you're having your wishbones, etc., powder-coated, ensure they leave all bearing surfaces/threads, etc., uncoated.
- Try not to get completely carried away in an orgy of dismantling, but stop and take pictures as you progress – it's amazing how much info isn't actually in the manuals and a few photos can help a lot.
- Happiness is reassembly.

3.7 The Rear Hubs

So, it was time to sort out the rear hubs. This was a job I had been awaiting with some trepidation. All I knew was that I needed end-float and pre-load - but exactly what were they, where were they used and how did I go about measuring them? It turned out to be relatively straightforward in the end, although obtaining some of the measurements proved difficult.

Basically there are two sets of bearings in the hub carrier, the main ones for the rear hub (axle) and a smaller set at right angles to the axle which enable the hub to rotate slightly (around the outer fulcrum shafts) as the rear suspension goes up and down. The axle bearings require end-float and the fulcrum bearings require pre-load.

End-float simply means that the bearings are slightly loose with a little play in them and pre-load means that the bearings are slightly tight with a little pressure on them. There is, of course, a set amount of end-float and pre-load which is measured by the use of feeler gauges and digital vernier calipers, and then physically set with shims and spacers.

So, I merrily pulled the hubs apart – a particularly dirty job, as the hubs are literally full of grease. The bearing races for the stub axles were difficult to get out, as they were very tight. I therefore popped the hub carriers in the oven for a while (Gas mark 6 for 10 mins is recommended!) and as the carriers are alloy and therefore expand more readily than the steel races, the races just fell out. Egon Ronay recommended (with a Dunlop star?) but a dish best prepared when certain people are out for the day!

Having cleaned up the hubs, I took them to the local machine shop as I couldn't get the old bearing races off the shaft (see photo 3.7-3) so I thought I'd get them to assemble the axle at the same time. Having done this, I tried to set the required end float on the axle, which is obtained by measuring the difference between the bearing race and the inner axle shaft. When this has been measured, a spacer is added to ensure the correct clearance (between two and six thousandths of an inch). To obtain this reading I bought a digital vernier caliper. However, I found it virtually impossible to get a proper measurement because, to get an accurate reading, the caliper had to be vertical. If I accidentally tilted the instrument whilst measuring, the

3.7-1 *Left: Baking the hub carriers gently at gas mark 6!*

The new bearings for the hub/stub **3.7-3** *axle. Note the old bearing still on the stub axle that wouldn't come off and required the services of the local machine shop to shift it. They then assembled the hub for me with the new bearings in*

Attempting to measure end float **3.7-2**

reading changed dramatically (since we're dealing with thousandths of an inch). I also discovered that the reading wasn't uniform anyway and varied around the bearing; so getting an accurate reading was impossible.

Having finally settled on the most accurate reading I could, the whole process was rendered irrelevant anyway when it was pointed out to me that the bearings had been fitted too tightly by the machine shop and needed to be loosened. Loosening them slightly changed the whole reading and I had to start the whole process all over again.

I did get measurements eventually, but when the hubs were fitted with the requisite spacer and the rear wheels put on, the amount of play didn't seem right. I decided I would have to set them again, using trial and error, when I came to check the tracking/camber/toe-in/ride height at the end of the restoration as they both seemed to have too much play in them (which you can only really assess when the wheels have been refitted and you can rock them).

Incidentally, I was particularly worried about the camber angles/toe-in, etc., generally as the car was

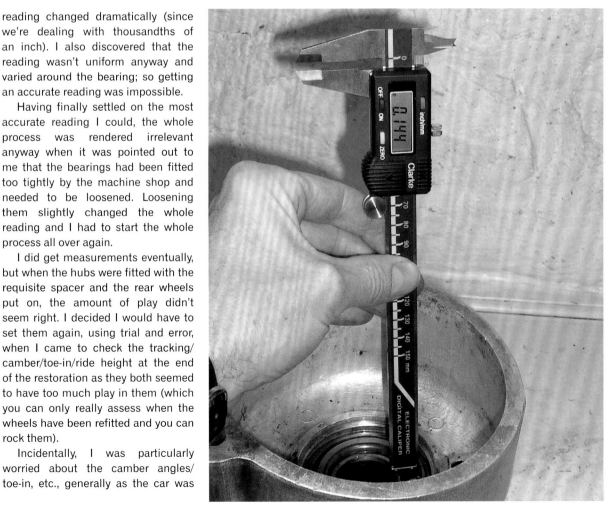

being assembled with new discs and a new differential in a different body shell. I feared that the final set-up of all the various adjustments wouldn't be too easy and much disassembly and changing of shims might be necessary (although I was looking forward to this as it would mean the car's nearly finished!).

The pre-load on the outer fulcrum shaft is easier to measure. You require a pre-load equivalent to one thousandth of an inch. To achieve this, bolt the shaft up with extra washers and spacers on the ends and with too many shims in the middle (see photo 3.7-5) and measure the gap left on the

outside. Remove shims to the value of the gap plus one thousandth of an inch and 'hey presto!' you have the correct pre-load.

One unexpected problem I encountered was with my feeler gauges. A tool as simple as this had me stumped. I kept getting the strangest of readings when I checked and double-checked my measurements. I simply couldn't understand it; sometimes the readings appeared accurate, at other times completely nonsensical – until the penny dropped. My feeler gauges are double sided, with imperial on one side and metric on the other. At times I was accidentally using the metric

3.7-4 *This is the order for reassembling the fulcrum shaft bearings*

3.7-5 *Fulcrum shaft made-up with extra spacers and washers to enable measurement of pre-load. Shims are inserted in the gap in the middle of the shaftrings*

gauges without realising it, hence the incomprehensible readings. (Doh!)

The hub was finally slotted onto the half shaft and bolted into position with shims either side to ensure that it was centred properly. See Photo 3.7-6 – note the use of the correct side of the feeler gauges! One slight modification made to the hubs was blocking off the 'breather' hole for the fulcrum shaft. Everyone I spoke to agreed that there was no good reason to have this and all it did was allow grease to escape when greasing the hubs. All I did was to screw a self-tapping screw into the hole and then snap the head off – hole blocked. See Photo 3.7-6 again. Finally, I fixed the rather odd looking UJ covers on the drive shafts with stainless steel hose clips and the rear axle unit was almost finished!

One general point I want to make is about nickel-plating and powder-coating. I decided at the start of the restoration to either plate or powder-coat *all* parts (or replace them with stainless steel where available/suitable) but there is a slight problem with this: if the parts are a bit rusty, all

Shims

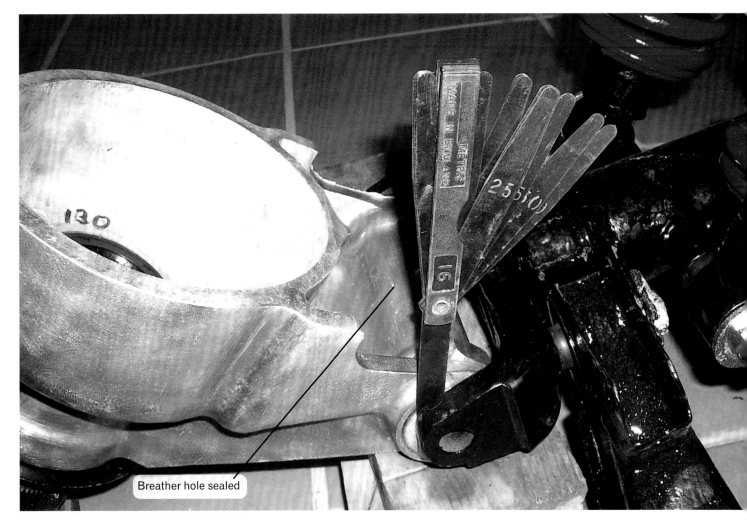

Breather hole sealed

Measuring the gap between hub **3.7-6** *carriers and wishbone so shims can be added to centralise the hub.*

the imperfections still show slightly on the powder-coating and very much on the nickel-plating, even if the parts have been grit blasted. If you want parts to look really good, you need to buy new ones and paint/plate them. This was particularly true of the UJ covers which were thin metal and very rusty. I had them blasted and then plated. The result was poor as the surface was so pitted. I therefore had them powder-coated on top to hide the worst. They're still not good but, as they're virtually invisible when on the car, it doesn't matter too much; my criterion was that they shouldn't rust in future. With more visible parts, it's advisable to buy new ones or they'll still look pitted. With chroming it's worse as the polishing process removes the pitting – along with most of the metal! This means, for instance, that bolt heads become rounded and a lot smaller size than they should be!

Lessons learnt:

- End float is used on the rear axle bearings and should be between two and six thousandths of an inch.
- Pre-load is used on the outer fulcrum shaft and should be minus one thousandth of an inch.
- You need a dial gauge to measure the end float properly (which I don't have).
- End-float is a straightforward principle but is hard to actually achieve (and I still haven't) although it's possibly best done by trial and error anyway.
- It is advisable to block-off the breather hole in the hubs to enable more effective greasing.
- Hubs loosen nicely at gas mark 6.
- Always triple check measurements – you might be using the wrong feeler gauges!

3.8 Back Axle Re-fitting

The rear axle unit was almost finished! All that remained to be done was to fit the handbrake operating mechanism, the bottom plate and the brake pipes. Fitting the bottom plate was pretty straightforward, it was just a case of ensuring all the bolt holes lined-up properly, which meant a certain degree of levering and gentle persuasion but, other than that, there were no problems. I used stainless steel nuts and bolts for this which, I think, should be strong enough to deal with any stresses in this area – time will tell.

The handbrake operating mechanism was slightly more complex. I'd dismantled it ready for plating and, as ever, on its return I couldn't work out how it all went back together. A quick visit to my local E-type garage and, a few photos later, all was well and the mechanism was bolted to the cage using stainless steel bolts. (One of the original bolts had rusted solid and the captive nut it screws into in the cage had broken free and was turning so I'd had to saw it off. I'd then had to break open the cover holding the captive nut, replace the little square captive nut with a new one and weld the cover back down again before having the cage powder coated). I also re-plated and re-fitted the handbrake lever inside the car, together with the handbrake cable so that, when the axle was fitted, I would be able to secure the car on the handbrake, as necessary.

I finally turned my attention to the brake pipes and fitted a new set of Kunifer pipes. The only real problem I had here was bending the pipes properly as my pipe-bending tool doesn't seem to be much good and some of the bends aren't quite as neat as I'd like them to be. I think maybe I haven't worked out how to use the tool properly. I also wasn't quite sure where to run some of the brake pipes but, as there doesn't appear to be any uniformity over this, I ran them where I thought best, ensuring that they weren't rubbing at any point. I also fitted extra remote bleed nipples on both calipers, near the bottom of the cage, to allow for easier bleeding. This seems to be a pretty standard modification that should work OK (note the word *should* here. In any situation to do with classic cars or anything mechanical *NEVER* use the word *will* until you have checked it is indeed working properly as you are

3.8-1 *Left: The completed back axle unit ready and waiting to be fitted. Note: the remote bleed nipples for the rear calipers on the lower front edge of the cage*

3.8-2 *The axle, held in place with a trolley jack and surrounded by numerous lumps of wood in case of accident, is slowly offered up to the body shell. The special 'V' mountings are already loosely bolted to the body*

simply courting disaster. This is also true of household plumbing, electrics and anything you're doing when your wife is watching!)

It was finally time to fit the axle to the body - a momentous occasion as it marked a milestone as this was the first major bit of reassembly to take place. I duly enlisted the help of Chris from next door for this. I'm not sure if it is possible to attach the axle to the body on your own, but I certainly wouldn't recommend it. We jacked the car up as high as we could to give us room to work (so important) and then manoeuvred the axle assembly carefully using a trolley jack and lots of wood until it was under the body. I realised just in time that one job that required to be completed before fitting the axle was to attach the petrol pipe

to the union through the rear body. I think it would be nigh on impossible to connect the pipe with the axle in place.

We decided that the best technique was to loosely fit all the Vee mountings to the body first (together with the original spacers - despite this being a different body shell, the spacers appeared to be required) and then mount the axle to them. This worked for us. Actually bolting the axle in position was difficult, but with a little patience, a variety of odd-shaped spanners, a carefully applied crow bar and various amounts of pressure on the trolley jack, it was finally in place. The crow bar also came in handy after we'd managed to tighten the final nut on one of the rear mountings with a ring spanner (by what seemed like

100th of a turn at a time, due to the restricted amount of space to move the spanner). Now that the bolt was finally tightened we couldn't get the spanner out! After various fruitless attempts, we simply applied subtle leverage with the bar in the right place and retrieved our spanner (the Vee mountings are rubber and therefore have just enough give in them).

One other item of note is the fitting of the bolts that hold the top of the shock absorbers in place. One school of thought is that the bolts should be fitted from the inside out so they can be removed with the cage in place. If they are fitted from the outside in, the bolt can't be removed as it fouls on the bodywork. As a result the shock absorbers can only be replaced by dropping the rear axle. I decided not to do this, however, as I thought that even with the bolts fitted from the inside it'd still be as hard to remove

the shocks in situ as it would be to drop the whole axle. Bolting the radius arms to the cups on the rear floor initially looked impossible, as they were nowhere near each other. However, applying the jack to the rear suspension and lifting the axle unit a fair amount worked a treat and they lined up without a problem.

The next job was to connect the handbrake, which I did, but, as you can adjust it in so many ways, I'm not sure it is at its optimum setting, although it seems to work OK. I finally bolted the rear anti-roll bar loosely in position. This will have to be fully tightened later when the full weight of the car is on it as otherwise the bushes could be damaged if it were tightened now. The best thing about the whole procedure was that the body shell suddenly began to look like a car again! Two wheels on my wagon!

3.8-3 *With the back axle in situ and the rear wheels back on the body shell, it suddenly started to look like a car again!*

Lessons learnt:

- The Jaguar rear axle assembly is incredibly heavy.
- Don't forget to fit the petrol pipe first.
- Having a friend on hand (preferably one with some mechanical aptitude) to assist with jobs like these is invaluable.
- Patience is a virtue (especially when trying to line up and bolt the rear axle to the Vee mountings).
- Don't tighten anti-roll bar bushes until they take the weight of the car.
- Never confidently announce that anything you're working on *will* work as you're courting disaster.

4.1 Time To Assess The State Of The Engine

There are times in life when everything goes smoothly and according to plan and the path ahead seems clear - and then there is the E-type engine. Why is it that just when you allow yourself to think the worst is over and that from now on everything's going to be straightforward, does the opposite apply? In the case of E-types, it's all to do with the fact that they're old and have often suffered so much abuse in the past, one way or another, and trying to undo previous attempts at 'restoration' is far worse than refurbishing a hitherto untouched car. And so it was in the case of my E-type engine.

When I bought the car, the engine appeared to be OK apart from a large oil leak from the cylinder head. I rather naively wasn't too worried about this

as I saw it as only one problem that was relatively easy to fix. (What I hadn't realised at the time was how significant such an oil leak was, both in terms of the health and usability of the cylinder head and as a sign of the poor health of the engine generally. Instead I'd just thought of it as an oil leak that could be fairly easily sorted.) I therefore decided to remove the cylinder head for inspection and rectification. At the time I didn't have the resources to do the job myself, nor the wherewithal to pay a decent garage to do the job, so my local garage did the work for me.

When they removed the cylinder head, they found that not only was the cylinder head badly warped (causing the oil leak), but the engine block was also cracked between several of the cylinders. The cracked engine

block was a very serious problem that could only be rectified by specialist machining with the engine out of the car and stripped down. Suddenly my simple cylinder head repair wasn't looking so simple or so cheap. The only course of action was to pay the garage to remove the engine from the car, strip it down and have the block mended. The engine was duly removed and we had the block stitched and skimmed as well as skimming the cylinder head to try and cure the original problem. See Photo 4.1-2 showing the engine out of the car in my local garage – almost as small as my own garage.

We also had the crankshaft reground as a matter of course as, with the engine out, it would have been a false economy not to have taken the opportunity. For the same reason I

4.1-1 *Left: An engine block in mid restoration with non-original core plug restraining straps in place*

My car in the local garage with **4.1-2** *the engine removed*

considered having the engine re-bored but it was judged that the cylinder bores were fine and didn't require re-boring even though they had never previously been re-bored and were still standard size. All that was deemed necessary was a new set of piston rings to bring the cylinders back up to scratch.

However, a set of standard size piston rings proved to be unobtainable and so a whole new set of standard pistons were called for! New timing chains, new valves, new valve guides and new bearings were also fitted throughout, as again not to do so appeared false economy. Removing and rebuilding the engine is such a major operation that a few (!) extra pounds spent on bearings, etc., is well worth it. The work was duly completed and afterwards the engine ran well with no oil leaks and good performance although it did still seem to use a lot of oil.

Following this engine rebuild, I had covered less than 3000 careful miles before taking the car off the road for my full restoration. So, I thought that the engine would still be in good condition and require little further work. My plan was, therefore, to simply strip the engine down to check all was well and then reassemble it. Unfortunately this wasn't to be.

On stripping down the engine, the first thing that became obvious was how much sludge and dirt there was in it. The bottom of the sump was covered in about ¼ inch of thick black sludge and the rest of the engine wasn't much better. See Photo 4.1-3. This level of dirt did not bode well, nor did the oily deposits on the piston crowns and on the back of the valves and the valve stems.

On further inspection it became clear that the engine was in a generally poor state. The dirt in the engine combined with poor workmanship during the rebuild had rendered many parts, old and new, useless. I went on to discover that the oil pump had a very stiff spot when turned. On taking it apart it was obvious that a relatively large foreign body had been sucked through the pump (which works on very tight tolerances) and had left large gouge marks in the rotor vanes on its way through. Needless to say, the pump was beyond repair. See Photo 4.1-4 of the damaged oil pump rotor. The newly ground crankshaft was scored (and full of sludge as it hadn't been cleaned out previously) and all the new bearings throughout the engine were already worn to excess.

Not only this, but the engine had obviously been burning a considerable quantity of oil. (I do remember seeing the odd cloud of blue smoke, but I was in denial - the engine had been so comprehensively rebuilt, it couldn't be burning oil, could it?) Further investigation revealed that while the cylinders appeared to be OK, although they were within tolerance at the top, they were oval and oversize at the bottom. A re-bore and another new set of oversize pistons were called for.

On removing the sump, it was found to be full of thick black sludge

Then came the really good news. In one of my manuals it says that if the XK engine has a weakness, then it is the cylinder head, which tends to warp due to overheating and general neglect of maintenance (rather reminds you of Triumph Stags, doesn't it?). On inspection of the head it was deemed that so much metal had been skimmed off the cylinder head in an attempt to stop the oil leak during the previous rebuild, (together with the skim of the block following repair of the cracked waterways) that the compression ratio was way too high for the engine to run properly, especially on today's lower octane fuels. The head was therefore deemed to be scrap. Oh, joy. In fact, the only part to survive from the previous rebuild were the timing chains that seem to have avoided the worst of the carnage. See Photo 4.1-5 of the dismantled head and pistons before I realised they were damaged beyond repair.

My idea of a quick strip-down, check and reassembly hadn't quite worked out. (No surprises there) Not only did all the parts I'd replaced and reconditioned before need to be replaced and reconditioned again, I also required a new oil pump and a little item called a cylinder head. So, who was to blame? Was it the garage I'd employed to rebuild the engine a few years ago, and who had obviously not done a proper job? In fairness, no, not really. At the time I'd been desperate to get the car driveable (it leaked so much oil that it was virtually un-driveable – although it passed the MOT without a problem) and I had no facilities to do the job myself and very limited funds available to pay someone else to do it for me.

The garage therefore had done what I'd asked – to rebuild the engine in order to stop the oil leak, without breaking the bank. They had also repaired essential items (the engine block), in order to get the car back on the road, but that was all. In retrospect it is easy to say that I should have had the engine rebuilt by a marque specialist in the first place who would have sorted it out properly. But as I didn't have the funds for such an undertaking, that's far easier to say than actually do.

The lesson here is a simple one: E-types are damned expensive cars to restore and maintain, but if you try to cut corners and do things on a budget, you are simply asking for trouble. I return once again to my motto: *Do the job once and do it properly*. Putting new parts in an old engine – or suspension, or braking system, etc., that has not been properly overhauled will always have the same result: the new parts won't cure the fault, they will wear out very quickly and the whole job will have to be done again, properly, in the near future.

 4.1-4 *The vanes of the oil pump are showing damage from a foreign body*

Lessons learnt:

- E-types are expensive, no matter how old or how new.
- Don't just put new parts into worn-out systems: they won't work.
- Cut corners at your peril.
- The cylinder head on the XK engine is a weak point.
- Remember how lucky you are to have such a character-building hobby!

My old cylinder head and pistons **4.1-5**
before being discarded

4.2 Rebuilding The Bottom End Of The Engine

After recovering from the rather bad news regarding the state of the engine, it was time to get on with (re)reconditioning it. The block was sent away to be re-bored (+20 thou. as there were/are apparently no +10 thou. pistons available) and the crankshaft was sent away to be reground (again) and balanced together with the flywheel, which was also lightened. The whole balancing/lightening process was an expensive one, but one that will hopefully be worth it in terms of the smooth running of the engine. I had the crankshaft sludge traps unscrewed and cleaned out as well, as this hadn't been done previously - needless to say they were full of sludge – and gave the oil ways a good clean as well. See Photo 4.2-1 of the reground, lightened, balanced and

4.2-1 *My reconditioned crankshaft in place with new sludge trap plugs fitted, sealed and centre-punched to keep them secure*

cleaned-out crankshaft.

At this point I also took the decision to fit a rear crankshaft seal conversion to enable the fitment of a proper oil seal in place of the original rope item. I knew that this involved irrevocable machining of the crankshaft to accept the new seal, which I thought was an acceptable modification if it meant an end to oil leaks from the rear of the engine. I should also mention at this point that I used engine assembly oil throughout reassembly as this is designed to provide the best protection for the engine during initial start-up before oil pressure is established.

However, what I didn't realise at the time was that, even with the machining of the crankshaft, it is necessary to cut the new seal in half to enable it to be fitted over the flywheel flange and is

4.2-2 *Lefy: My new rear crankshaft oil seal in place with ends SuperGlued together*

My lovely new pistons with con **4.2-3** *rods attached, waiting to be fitted to the engine*

then Super Glued (yes, Super Glued!) together again when it is in place, thus making this modification a lot less clear cut than I had thought. Apparently it has been known for the new seal to fail spectacularly when the rebuilt engine is restarted requiring the whole engine to be stripped down again. There's no way of knowing if the seal is OK before this. I was now looking forward to restarting the engine with some trepidation! Anyway, whatever the case I've now got an engine that is in some small measure held together with Super Glue! Would I have made this modification if I'd fully understood the potential problems to begin with? Well, 3000 miles on and all appears well - great relief. See Photo 4.2-2 of the fitted oil seal conversion.

I then weighed all the con. rods with a view to balancing them but discovered that they were in fact already nearly identical in weight. I was ready to shave a little metal from the bottom of the rods, but this proved unnecessary. The block returned from machining and I was surprised to find that the bores required extensive cleaning before the pistons could be refitted as they were covered in fine filings from the re-bore. Without cleaning, the engine would have suffered extensive premature wear. The new +20thou pistons (see Photo 4.2-3) were fitted

after I had gapped all the new piston rings by placing them in the cylinder bores and checking the gap in each ring with feeler gauges. See Photo 4.2-4. The crankshaft was refitted with all new big end and main bearings. See Photo 4.2-5 of my old big end shells after only 3000 miles. I decided to fit new big end bolts (later type ones from an XJ6) to be on the safe side as the originals were by now looking a little tired. Finally, the distributor drive and

4.2-4 *Gapping the piston rings by inserting them in the top of the cylinder and filing the ends down as necessary*

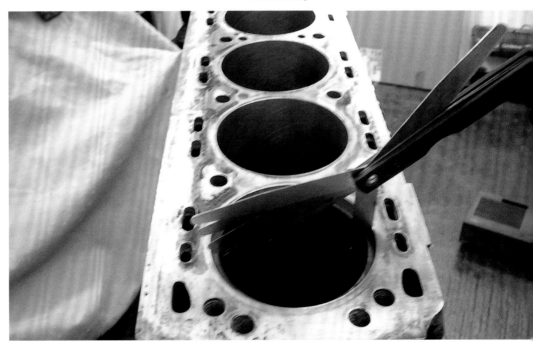

oil pump were fitted with the requisite pipework and the bottom end was finished. See Photo 4.2-6.

I then trial-fitted the sump – and it wouldn't fit. It just didn't sit on the block properly. For a while I was stumped. I looked at it several times, but all seemed to be in order – until I finally realised my error. I had fitted the oil pump feed pipe incorrectly. If you look carefully at Photo 4.2-7, you can see that I've fitted the central pipe clip upside down so the pipe's further away from the crankshaft than it should be. Simple errors like this can induce major puzzlement and make one worry that you've made similar errors that haven't yet been discovered.

While working on the bottom end, I discovered that, as mine was a later Series II engine, I could apparently fit an up-rated front crankshaft seal from a later XJ6. If you look at Photo 4.2-11, you can see the new seal at the top, which includes an up-rated outer seal with an inner 'O' ring seal to provide a superior seal, and the original underneath.

Next up was the timing chain assembly. All that was required was to replace the various chain tensioners including the hydraulic chain tensioner

4.2-7 *The crankshaft and oil pump in place - with incorrectly positioned oil feed pipe*

A standard spanner adapted to **4.2-8** *reach the timing chain tensioners*

as a matter of course. The only problem here was getting at the nuts holding the lower tensioner in place – they are situated directly behind the timing chains and there is no way an ordinary socket or spanner will reach them. I was fortunate enough to be able to borrow a spanner that had been carefully bent at right angles to create a cranked spanner enabling the nuts to be tightened with the guide in the correct position. See Photo 4.2-8. I then fitted a later type hydraulic tensioner, which was a direct replacement for the earlier type. See Photo 4.2-9 of the chains and tensioners loosely in place.

I polished the timing cover and fitted it to the front of the engine together with the original water pump which I deemed to be good enough not to require replacing, and prepared to fit the sump. For the second time, the sump wouldn't fit. This time because my new front 'wonder seal' on the crankshaft from an XJ6 would in fact *not* fit when I was informed it would. Why not? Probably another anomaly from Jaguar. According to the engine number, the seal should have fitted, but then my engine should also have the timing pointer on the side of the sump (late Series II FHC without power steering) not at the bottom where mine most definitely is. It's just another of those little anomalies that no-one can really explain and was probably due to there being a few spare sumps/

The timing chains and tensioners **4.2-9** *in place on the engine*

crankshaft pulleys from slightly earlier power-assisted cars being used up on the day my engine was built.

Anyway, whatever the case the new seal became squashed and deformed as I tightened the sump, so the whole lot had to come off again to fit a standard seal. See Photo 4.2-10 of the sump refitted but with a crushed front oil seal. Luckily I had elected to only put gasket sealant (I used Blue Hylomar throughout the engine) on one side of the gasket in case they ever needed to be taken apart again (in this case rather sooner than I'd bargained for), so this was a relatively straightforward job. I was also able to at least retain the later machined bush with the 'O' ring inside it. See Photo 4.2-11 of the old and new front oil seal. Finally, I painted the block with some special engine paint and fitted a new set of core plugs which I cemented in place with Araldite.

The engine was now beginning to come together and it was time to turn my attention to the little matter of the cylinder head, which took more time and effort to get right than all the other parts of the engine put together.

4.2-10 *Sump fitted with later type front oil seal which didn't fit*

The new later type oil seal **4.2-11**
assembly at the top of the picture together with extra internal oil seal; the old original oil seal assembly is shown below

Lessons learnt:

- If you're going to fit a modification, make sure you know exactly what it involves, what the pitfalls might be and whether or not it's reversible.
- Just because a part is supposed to fit your car, it doesn't mean that it will.
- You need a cranked-head spanner to tighten the lower timing chain tensioner.
- If something doesn't look right or it doesn't seem to fit properly, it usually means there's something wrong.
- My engine is held together with Super Glue!

Dunlop Aquajet - the right radial for your E-type

Jaguar chose the rain-defying, road-hugging Dunlop SP Sport Aquajet as the original-equipment radial for its astonishing E-type. The Aquajet is still made in England and is available exclusively through Vintage Tyres.

Branches at Beaulieu and Bicester Heritage.

VINTAGE TYRES
FOR CARS AND BIKES FROM THE 1890s TO THE 1990s

EST. 1962

★ Trustpilot ★★★★★

01590 612261   sales@vintagetyres.com   vintagetyres.com

AVAILABLE IN 185VR15 AND ER70VR15 (205/70VR15) SIZES.

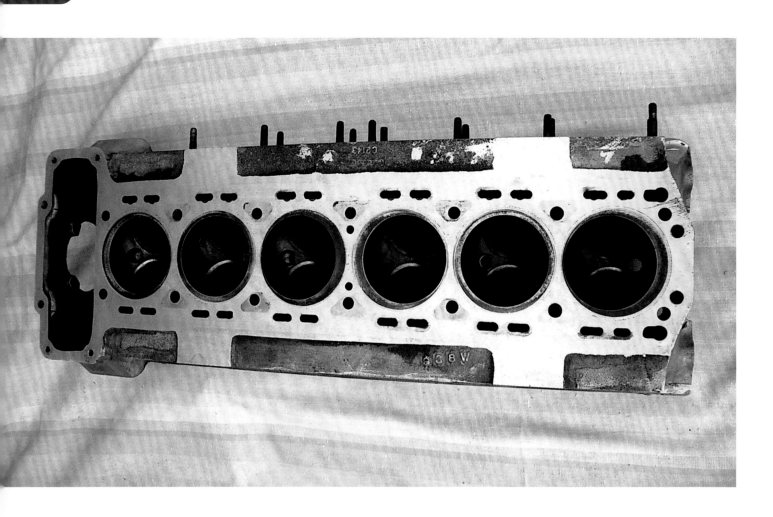

4.3 The Cylinder Head

With the engine block generally finished and the timing chains in place, it was time to turn my attention to the cylinder head. My old head (which I'd previously had completely reconditioned) had been consigned to the scrapheap as too much metal had been skimmed from it in an attempt to straighten it, which in turn meant that the compression ratio would be too high. I therefore sourced a decent second-hand replacement head which I think was for a slightly later car (an XJ6 possibly?) but which definitely fitted my engine block – a later Series II engine with two extra holes at the rear of the head to improve cooling. See Photo 4.3-1 of my old cylinder head and Photo 4.3-2 of the replacement one – at this point the old one looks a lot better than the new one before it was dipped and cleaned. However, if you look closely at Photo 4.3-1, you can see that so much has been skimmed off the face, metal has been taken off the main casting.

This second head needed reconditioning itself and so it went off to the machine shop to be skimmed and to have new valve guides fitted. When it returned, I have to say that I was slightly dismayed to find that it, too, had required a substantial amount of metal to be skimmed from the bottom face in order to get it flat, but not as much as my previous head, and it was deemed to still be within acceptable limits. The engineers had also checked the alignment of the camshaft bearings on top of the head, as these sometimes need re-machining as well (if a head warps, the whole head can twist, including the camshaft bearings which then have to be re-machined) but they were apparently OK on my head and didn't require any work.

I also had the head dipped in a caustic solution to get it clean. However, on retrieving the head I wasn't happy with the cleanliness of it and spent many, many hours polishing it up with a variety of proprietary cleaners, most of which proved ineffective. In retrospect I should have had the head bead blasted (vapour blasted?) which would have saved a lot of unnecessary work. I also painted the top of the head silver, which was the correct colour for my car. In this instance, I wanted to use special paint specifically designed for this application, but it proved to be temporarily unobtainable so I used Hammerite instead which I hope will

4.3-1 *Left: My old cylinder head after skimming, showing just how much metal required removing to get it flat*

My replacement (second-hand) **4.3-2**
cylinder head before fettling

last. (3000 miles on and it still seems OK)

I then set about re-fitting the valves. Firstly, I ground the valves in using fine grinding paste and then fitted my existing valves (which were almost new) to the head. This proved to be a fairly straightforward task, although locating the collets was rather fiddly. When all the valves were in place, I began the task of setting the required tappet clearance. I'd never actually set tappets on an overhead cam engine before and I was quite wary – if I'd have known what was to come I'd have been a lot more than just wary!

Firstly, I replaced nearly all of the tappets with new ones as they were showing signs of wear on their tops. I then fitted the inlet and exhaust camshafts in turn to measure the clearance and add the appropriate size shim to effect the correct clearance. As my engine was a later one with later camshafts (as signified by a groove cut round the ends of each shaft), it was deemed by various experts I consulted that the following clearances were required: 10 thou. Exhaust and 8 thou. Inlet. These figures are much lower than those stated in the manuals, so I hope they're OK! (Again they seem to be fine 3000 miles on) Trying to set the correct tappet clearance was where the problems began.

I measured all the clearances and found that many of them were so small that even with the smallest shim fitted (they go up in 1 thou. increments from 85 thou. to 110 thou.) the clearance was way too small - so small, in fact, that I had to keep taking the camshaft off and putting it back on again as I could only measure one valve at a time using a rogue 70 thou. shim that had apparently been specially machined to fit my old engine. I also found that,

4.3-3 *Removing tappets is made easy with a magnetic tool*

The source of all my troubles - the original tappets on the left and the replacement (thicker) tappets on the right

by moving the actual tappets around between valves, I was able to increase the clearance on the exhaust valves to within tolerance.

But what of the inlet valves? They all had too small a clearance for me to fit any size of proper shim. So, what to do? I enquired about getting some more thin shims made to fit my car, as with the 70 thou. shim from my old head, but I was informed this wasn't a good option and that such custom shims would be hard to come by. It was then suggested that I could grind a little off the valve stems to increase the gaps. I therefore removed the inlet valves and duly ground a little from the tops with a bench grinder. The results were clearly disastrous. Firstly, the tops were no longer flat and smooth, but were ground at irregular angles (I would have needed a lathe to get them truly flat) and secondly it dawned on me that valves are case hardened (or chill hardened?) so by grinding them down I had removed this hardened layer rendering the valves useless. Those who had advised me on this course of action quickly confirmed this and apologised for giving me such flawed advice. I bought another complete new set of inlet valves and fitted them - but the shimming problem remained.

Finally, and after much work fitting and re-fitting valves and camshafts, the cause of the problem dawned on me. Some of the clearances were OK, but not others and some clearances which initially appeared to be OK suddenly weren't, and vice-versa. So why was this? What was the common denominator?

A shim being fitted to the top of the valve stem. Shims go up in thickness from 85 thou. to 110 thou.

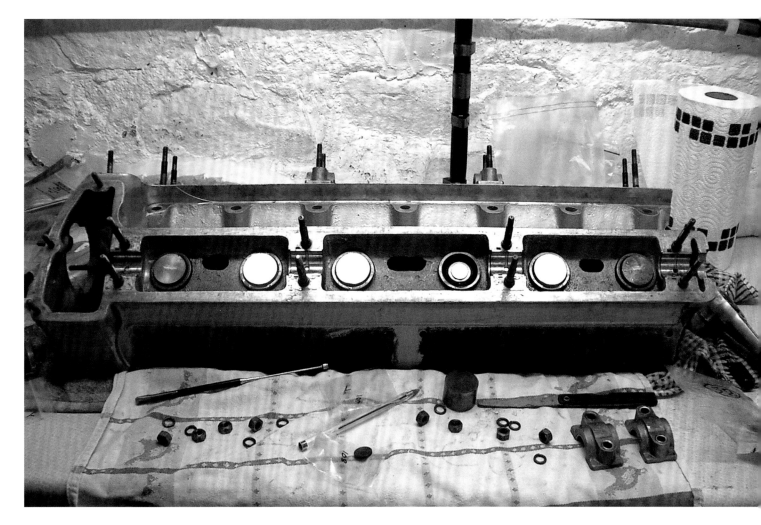

It was the replacement tappets!

I had already discovered that by moving the tappets round between different valves the clearances changed dramatically. I then realised that the clearances were within tolerance with the old tappets, but not the new. The replacement tappets were not original old stock but had been remanufactured and obviously made to the wrong specification - a little bit thicker than the originals - and it was these that were the problem. I sourced some decent second-hand original tappets and 'hey-presto!' the problem was solved and all valves were suddenly within tolerance. See Photo 4.3-4 of the old and new tappets (upside down for the sake of the photo). I finally fitted the requisite shims to the valves and the head was eventually ready to be fitted to the block. See Photo 4.3-5 of a shim in place on top of the valve before the tappet is fitted over it. Each shim is stamped with its thickness.

This whole episode had been infuriating, dispiriting, time-consuming and annoying (I lost count of the times I had to assemble and then remove the camshafts from the head) but at least I'd solved it in the end and I'd learnt a lesson regarding remanufactured parts: they're generally good quality and fit well, but not always!

4.3-6 *Fitting the tappets and shims to the head*

Lessons learnt:

- If something isn't right, don't try to sort it by short-cut solutions (such as doing stupid things like grinding the heads off valves). Find the cause of the problem and sort it properly.
- Replacement (non-original) parts are a great boon to the restorer – but check they fit properly first.
- Patience is most definitely a virtue.
- Take the advice of experts, but ultimately you have to make your own choices/decisions.
- Use a magnetic tool to remove tappets from the head.
- Finally solving an infuriating problem is very satisfying.

4.4 Fitting The Cylinder Head To The Engine

With the cylinder head completed, it was time to fit it to the engine block. This involved fitting the cylinder head studs, tightening the head down and setting the valve timing. I had eventually finished setting the tappet clearances and, having done so, both camshafts were fitted for the final time (I must have fitted each one at least 20 times previously during my efforts to set the tappets), roughly in Top Dead Centre position – as denoted by the notches in the camshafts for the setting tool (full details below) – and from then on they could not be rotated to prevent inlet and exhaust valves fouling each other.

I finished fitting the cam chains with their new guides and tensioners and held the camshaft sprockets temporarily in place with clips (see Photo 4.4-1). I then fitted the timing cover, water pump and associated pulleys. The 'P' clips holding the camshaft sprockets in place allowed me to rotate the engine (after a fashion) without the timing chains getting tangled up – although I did still manage to achieve this when one of the chains jumped its sprocket (no tension on the chain) without my realising and jammed itself solid down inside the timing cover. Carefully turning the engine backwards and judiciously pulling on sprockets and teasing links out one by one eventually remedied the situation.

I then fitted the cylinder head studs. Much has been said about studs and their suitability for such a job – they are subjected to massive stretching forces and intense heat, and are permanently immersed in coolant. (Being a later engine, mine is known as a 'long stud' engine as the studs go right down through the block, as opposed to a 'short stud' engine where the studs screw into the top of the block and do not go down through the waterways. I believe the longer studs reduce stresses in the engine block) All I can say is that when the engine had previously been rebuilt, some 3000 miles previously, I had had new studs fitted from a reputable supplier. Since then I had scrupulously maintained the correct mixture of antifreeze and water in the engine. However, if you look at Photo 4.4-2 you can see quite clearly how one of the studs had seriously corroded – all the other studs appeared to be fine. I made a few enquiries regarding fitting up-rated studs as I

4.4-1 *Left: The camshaft sprockets held temporarily in place with 'R' clips*

A badly corroded cylinder head stud **4.4-2**

was sure I'd heard there were some available, but my efforts to track down these proved fruitless and I elected to use the original studs, replacing only the corroded one. I only hope that this was in some way a rogue stud and that they are now all OK.

Fitting cylinder head studs may appear to be a simple job, but isn't quite as straightforward as it first seems. The studs are supplied over length and have to be cut down to the required size on fitting. If there is too much stud showing above the cylinder head when you tighten down the domed cylinder head nuts the nut will simply tighten on the top of the stud, not the cylinder head, giving the appearance that it is torqued down when in fact it isn't. So when you think your cylinder head is nicely tightened down, it may in fact be loose. Conversely, if there is too little stud showing, there may not be enough thread to satisfactorily tighten the nuts down to such a high torque and the studs may either loosen or the threads give way completely.

On initially fitting the studs, I found a massive difference in the lengths of each stud, which coincided with how far the stud would actually screw into the block. Some studs screwed right down whilst others would only go in a few turns before binding. It took a lot of swapping studs round, getting them to seat as deeply as possible by screwing them in with the help of two nuts locked together, and cutting down

the new stud before they were all in place and all at the correct height. See Photo 4.4-3. It is worth noting that four of the studs are longer than the others as these have the lifting brackets fitted to them.

I fitted the head to the block and torqued the cylinder head nuts down, as per the manual. I torqued them down to 54 lbs knowing that I would later torque them down to 58 lbs when I'd run in the engine. My only problem was how to torque down the six nuts

The cylinder head studs finally in place **4.4-3**

on separate studs around the front of the engine (with copper washers underneath them), a couple of which I couldn't get a socket on, only a spanner. I therefore had to guess the torque of these. I still don't know how to get a torque wrench on to these nuts.

A big challenge came after I'd finally fitted the head to the engine, one that I'd been both relishing and fearing – setting the engine valve timing. I'd heard and read much about this procedure and was rather concerned as various people had told me how crucial it was to get it right. One of my main concerns was establishing Top Dead Centre (TDC) on number 6 cylinder (Why, oh why, did Jaguar decide to use their own numbering system and call the front cylinder No. 6 when everyone else – including me – calls it No. 1?) I can't tell you the amount of confusion it's caused me during the course of the engine rebuild as several times I've forgotten and fitted items in the wrong order or done some other silly thing.

I've had to make a big sign in the garage that says, "No. 6 at the front, No. 1 at the rear". Even writing this now, I still got confused and had to go back and change it! At this point Ken Jenkins, my local Jaguar expert, who had been following the restoration with interest, volunteered to come and help. This was a massive boon as I was now able to undertake the work with the confidence that with Ken there it would be completed properly. See Photo 4.4-4 of Ken working on the engine.

Having slightly tensioned the top timing chain, we set TDC using the timing marks on the crankshaft pulley. This meant that the camshaft sprockets were now in the correct position to bolt onto the camshafts. We then lined up the camshafts using the special setting tool (see Photo 4.4-5) so that they too were now in TDC position. The holes on the sprockets are then lined up with the threaded holes in the camshafts by the simple device that the camshaft sprockets are not one piece but two pieces held together on splines. With the two pieces apart, the centres of the sprockets can be rotated without rotating the outer sprockets with the chains on. When the holes in the sprocket centre line

4.4-4 *Ken Jenkins helps to set the valve timing*

The camshaft setting tool in **4.4-5** *position*

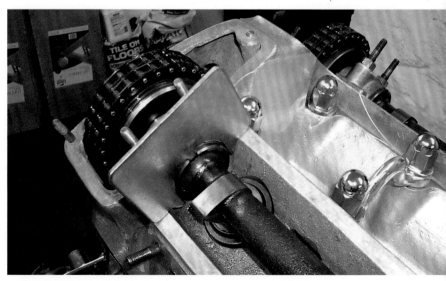

up with the threaded holes in the ends of the camshafts, the two pieces of the sprocket are re-engaged on their splines and bolts screwed through the sprockets into the camshafts – the camshafts and sprockets are now bolted together - at exactly TDC. See Photo 4.4-6 of the holes in the sprockets, ready to receive the fixing bolts.

Having successfully completed this

The inner section of the camshaft **4.4-6** *sprockets is rotated until the bolt holes line up with the camshafts*

4.4-7 *The entire engine was now beginning to take shape, being painted and plated, and with the cylinder head and water pump fitted - an item later found to be faulty*

4.4-8 *Cam covers were powder-coated and then the raised ribs were sanded down to expose the alloy which was then polished*

operation, we checked the tension on the timing chain and rechecked the timing on both camshafts. Everything seemed to be in line still so we tightened it all up, fitted locking wire to the bolts holding the sprockets onto the camshafts, and the job was complete. I subsequently polished and fitted the cam covers, which I'd had repainted. (On Series II cars you can get the covers powder-coated. They come back *covered* in paint. You then gently sand the ribs down to expose the metal and then polish this up – not quite the finish of a Series I cam cover, but not bad.) See Photo 4.4-8 from slightly later in the restoration.

By now the engine was actually beginning to look like an engine again. I must say that I was pretty relieved to have finished the engine rebuild. It had taken much longer and proved more difficult (and far more expensive!) than I'd anticipated with many unexpected problems. On the plus side, at least I knew the engine was now completely and properly reconditioned and I had learnt (if not mastered) how to rebuild an XK engine, including the mysterious art of setting tappets and valve timing on such an exotic and iconic piece of automotive history.

Lessons learnt:

- Cylinder head studs need to be fitted carefully.
- If you can find up-rated studs, I'd use them for peace of mind.
- When you torque down the head, follow the pattern in the manual. On my head I initially torqued the studs down to 54 lb f ft and I will re-tighten them to 58 lb f ft after the engine's done a few hundred miles.
- Cover your shiny, new, chromed cylinder head nuts with rag before tightening to avoid damaging the chrome.
- If someone with experience is available, use them – books and manuals are OK, but nothing beats having a real person in the garage with you to give help and advice as necessary.
- A metal-polishing kit was definitely one of my better buys.
- On Jaguars, No. 6 cylinder is at the front.
- On all other cars, No. 1 cylinder is at the front.
- Or is it the other way round (!!??).

4.5 Engine Ancillaries

With the main part of the engine now completed, it was time to turn my attention to the ancillaries: in this case, the carburettors and manifolds. My first problem was of my own making. In search of perfection, I decided to remove the two short pipes to the rear of the inlet manifold (one for water, the other for vacuum – I think there's only one on earlier cars, but I'm not sure) and get them plated. Although they screw into an alloy manifold, they were both seized solid. I eventually got the vacuum pipe out but, having finally found a long enough socket to fit the water pipe, it sheared off when I applied considerable force. Marvellous. See Photos 4.5-1 and 4.5-2 of the resulting mess. The machine shop that I had used in Sheffield for the previous 25

odd years suddenly closed down and, being unfamiliar with other engineers, I decided to have a go at removing the remains of the hollow tube myself.

I eventually got the remains out, but did considerable damage to the thread in the manifold at the same time. I purchased a new pipe and had both unions chrome plated. I've sealed the new one in with thread seal and ptfe tape, so I hope it'll be OK.* I also polished the inlet manifold using a polishing kit fitted to my bench grinder, and I'm rather pleased with the finish. It takes a bit of time to master metal polishing, but the results are worth it.

Meanwhile I turned my attention to the exhaust manifolds. What to do with them?

• Paint them.
• Have them re-enamelled (or buy new

ones already enamelled).
• Buy a set of stainless steel replacements.
• Have them ceramic coated.
• Have my existing ones plated.

I decided against painting because that wasn't permanent enough. I didn't go for the enamelled option because (rightly or wrongly) I was worried about them cracking if they got wet whilst hot. I was close to buying a set of stainless steel replacements but finally decided against this as: a) they are quite expensive, b) they don't increase bhp as the existing manifolds are quite adequate, and c) they tend to turn blue and don't look too good after a while. I enquired about having them ceramic coated (which looks good, keeps heat down significantly and

4.5-1 *Left: The inlet manifold with sheared off water pipe*

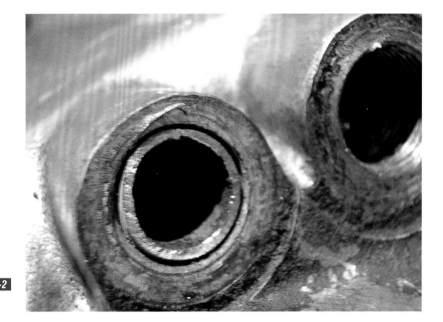

The remains of the water pipe **4.5-2**
firmly embedded in the manifold

My replacement exhaust **4.5-3**
manifolds blasted and
nickel-plated with stainless
steel studs fitted

doesn't crack) but this was also too expensive. So, I finally decided to have them nickel-plated. Brian Perkins at Prestige Plating showed me his E-type with plated manifolds and they didn't look too bad. The plating turns grey after a while, but still looks OK.

Nothing is ever straightforward, however, and the first thing that happened was that my exhaust manifolds were deemed to be scrap. Both sets had been welded at the bottom flanges where the studs to the down pipes fit and I was advised that the best thing to do was bin them. I was duly supplied with some good second-hand ones as a replacement. The

first thing I did was to have the studs replaced with new stainless steel ones at my newly-found alternative machine shop and then have the manifolds shot blasted clean, after which they were rushed to the platers as quickly as possible to try and prevent oxidisation and were duly plated. The result is good, but bear in mind that after the engine's started they will tarnish with the heat and turn a dull grey colour. See Photo 4.5-3 of the brightly plated manifolds.

I also replaced all inlet and exhaust manifold studs with stainless steel ones (available from SNG Barratt) although the lengths of the exhaust manifold

studs was something of a conundrum. They come in two sizes, short and long, but there's something like 13 long ones and 3 short ones. Where the three short ones are supposed to fit is something of a mystery. If there were 13 short and 3 long, this would make more sense: longer ones for the studs having the gearbox breather and dip stick attached to them. But the other way round, with 13 long and 3 short? No-one I spoke to could shed any light on the matter, so I bought another 3 long ones and had them all the same length. Sorted.

Finally, I rebuilt the carburettors. Firstly I had them all vapour blasted. Some people don't recommend this as

debris can be left in the fine cavities in the body of the carbs, but mine seemed to be OK on return from the blasting, and I also gave them a good session with carb cleaner to make sure. While the bodies were away being blasted, I was very busy with my metal-polishing kit on the dashpots.

I bought the requisite three servicing kits for the carbs (I was intending to buy the full rebuild kits, but was told that this was hardly ever required) and set about reassembly. See Photo 4.5-4 of one of the carbs awaiting reassembly together with the linkage system and a yet-to-be-plated petrol pipe. Using my various manuals, the instructions supplied with the kits and my extensive photos of the carbs being dismantled, I found the reassembly fairly straightforward (photos of what parts looked like before and during dismantling really *are* such a great help). However, there's one thing worth remembering: the float chambers are on the right on the front two carbs, but on the left on the rear carb. (I'm sure you can guess how I found that out!) Also it's important to establish which is the front carb as that has the vacuum take-off for the distributor fitted to it. A crucial check is to ensure the needles are centralised in the main jets, as otherwise even well reconditioned carbs will never work properly if they aren't. See Photos 4.5-5 and 4.5-6 of the completed carbs.

One slight modification I decided to

make in this area was to just use bell mouths with wire mesh (gauze) at the ends instead of the standard big air filter system. I've always loved simple bell mouths with gauze so I opted for these. I've always thought the big air box unsightly and ungainly. My belief that I didn't need a proper air filter was supported by the fact that I wasn't going to be doing that many miles and that anyway many of my old British motorcycles never had air filters fitted and they seemed to go OK.**

As ever, however, this wasn't as straightforward as anticipated. When

I received the new bell mouths, they were finished with rather cheap metal plates drilled with holes, similar to a colander, instead of having nice wire mesh over the ends. Not only this, but I was later advised that they didn't work too well at high speeds as the holes were too restrictive. As a result, I opted to fit open bell mouths, which have removable, foam filters. This will give me the best of both worlds, I hope, in that I can put the filters (socks) on for normal driving, but take them off if I want to show off my shiny new engine bay. See Photo 4.5-7 of the carb

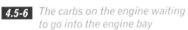

The carbs on the engine waiting to go into the engine bay

Different bellmouths with the **4.5-7** 'gauze' one on the left and the open one on the right

trumpets and the foam air filter and Photo 4.5-8 of the foam filters in place.

In order to facilitate this change, I needed to fit new jet needles of a slightly different size to standard. The recommended needle for running the engine without filters was an 'O' with an altered profile to cope with the increased airflow from open carbs.

With the carbs fitted to the inlet manifold the final job was to fit all the linkages for the throttle and the choke (pictures from an assembled car are very much a necessity here) and the job was virtually completed. I decided to chrome all the linkages and screws and springs on the carbs in order to achieve a quality finish. You can buy stainless steel linkages but these are very expensive and the chrome plating looks good. You will also almost certainly have to replace the bush on the main spindle where it sits in a bracket on the bulkhead. The original bushes aren't available but ones to fit a Series III (Stromberg) do the job. The spindle doesn't want to be tight in this bush (don't forget how much the engine rotates under load) but it doesn't want to be totally slack either.

*3000 miles on - so far so good

**Likewise, the carbs work well without the original air filter but are *rather noisy* - especially if you run the engine without the foam filters on!

The foam air filters in place over **4.5-8** the bellmouths. The logos stand for Piper Cross

Lessons learnt:

- If a stud can shear off, it generally will.
- There's no definitive answer to what to do with exhaust manifolds – the choice is yours!
- Rebuilding carbs is fairly straightforward, but do take pictures of the dismantling process to make life easier.
- Items you remember fondly from 30 years ago may no longer be available.
- Beauty is in the eye of the beholder.

5.1 Preparing The Bulkhead

With the engine block finished, it was time to sort out the bulkhead and gearbox, and get ready to refit the whole assembly to the body shell.

The first thing I did was to ensure that all the work required inside the bulkhead was completed. This included fitting the heater transfer pipes, the vacuum transfer pipes, the windscreen washer pipes and the windscreen wiper rack. It is very advisable to change the heater transfer pipes for new ones (preferably copper ones that are now available), as these pipes are virtually impossible to replace later on. I have been told that they were the first part of the car to be assembled on the production line when they were new and I can well believe this. Even with the body shell totally stripped, it's

really difficult to fit the pipes inside the bulkhead. One of mine had indeed ruptured previously and a rather ugly temporary rubber pipe going round the back of the engine had been used to replace it.

My car also has vacuum transfer pipes fitted in the bulkhead. These connect the brake servo unit with the vacuum tank and master cylinder. (A pictorial of this arrangement can be seen on Plate 34 of the *Series II Parts Catalogue*) These pipes only seem to have been fitted to certain cars, however, with some having the pipes running behind the engine, secured to the front of the bulkhead. Unfortunately, despite enquiring of several knowledgeable people, I still have no idea why different cars have different arrangements.

Pop rivets, which are hard to attach as the pipe itself gets in the way of the pop rivet gun, secure the pipes to the bulkhead, but I managed to fit them eventually. Ideally you should use a rivet gun with a long thin nozzle so it clears the pipe itself and allows you to ensure the pipe doesn't get in the way and the pop rivets are securely in place.

The next job was to fit the windscreen wiper mechanism inside the bulkhead. The wiper mechanism is a real struggle to fit, especially as you don't want to scratch your new paintwork! However, with a little coaxing it does go in – honest! Ensure that the little oval rubber seals under the wheel box escutcheons fit properly as they'll probably leak otherwise. Also first check that the various holes in

5.1-1 *Left: Not my car but this shot shows the wiper rack and one of the heater transfer pipes visible inside the bulkhead*

5.1-2 *Trial-fitting the engine frames to the bulkhead is very important as neither the bulkhead nor the engine frames will move! Note the absence of transfer pipes at this point - just holes in the bulkhead on this example*

You need to be completely certain that the washer nozzles are fully tightened in the correct position as trying to tighten or adjust them later on is a real nightmare 5.1-3

the top of the bulkhead (for the wiper escutcheons and washer jets) are large enough. I found that mine had closed up with the various layers of paint and filler applied whilst prepping the bodywork and needed to be carefully enlarged.

I had heard that you should fit rubber 'O' rings under the windscreen washer jets to stop them from working loose (as most people are no doubt aware, it's almost impossible to tighten them up later on). However, after consulting various experts, I opted to stick with the original fibre washer – although I broke one of the nipples trying to tighten them up too much – but do try and get them tight, and facing the right way! If you have to alter the direction of the jets later on you will almost certainly loosen them.

I decided to fit heat-reflecting matting to the inside of the gearbox tunnel in an effort to reduce the in-car temperature from the customary 'roasting' to a more comfortable 90º centigrade. I used self-adhesive reflective matting from a company called Agriemach Ltd (Tel: 0044 (0)1342 713743) which hasn't fallen off so far! (After 3000 miles I am happy to report that it is very effective and has remained firmly in place so I would definitely recommend it)

Lessons learnt:

- Ensure that all pipe work and preferably the wash/wipe system are fitted to the bulkhead before you do anything else to the body shell.
- With the engine out, you can fit such items as heat-reflecting matting to the gearbox tunnel.

5.2 Rebuilding The Gearbox

I then turned my attention to the gearbox. I took the decision to keep the original 4-speed box for the following reasons:

- The later E-type 4-speed boxes are good gearboxes.
- In order to convert to 5-speed, you either need to fit an old Getrag box or a much more expensive modern one such as a T5. Getrag gearboxes are, I believe, all second-hand from old BMWs and are rarely rebuilt due to the specialist equipment required. I have heard various stories of problems with them. New boxes such as the T5 are simply very expensive.
- Although having 5 speeds would be nice, I think that a well built 4-speed box will suit my requirements better than a potentially dodgy 5-speed.
- It is very difficult to fit overdrive units to shorter wheelbased cars. (Ideally I'd love 4 gears and an overdrive. I got used to this on my old Triumph Vitesse and I do miss it) In order to get them to fit, you have to enlarge the gearbox tunnel which isn't an easy job. I believe that there is room to fit them to 2+2s without altering the bodywork as they were made to take the larger auto boxes. The only modification required is to shorten the prop shaft.

I therefore decided to rebuild my old gearbox. This was another job that I was rather worried about tackling (along with the rear diff.), as I'd heard they were difficult to get right. I consulted Ken Jenkins and he immediately told me to get a specialist to recondition it for me, as I probably wouldn't get it right! (He obviously knew me better than I thought!) I didn't need telling twice as this was another job that I didn't have to do – I'd enough on as it was and this seemed an ideal excuse for me to lighten my workload.

The gearbox was duly despatched to a specialist and returned a month or so later looking very clean and hopefully as good on the inside as it was on the outside. The main drawback of this little departure was the £700 it cost to have it done, but it was a load off my mind. (The other problem is that now, after driving the car for 3000 miles, I am still having major problems with intermittent heavy oil leakage from the rear seal of the gearbox which no-one seems to know the cause

5.2-1 *Left: My original gearbox rebuilt by a specialist and mated to the engine with a new clutch assembly. Unfortunately the gearbox continues to give me problems*

5.2-2 *Rebuilding the gearboxes built by Moss and in-house by Jaguar is really a job for a specialist and not the DIY guy at home*

5.2-3 *This shot shows a Jaguar gearbox, minus the bellhousing. The Series II 'box was a great improvement over the very slow SI gearbox*

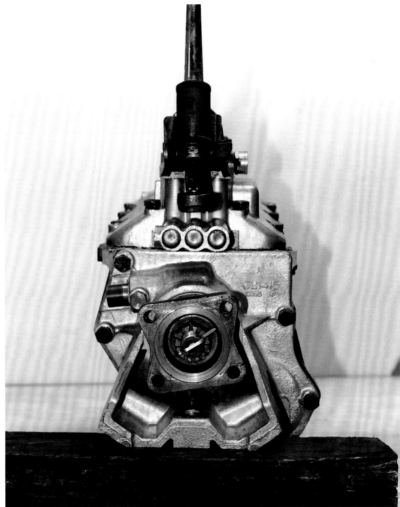

of – exceptionally bad news – it's an engine out to job to correct even if we can identify the cause of the problem which is by no means certain)

Finally, I had new UJs (universal joints) fitted to the prop shaft. It is impossible to remove the prop shaft without first removing either the engine and gearbox or the whole rear suspension. It is therefore very advisable to recondition the prop shaft whilst the engine is out. I also realised that the prop shaft doesn't actually run in a straight line as the rear differential is slightly offset. The importance of properly functioning UJs is, therefore, paramount as they are working hard for a living. In my case I discovered that one of the UJs was partially seized and in need of replacement anyway. I tried unsuccessfully to remove the old UJs as they were rusted in and it proved beyond my capability to free them. I therefore took the shaft to the machine shop where they fitted my good quality replacements for me – once again, fitting cheap UJs is a complete false economy as if they go wrong it's engine/gearbox or rear suspension out again. At the same time, I had the prop shaft balanced.

Lessons learnt:

• Recondition the prop shaft as a matter of course – but don't forget to put it back again!

5.3 The Clutch

My next job was to fit the clutch. I initially toyed with the idea of refitting the old clutch as it was fairly new and this would have saved me money. I'm very glad I didn't do this as, in retrospect, I'm not exactly sure how old the clutch was and it was actually in a pretty poor state – it would have definitely been a false economy. I therefore looked at the different options. To my surprise, I discovered that there was a bewildering array of different clutches to choose from. There were three options I considered:

- An original replacement item
- A full racing clutch
- An up-rated 'fast road' clutch (also known as a green clutch I think)

The problem with the standard clutch is down to the fact that mine is a Series II car and that Jaguar in their wisdom decided to fit a slightly smaller clutch to the later Series I and Series II cars (9½" instead of 10") as an economy measure. This means that if you drive the car really hard you can induce clutch slip, or worse. I immediately discounted the full racing clutch - as the name suggests, it's for racing only. I therefore decided to go for an up-rated clutch. However, due to the cost implications, this decision was soon reversed and I ended up with a new standard clutch. (The gearbox rebuild had made rather a mess of my budget) I reasoned that the standard clutch was OK for normal road use and as I don't drive like a nutter (any more) then the standard one was OK. (This has since proved to be the case although the car does suffer from slight clutch judder when pulling away

which is slightly worrying)

Although everything went roughly according to plan with fitting the new clutch and attaching the gearbox to the engine, minor problems, that were potentially major, did crop up. Firstly, there is a little grub screw that holds the clutch fork (which in turn holds the clutch release bearing) to the bell housing on the gearbox. On attempting to remove this rather small and insignificant little screw, it decided to shear off flush with the fork. I tried various methods to try and remove it, but without success. In the end I welded a blob onto the end of it which enabled me to get a hold on it and was able to unscrew it with a pair of pliers. I think that the heat generated by the welding process also helped quite a bit in freeing it. See photo 5.3-2 of the

5.3-1 *Left: Near Disaster! I very nearly bolted the gearbox to the engine before tightening the main oil gallery plug. The loose plug is seen at the rear of the engine with a loose copper washer around it. Just spotted at the last minute!*

clutch fork with the sheared-off grub screw in two parts.

Secondly, I was just about to bolt the gearbox to the engine block when, at the last moment, I realised that I'd forgotten to tighten up one of the main oil gallery plugs. When the engine was bolted to the engine stand, it had proved impossible to tighten up this particular plug as the stand was in the way. Having removed the block from the stand, I'd forgotten all about it. Only as I was about to attach the gearbox did I remember it. This was potentially a very serious error that could have led to the destruction of the engine through loss of oil and oil pressure. Thank God, I spotted it just in time. See photo 5.3-1. (The end spigot of the gearbox main shaft was greased [as in the picture] to prevent squeaking when the clutch is disengaged with the car not moving)

Other jobs that were tackled at this point were the rebuilding of the clutch slave cylinder (later to prove futile – the slave cylinder began leaking badly very soon after the car was on the road and had to be replaced. As with most of the hydraulic parts I reconditioned with new seals, etc., the problem appeared to be a badly worn/corroded cylinder which leaked fluid past the new seals – copiously) and the fitment of a spin-on oil filter conversion that should make oil changes easier in future. I then filled the engine with relatively cheap 15/40 engine oil for running-in purposes. (In retrospect I shouldn't have done this but used a proper running-in oil instead from such as Millers or Castrol) I'd already had the starter motor reconditioned by Lucas (along with the alternator) but to be honest they seem to have done a poor job that appears to have involved little more than stripping down and repainting. I hope that they prove me wrong and that both items work properly. (So far so good)

Above: The component parts of **5.3-3** *the slave cylinder showing the old and new seals. Despite this, the slave cylinder failed almost immediately when the car was on the road and was replaced with a new item*

Top: My clutch fork and sheared **5.3-2** *grub screw. I removed the broken stud by welding a blob on the end and then extracting it with pliers*

Lessons learnt:

- Check, check and check again that all nuts, bolts, etc., are properly tightened before reassembling an item that can't be re-tightened later.
- Be prepared to change plans as circumstances (and usually budget) dictate.
- Before fitting new seals to hydraulic units, check that the main cylinders aren't corroded.

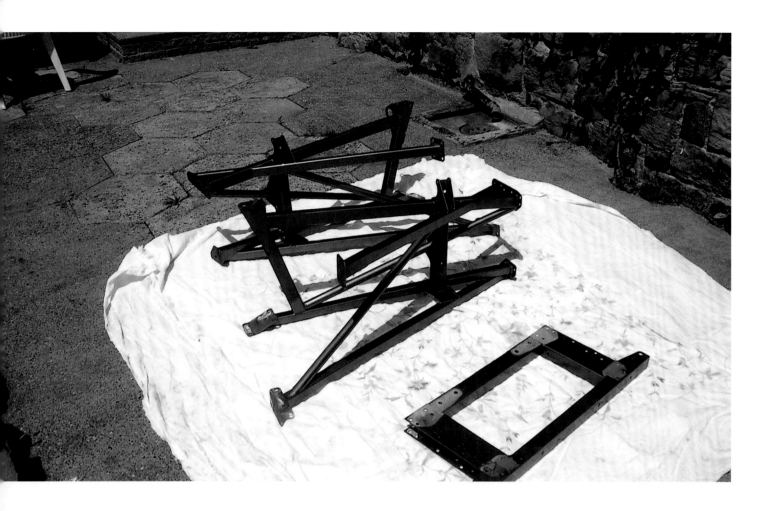

5.4 Engine Frames - A Sad Saga

Just as I was about to refit the engine and gearbox assembly, I discovered a major problem with my engine frames. Although they appeared to be in excellent condition when I purchased them with the body shell, I later discovered that one of them had been mended. The left hand engine frame bolts to the bulkhead underneath the battery tray - which is often its undoing. The battery tray on E-types has a small drain hole immediately above the engine frame that should have a short drain tube attached to it allowing water and excess battery acid to drain harmlessly away underneath the car.

However, on many E-types – even restored ones – I have noticed that this small and seemingly insignificant tube is missing, allowing battery acid

to drip straight onto the engine frame where it bolts to the bulkhead, which is already in a fairly exposed position near the floor pan. This is a recipe for disaster, causing the engine frame to corrode and weaken even faster. (Check your battery tray drain pipe now! – although I'm not sure if all models should have one)

This had obviously happened in the case of my body shell and I'd failed to notice the repair when I bought it. The repair is in the form of a short sleeve brazed over the strut and onto the mounting bracket. This repair appears to have been carried out quite professionally and is definitely brazed, not welded. The question is, however, can engine frames be repaired at all, no matter how professionally? This is a question

I have devoted an inordinate amount of time to in recent months, but as I have no knowledge of metals and molecular structures, etc., I have been totally reliant on others to help me with the answer.

My understanding as a complete layman is this: the properties of the special metal used for the engine frames of an E-type changes when under extreme heat (e.g. when being brazed, which is the main reason why it's brazed instead of welded as the process isn't as hot). The resultant change in the molecular structure (?) of the metal causes it to become brittle and it can therefore crack.

Initially, however, the first people I spoke to all thought my engine frame was OK and the repair a good one so I went ahead and completed the

Left: I removed the frames from the body and painted the parts not yet sprayed as well as filling them with rust proofer

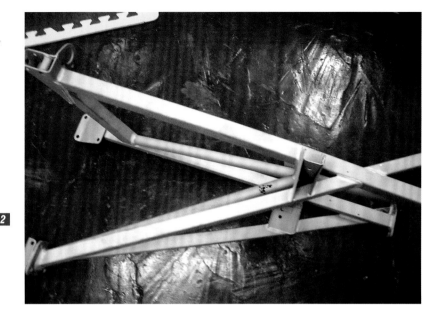

After blast-cleaning, on first viewing the replacement frame looked as good as new **5.4-2**

final fitting of the bonnet and had the whole lot painted. Later opinion went against this and advised that engine frames should *never* be mended (certainly with a sleeve like mine) and it would be foolhardy to fit the mended engine frame to my car.

I therefore took the decision to replace the engine frame on the grounds that if there was any doubt, then this was the correct course of action. However this proved to be far from straightforward. First of all I was directed to Urich from *E-type Fabrications* (Tel: +44 (0)1325 481819) who builds new engine frames, and

ordered a new one from him. However, Urich advised me that no two frames are ever identical and that I may need to adjust the bonnet to fit as a result of fitting a new frame. Having just spent several months getting the bonnet to fit perfectly and having had it painted, this wasn't what I wanted to hear. Also, new frames don't come cheap and I really didn't want to spend that much money on something I already had.

I canvassed more opinion on the matter and as a result reversed my initial decision and decided to stick with my existing frame after

all. I therefore rang Urich with great embarrassment and cancelled my order, which to his great credit he accepted without quibble or criticism.

Shortly before I was due to fit the engine, however, I changed my mind again! Following further talks with more experts, I had a crisis of confidence and decided to indeed change the frame on the simple premise of 'better safe than sorry' - but there were still the issues of cost and getting a good fit to be addressed.

At this point, I went to the excellent

5.4-3 *A closer inspection revealed considerable corrosion in an unlikely place*

E-type Club technical seminar at CMC and by chance they had what appeared to be a decent second-hand engine frame for sale at a reasonable price. They were incredibly friendly and helpful and, whilst there, I was keen to buy it - but they refused to take my money! Instead they insisted that I brought it home and had it blast-cleaned first to ensure that it was sound underneath all the layers of paint, etc., before paying. It has been known for apparently sound frames to be found to be rotten after proper inspection.

So I brought the frame home and had it blast-cleaned. After this, it was revealed that, sure enough, in the most unlikely of places, the frame had rusted through! What appeared at first glance to be a totally sound and rust-free frame, in fact wasn't (see photo 5.4-3). CMC were right to be circumspect. They immediately took the offending frame back without question. During the course of the rebuild, I have found them to be very helpful and understanding of the plight of the home restorer and have tried to be of assistance where others might not have been as ready to do so. I, however, was back to square one.

You will probably not be surprised to hear that shortly after this episode I changed my mind *again* (!) and decided to fit my original frame after all, for the following reasons:

- As ever, there was no consensus between the experts I spoke to as to whether the frame was serviceable or not - so maybe it is!
- I couldn't really afford a new one.
- A new/replacement one might not fit properly and therefore, in turn, the bonnet wouldn't fit either.
- I reasoned (probably incorrectly) that if the frames were brazed together in the first place then you must be able to braze them to mend them.
- Urich used to mend broken frames, rather than just supply new ones (although I think he replaced the whole strut in question) but doesn't any more for various reasons – so they *can* be mended!

5.4-4 *My original frame with sleeved tube next to the replacement before it was cleaned*

My original sleeved frame back **5.4-5**
in situ

I therefore refitted the engine using my original frame. I'm quite sure that I will live to regret this decision! For a start, I will have to point this repair out to the MOT tester and inform my insurers of it and it may be that one or both of them might not be happy with it. There is also the possibility that those who told me that it will crack are right and I'll have to replace it anyway. If I do need to replace the frame in future, it will be a very big job and I'll be kicking myself for ever and a day, but it's done now so that's it.

I can't quite believe I've written this entire section just about one engine frame, but it's such an important issue it needs serious consideration. It's the one area of the rebuild that doesn't fit into my 'do it once and do it right' philosophy, but time will tell if it was the correct decision - or not. (3000 miles on all seems well, touch wood!)

Lessons learnt:

- If your engine frames are suspect, replace them *before* fitting and painting the bonnet as no two frames are identical.
- Engine frames can appear to be in good condition when in fact they aren't – at the time of writing the newest original frames are 36 years old and they can be nearly 50 years old – long past their 'use by' date.
- As far as I am aware, there is no definitive answer as to whether or not you can mend engine frames.
- Check your battery tray drain pipe is in place.
- 'However' is the commonest word in the DIY restorer's vocabulary!

5.5 Refitting The Engine And Gearbox Assembly

Having finally decided to re-use my original engine frames, it was time to refit the engine and gearbox assembly. I utilised my wonderful engine crane for the fourth and final time (engine out, rear suspension out, rear suspension in, engine in) – considering the expense you don't get much use out of it for your money, but you can't manage without one! I managed to refit the engine to the body by locating the engine and gearbox in the correct position on an engine hoist and then reassembling the engine frames around it. I also fitted up-rated engine mounts as I'd had standard remanufactured ones fail on me in the past.

Refitting the engine by swinging the unit into position and then bolting the frames around it proved to be a fairly straightforward method of engine replacement, but even without the engine frames in the way it wasn't easy to manoeuvre the engine into the correct location – how people manage to put an engine back in from the top with the frames still in position I don't know – it must be a very difficult job that requires enough headroom to lift the engine at a fairly severe angle and the car needs to be a fair way off the ground too. Those who have already done so, I salute you! The other method of engine removal/replacement is from underneath. Most people tell me that this is the most straightforward method with the engine frames in place. The main problem here being to get the car high enough in the first place to allow room for the engine to

5.5-1 *My newly assembled engine and gearbox are offered-up to the body shell with the engine frames removed. Note the reflective insulation on the gearbox tunnel*

exit underneath – access to a pit or even better a car lift would come in very handy!

In order to fix the engine frames to the bulkhead, I'd bought a complete new set of engine frame mounting bolts and had them all nickel plated as they are high tensile bolts and so stainless steel ones cannot be substituted. Bolting the frames to the bulkhead was relatively straightforward, mainly because the whole caboodle had previously been

Bolts For Front Frames

The correct order for the different engine bolts varies slightly according to model, but here is the basic order for the front engine frame bolts:

- There are 20 mounting bolts in total.
- There are four 2½ inch (6.35cms) bolts per side (eight in all) that bolt through the bonnet hanging frame, the picture frame and the engine frames at the top.
- There are three 2 ³/₈ inch (6.03cms) bolts per side (six in all) securing the lower front fulcrum blocks.
- There are two shorter 2¼ inch (5.71cms) bolts either side that go at the bottom of the picture frame on the inside, passing through the oval shims (four in all).
- There are two 4 inch (10.16cms) long bolts one either side that go through the lower fulcrum block and the anti-roll bar mountings. See Photo 5.5-2.

All bolts are inserted facing rearwards with their heads towards the front of the car except the two outermost at the bottom of the picture frame. These two bolts (holding the fulcrum block in place) have to go in the other way round as they can't be inserted from the front. See Photo 5.5-3.

The two outer bolts at the top of the picture frame, attaching the bonnet-hanging frame, must be inserted at the same time as the bonnet-hanging frame as they can't be inserted later (the bonnet hanging frame is in the way at the front and the engine frame at the back). See Photos 5.5-4 and 5.5-5. CMC tell me that there should not be any washers under the heads of the bolts, but that there should be a washer and a lock washer under the nyloc nut ... but I didn't fit any to mine and I'm unsure if they were used orginally.

5.5-2 *Very long bolt (top right) going through the anti-roll bar mounting and the lower fulcrum bush*

5.5-3 *Lower fulcrum block bolt inserted from the rear*

5.5-4 *Outer bonnet stay mounting bolt must be inserted at the same time as the stay as it can't be inserted afterwards – don't forget the radiator mounting brackets! (Series II)*

5.5-5 *...the same goes for the other side!*

5.5-6 *Engine in place! The venerable XK engine is one of the E-type's finest attributes. It gives the cars a good deal of performance, superb torque, utter docility and smooth refined power. It is a brilliant engine which is strong and gives reliability and long life, making E-types very practical and satisfying classic cars to own and, above all, enjoy*

bolted in position so I knew it fitted OK. Needless to say, it is imperative to trial-fit the engine frames, etc., before spraying the car in order to check that they fit - just a fraction of an inch out and the bolt holes simply won't line up – and you need to have trial-fitted the bonnet!

With the frames bolted to the bulkhead, I turned my attention to the picture frame at the front which I initially fitted only roughly as you can only tighten the bolts fully with the bonnet frame in place. At this point, I discovered I had a very confusing set of bolts of varying lengths – the problem being which ones went where?

I slowly began to establish where each bolt should be located, but this wasn't an easy task as it only became clear if a particularly long bolt was required when the associated part that dictated the use of a longer bolt had been identified – and this was often some time after I'd put the bolt in a different position and so had to unbolt it and move it. This was aggravated by the fact that some bolts can't be removed without removing the whole bonnet frame as the frame itself is in the way. For this reason, I was forced to take the bonnet frame off and remount it no fewer than three times – and even now I still don't think I've got all the bolts in exactly the right place. It is also worth noting that the 'Fulcrum Block' (see Photo 5.5-7) which attaches to the front of the lower wishbone on the suspension fits inside the picture frame at either corner – failure to insert these before tightening the bolts leads to the two flanges simply closing up – guess how I know that?

If you look at one of my earlier efforts (see Photo 5.5-7 again), you can see I've managed to put the horn-mounting brackets on upside down (they looked OK until I put the anti-roll bar on!) and fitted the anti-roll bar mounting blocks inside out! Having corrected this minor error (see Photo 5.5-8), I later discovered I'd omitted the radiator stay mounting brackets (Series II and III only, I believe) from one of the bolts at the top of the bonnet stay – one of the bolts that requires the dismantling of the entire structure to remove. Typical. I was found to be feverishly muttering my mantra, "Don't worry, you'll do the whole job much quicker the second/third time around" but without much conviction – especially the third time I had to do it!

It is also worth noting that there are two little oval spacers that fit between the picture frame and the

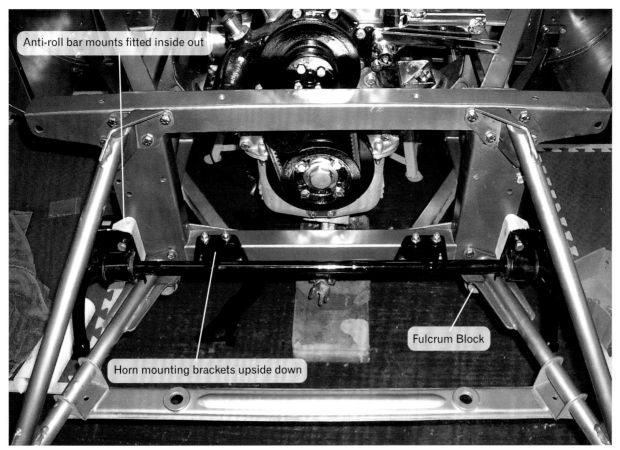

5.5-7 *Spot the deliberate mistakes!*

Anti-roll bar mounts fitted inside out

Horn mounting brackets upside down

Fulcrum Block

5.5-8 *That's a bit better!*

5.5-9 *The picture frame assembly finally complete with radiator-mounting brackets, anti-roll bar brackets correctly positioned and the horn mounting brackets the right way up*

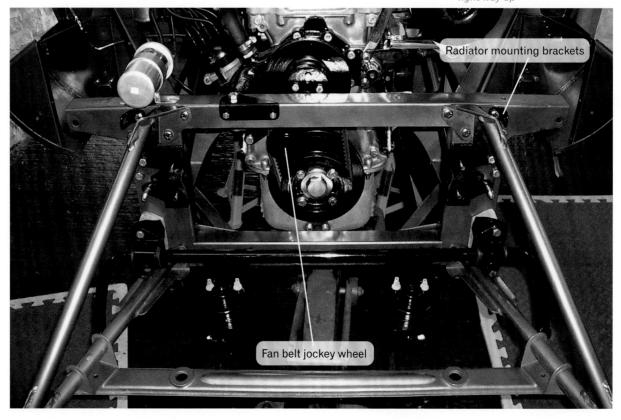

Radiator mounting brackets

Fan belt jockey wheel

engine frames, one on each side at the bottom of the frame and secured by the horn-mounting bolts. These ensure a proper fit between the frames and the picture frame and could easily be overlooked. I only realised that they were there as I'd left them semi-assembled when I'd stripped the car down (see Photo 5.5-10 of typically rusty and battered horn-mounting brackets and spacers, anti-roll bar mounts, steering rack mounts and radiator stay brackets, prior to blast cleaning and powder-coating).

One other small item of note is the jockey wheel (see Photo 5.5-9) used on the fan belt to maintain tension. If you look carefully into the groove of this sealed item, there is a small grub screw that can be undone with an allen key. I had been told that you could then fit a small grease nipple in its place and grease the bearing. However, having removed the grub screw, I couldn't find a grease nipple that would fit (the groove is too narrow), so I simply

sprayed lithium grease down the hole and replaced the grub screw. I don't think that this is as good as greasing, but better than nothing. Incidentally, my problems with the picture frame bolts has reminded me that the bolts that hold the water pump on are also all of uneven lengths, but you can work out which one goes where quite easily as all the holes in the water pump body are of lengths to match the bolts.

I eventually mounted everything, including new polyurethane steering rack mounts that I hope will help to make the steering slightly more positive. Alternatives are to fit ones of either original specification or which are completely solid. The original ones are more forgiving (not as many bumps, etc., transmitted to the steering wheel) but not quite as precise. The solid ones are for racing only and I think they'd be very hard to live with on the road. The main thing is to check they are properly laminated together as problems occur when the sandwich starts to delaminate.

5.5-10 *Picture frame fittings – anti-roll bar bushes, steering rack mountings and horn brackets prior to being refurbished*

Lessons learnt:

- If you are going to dismantle your engine frames, take careful note of where all the bolts and their associated fittings go before beginning dismantling.
- If you assemble something and it doesn't look right, it probably isn't.
- Make sure you choose the right steering rack mountings for your requirements.
- When reassembling something for the third time, remind yourself just how much you're enjoying it!

5.6 The Distributor

With the engine bay beginning to take shape, I turned my attention to the distributor. I'd read an article by CMC (Classic Motor Cars) regarding overhauling distributors and so decided to tackle mine, fitting new springs that control the rate of ignition advance, and also fitting electronic ignition. I had looked at fitting a brand new electronic distributor as they are supposed to work very well. However, for reasons of cost (they're not cheap) and the fact that for some reason they only currently make them with a red distributor cap, I decided against it. I duly removed the old springs from the distributor (they didn't want to come off!) and fitted the new ones which did require the distributor to be stripped down, but were easy to fit having done so.

I'd also previously purchased a Lumenition kit as I wanted to fit electronic ignition, but without the associated extra box that most kits require to be fitted somewhere outside the distributor. The Lumenition kit fits completely inside the distributor and so keeps the original look. An easy-to-follow set of instructions came with the system (eventually - see below) and I had no problem fitting it. Roughly it went as follows: I removed the points from the base plate and sawed off the dowel that locates the points as it's in the way of the new electronic module. This is the only major drawback to the system – it is irreversible. If I ever wanted to revert to points at any time, I'd need to fit a new base plate (this eventuality occurred rather sooner than expected!). I also removed the

old wire that goes from the points to the ignition coil and the plastic shroud that accompanies it. I then screwed the electronic module to the base plate along with the associated new wiring (yes, it even comes with a little cable tie!). See Photo 5.6-4. Next, I fitted the 6-point rotor on the main shaft and refitted the rotor arm on top of that and the job was complete. See Photo 5.6-5. The main thing to check is that the rotor is very close to the electronic module as, if they're too far apart, it won't work properly.

All of the above was fairly straightforward apart from three slight problems I encountered:

While fitting the new advance springs, I removed the entire advance unit to clean it to make fitting the new springs easier. In doing so, I

Left: The completed distributor with electronic ignition system – soon to be discarded

5.6-2 *The centrifugal ignition advance mechanism viewed from underneath with the springs removed*

inadvertently refitted it the wrong way round in relation to the bottom half of the shaft, which in turn fits into the engine and will only go in one way round. My ignition is therefore now 180º out. Rather than trying to rectify this by taking the new springs off (almost impossible without damaging them) and turning the shaft round, I re-wired my distributor cap to compensate by moving all the HT leads round 3 places. The ignition should therefore work OK. (Yep, works fine)

On refitting the rotor arm, I found it to be slightly wobbly as, with the new electronic rotor in position, the rotor arm didn't push as far down on the shaft as it used to. I rectified this with a little packing to hold it tight on the shaft and this seems to have worked.

On attempting to fit the electronic ignition, I initially found it very hard to follow the instructions, as they didn't seem to make sense. I was beginning to doubt my sanity and my ability to follow instructions when I suddenly realised the problem: the instructions were photocopied but, in my case, they'd only copied one side of a double-sided set of instructions, so I had pages 1 and 4, but not 2 and 3! I rang the company and they immediately despatched the missing pages, which meant that the instructions suddenly made a lot more sense!

I found that fitting the electronic ignition kit was pretty straightforward with clear instructions provided (eventually!). Fitting new advance springs was rather more fiddly, however, and required the dismantling of virtually the whole of the distributor (including the vacuum advance/retard unit which is a beggar to refit!)

Anyway, at least it got me away from the engine bay reassembly for a while so I was able to return to it refreshed and ready to tackle the front suspension.

New springs fitted to the ignition advance mechanism and inserted in the distributor housing 5.6-3

5.6-4 *The Lumenition module fitted*

Lessons learnt:

- You can replace the springs in the distributor to your requirements – but they are a bit fiddly to replace.
- New electronic distributors are available – but only with red caps.
- If you can't follow the instructions, it isn't always your fault!
- Lumenition kits fit completely inside the distributor and are maintenance-free. The question was - would it actually work when the time came to start the engine...?
- Check that new parts are available before modifying old ones in case you need the original part again.

The rotor arm fitted **5.6-5**

Do It Once, Do It Right. We know that the creation of your dream E-Type is just that – an investment – so we believe that only the best is good enough. Working with you throughout the restoration process, we ensure that your E-Type will emerge from our workshops as not just a perfect car, but *your* perfect car. Whether you want a factory original specification, or a range of discreet upgrades designed for modern roads, bespoke luggage set, hand crafted steering wheel, Classic Investments has you covered.

They don't write songs about boring daily drivers.

www.classic.investments   +44 (0) 7999 888 886   agris@classic.investments

5.7 The Front Suspension

When I had originally stripped the car down, I'd discovered that the right hand bottom wishbone was considerably bent (see Photo 5.7-2) and I'd been lucky enough to find a replacement at a Stoneleigh Spares Day (a must for anyone looking for that elusive part), albeit in a rather rough condition.

The first job was to dismantle the upper and lower wishbone assemblies, but they proved to be completely seized/rusted solid. I therefore took them to a local machine shop that had the necessary equipment to get them apart – but even then they had a struggle. With the parts returned, I removed the old suspension bushes from the six brackets and two fulcrum blocks, and the four bushes from the anti-roll bar links. I then sent the lot off for blast-

cleaning and plating or powder-coating as appropriate. On their return, I was faced with a veritable jigsaw of pieces that I had an idea somehow fitted back together (see Photo 5.7-1), but I wasn't sure how! Thank heavens for exploded diagrams!

The first thing I did was to fit all new polyurethane bushes to the suspension brackets (a polybush kit) in order to try and improve the car's handling and suspension. They come in different colours, each having a slightly softer or harder compound to suit specific requirements. I chose the black ones as these are recommended for normal road use, allegedly providing a firm but pliant ride. (I'm really pleased with the ride quality, taut but refined with no squeaks – I'd definitely recommend a polybush kit) To fit the polyurethane

bushes use hot soapy water that will allow the bushes to slide into place but then evaporate to allow the bushes to lock in position. If you use oil, it will continue to lubricate the bushes after they're fitted and allow them to spin which is not what you want to happen.

As I slowly reassembled the wishbones, I realised I was missing a fulcrum bracket. If you look at Photo 5.7-1, you can see there are only five such circular brackets in evidence. Somewhere along the line between the machine shop, the blast cleaners, the electroplaters, and myself, one had got lost. I was, therefore, forced to buy a replacement and get that plated before I could continue.

Eventually I managed to loosely assemble the top and bottom wishbones in roughly the right

5.7-1 *Left: Plated and powder-coated front suspension parts ready for assembly*

Bent original lower wishbone arm **5.7-2**

order, prior to fitting them to the car (see Photo 5.7-3). I then bolted the wishbones to the engine frames, which proved relatively straightforward, although the lower ones are a bit tricky, and then fitted the stub axle carrier between them. The stub axle carrier is attached to the two wishbones by means of two ball joints – an upper and lower one. The lower wishbone ball joint was simple to fit, as the original type that requires shimming has been superseded by a sealed for life easy-to-fit item and is a straight replacement for the old part. The top ball joint is still the original type, however, as the top wishbone forms part of the ball joint socket and this has to be shimmed. I found this quite straightforward (so far – see below). The ball joint comes ready supplied with a variety of different shims and you simply add or remove these until the joint feels quite stiff, but not excessively so, and that's it (see Photo 5.7-4).

There were two problems with this, however. The top plate of the ball joint is spring loaded to maintain pressure and this is, in turn, held down by a circlip. I found it totally impossible to fit the circlip while simultaneously pushing down the plate. To get round this, I used (misused) a ball joint separating tool to hold the plate in place whilst I fitted the circlip and this eventually worked (see Photo 5.7-5). The second problem was that as I'd had the wishbone plated and this forms the socket of the ball joint I'm not sure how this will wear in use as the plating may flake off and

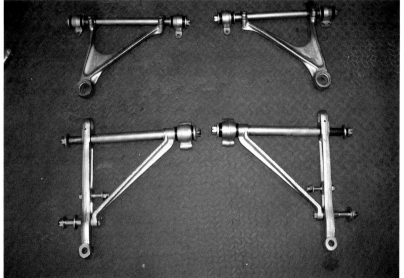

5.7-3 *Wishbones loosely assembled with new Polybush bushes in place*

create problems in the future. (So far so good, but I wish I'd also had the top plates plated as water sits on them and they've both corroded)

I fitted new stub axles to the carriers as my old axles showed signs of scoring where the wheel bearings had been spinning on them (the first stub axles to arrive, at great expense,

5.7-4 *Wishbones and stub axle carrier assembled. Note: the new 'sealed for life' bottom ball joint and the original ball joint in the wishbone at the top*

Refitting the circlip to the top ball **5.7-5** *joint using a three-legged puller to hold the top plate in position whilst I fitted the circlip*

were very poorly machined and, when I trial-fitted the front wheel bearings, they were found to be way too loose a fit – worse than the old ones they were meant to replace - and had to be sent back).

I also refitted the brake disc shields. I was in two minds over this. The shields aren't really necessary for occasional motoring and are rather ugly. Not only this, but they can actually induce brake fade as they prevent the discs from cooling down as fast as they could. In fact, if uprated calipers/ discs are used, it is recommended that they be removed for just this reason. However, they do incorporate the brake pipe mounting bracket and if discarded a replacement bracket has to be fabricated. I'm not sure if anyone supplies such a bracket.

Ideally, I would have liked to have fitted stainless steel shields, but I couldn't find anyone to supply these either (since then I've found that they are available from at least one supplier). I toyed with the idea of chroming my old ones but they were fairly badly pitted and I'd have had to buy new

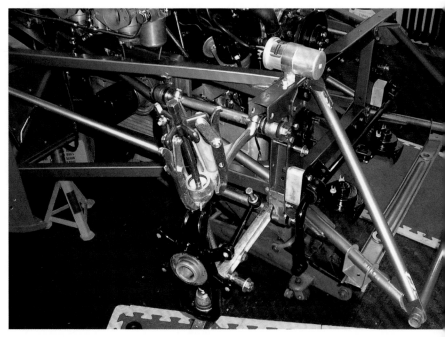

ones and then get them chromed, which was simply too expensive. So, in the end, I had my existing shields powder-coated black and fitted them. If something better turns up in the future, it shouldn't be too hard to change them (not got round to this yet). At this point, I also trial-fitted the calipers and brake pipes (see Photo 5.7-6).

My next big job was to fit the torsion bars: another job I wasn't looking forward to as it was one of those jobs that I'd heard so much about and wasn't quite sure how I'd cope with. In the end it wasn't *too* bad. My initial and major problem was setting the height of the bottom wishbone. This requires a special tool without which you haven't a hope. I therefore went and grovelled to those nice people at my local specialist and asked if I could borrow theirs. This was a big ask. Despite having spent considerable money there in the last few years, asking to borrow their special suspension setting

tool that they'd developed over time to provide the optimum ride height wasn't easy. However, after some initial hesitation, they agreed and I quickly fitted the setting tool in readiness for the torsion bars - although I had to partially dismantle the wishbones to fit the tool which bolts between the top and bottom shock absorber mountings (see Photo 5.7-7).

The torsion bars are handed and are stamped as such on the front ends. The problem here is that if the end has corroded, the stamps can be hard, if not impossible, to read. In my case the marks were still quite clear (see Photo 5.7-8). It's wise to check this before removing them from the car or mark them with different coloured tape as I had done (red and green, of course!) just to be on the safe side. To fit the bar to the car, you pass the rear splined portion of the bar completely back through its housing and then slide the bar forward, trying to line up the splines

5.7-6 *Fitting back plates, stub axle and calipers to the stub axle. Apparently stainless steel back plates are now available*

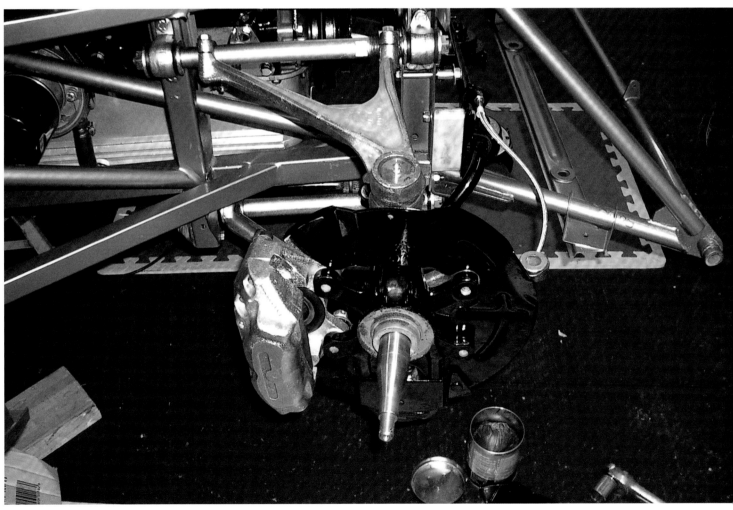

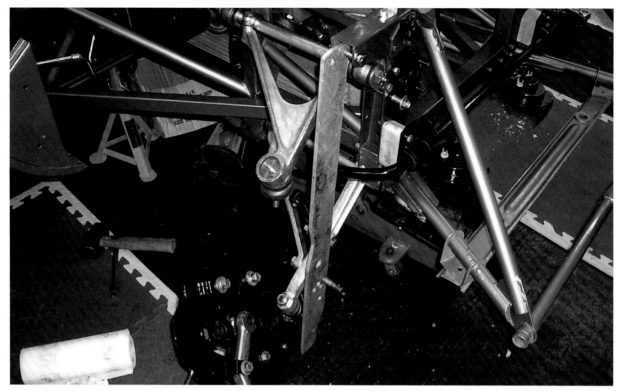

5.7-7   *Torsion bar setting tool in position using the shock absorber mountings*

Torsion bars are handed and **5.7-8**
stamped on the front end

on both ends of the bar with the splines on the housings. Keep turning the bar one spline at a time until the splines at both ends of the bar slide into their respective housings. The bar is made in such a way that the splines at both ends are slightly out of line with each other. So, by slowly rotating the bar, the splines will eventually line up with the splines in both housings. (Sorry if this sounds like gobbledygook but it's hard to explain – although it is in fact quite straightforward – and I didn't take any pictures - you don't always feel like finding the camera when wedged underneath the car covered in grease!).

The main problem I encountered was pushing the bars fully home. The splines lined up OK initially and slid half way home, but stubbornly resisted sliding fully in. I had to resort to some fairly heavy 'persuasion' to get them properly located. I was hoping that the ride height would prove to be right so I didn't have to go through all this again. (Ride height spot on after 3000 miles)

Lessons learnt:

- Replacement parts should always be checked for accuracy prior to fitting.
- Always check you've got all the parts you should have when collecting them from the machine shop, etc.
- Torsion bars are handed (mark them prior to removal in case the stamps are illegible).
- Having the correct tool to set the ride height is essential.
- Bent wishbones don't make for good handling.
- Stainless steel brake shields are available.
- Where there's a will, there's a way.
- Happiness is assembling nice new, clean and shiny parts.

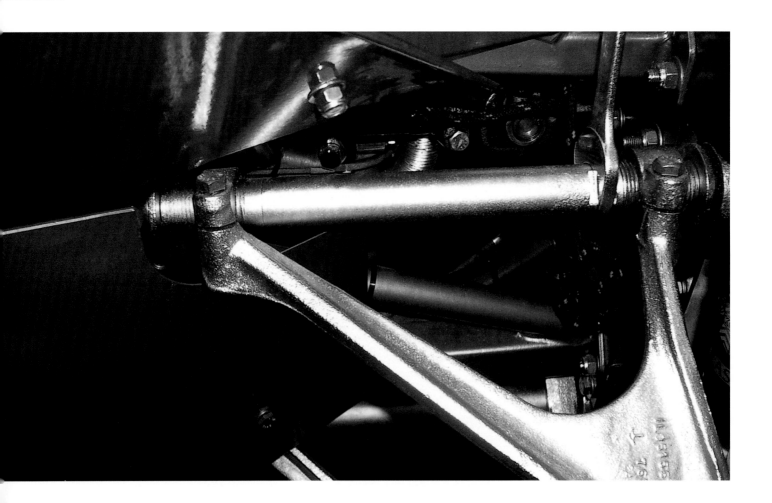

5.8 Front Hubs, Front Brakes And Steering Rack

With the torsion bars, front wishbones and axle carrier loosely fitted, I turned my attention to the hubs and brakes. In retrospect, I should at this point have set the camber and castor angles. However, I thought I needed to have the car with its wheels on the ground and loaded with fuel, etc., before I could do this. This proved not to be the case. Around this time, I returned from the second excellent *E-type Club* CMC technical seminar where, as usual, I found out all the things I *should* have done at the time, but will now be a lot harder to do! One of these jobs was to discover that the camber angle (how much the top of the axle carrier/wheel leans out from the vertical) and the castor angle (how much the top of the axle carrier leans towards the back of the car) can be done

with the car perfectly flat and with the ride height setting tool in place. There is no need to have the car loaded.

The camber angle is adjusted by adding or removing shims from where the top wishbone bolts to the engine frames, effectively pushing the top of the axle carrier (king pin) further away by adding shims and therefore increasing the camber angle or vice-versa. The angle can be measured with a camber/castor angle measuring tool held against the front disc.

The castor angle can be fixed by placing the set square up against the axle carrier and then turning the threaded top wishbone shaft with a spanner, which has the effect of moving the top wishbone backwards or forwards, and therefore the top of the axle carrier too, increasing or decreasing its angle

relative to vertical as appropriate. (See Photo 5.8-1 from later in the restoration showing how the top wishbone shaft is rotated with a spanner once the two pinch bolts have been slackened - as well as the two castellated nuts at the ends of the shaft, if necessary)

The recommended castor angle is 1½º positive (top leaning towards rear of car) and that for the camber is ½º negative (top leaning in towards engine).

As it is, however, I didn't set these and so I left myself a much harder job to do at a later date when all the accessories such as mudguards, wiring and brake pipes would be in the way and make for a much harder job. So, no change there then!

My next job was to replace the wheel bearings as a matter of course and

Left: Setting the castor angle by slackening the two pinch bolts and then rotating the top wishbone shaft with a spanner

One of the outer wheel bearing 5.8-2 *races showing signs of wear and bad pitting*

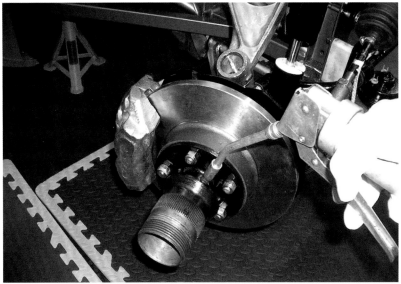

because the races were showing signs of pitting and wear (See Photo 5.8-2) The outer races have to be drifted out from the hub to replace them but, as I remember (it was quite a long time ago – well beyond my current memory limit!), they weren't hard to remove and came out quite easily, and the new ones were then drifted in to replace them.

After this, I bolted my new discs to the hubs. I fitted original solid discs rather than up-rated ones for the following reasons:

- When I bought the discs (a couple of years before, with the fanciful notion that I would soon be needing them!), up-rated discs were not available for Series II front brakes.

- I knew that up-rated discs were being developed but I thought the cost would be prohibitive (for some reason even standard Series II front discs are very expensive – look at some price lists! – so I wasn't sure how much the up-rated ones would be).

- Some up-rated discs (e.g. vented) do not improve braking *per se*, but help prevent brake fade under heavy use, so little advantage is gained in normal driving conditions.

- The Series II brakes are pretty good as standard and so I hope they'll be good enough as they are (but could do with more servo assist).

Having done this, I drifted the new inner ball race onto the stub axle and secured it with *Loctite* to try and stop

it spinning, slid the hub onto the shaft and finally fitted the outer ball race. The manual says to tighten the bearings until the hub feels "sticky" to turn and then loosen it off one or two flats. So, that's what I did, although exactly how tight 'sticky' is, is a matter of interpretation. I planned to check the bearings again after the first couple of hundred miles or so (along with all the other bearings/tolerances/adjustments, etc.) and adjust them as necessary. (They both needed considerable readjustment after the first hundred miles or so)

With the hubs fitted, I pumped copious amounts of grease into them; and then some more; and then some more; and then some more! It took a long time to fill them as the hub is

Greasing the front hubs. They 5.8-3 *both took a lot of grease before they were full*

basically just a hollow cylinder and I ended up using nearly half a tin of grease between them. (See Photo 5.8-3) And why does my grease gun suffer so badly from airlocks every time I refill it!

The calipers were then bolted on and checked to ensure that they were exactly parallel to the discs – if they're not, the brake pads will not be flat against the discs. Shims are available to adjust this, but both mine seemed to be OK without them.

Next up were my new 'Greenstuff' pads which are now manufactured with a special coating in order to try and eliminate brake squeal. (See Photos 5.8-4 and 5.8-5) This is the only upgrade I've made to the brakes. Let's just hope the brake pads work as well as most people (although not everyone) tell me they do. (Now very pleased with the brakes – sharp and without any squeal at all. However, they're still not up to modern standards, requiring considerably more pedal pressure. I'm currently enviously coveting the much larger servos fitted to modern vehicles!)

All that remained to be done was fit new braided stainless steel brake hoses and new front shock absorbers (yes, I know they're really called dampers but I, like most people, will always call them shock absorbers - so there!) I chose Konis for the same reasons I fitted them to the rear suspension. All the shock absorbers on the car were pre-set to one setting up from softest (I think there are three or four settings) which were set by the garage I bought them from. The front anti-roll bar was attached to the drop links and that was about it. (I'm really pleased with the ride quality on the car and I think this is mainly down to the shock absorbers. I would class my Konis as excellent)

I decided to keep the whole steering/suspension set-up close to original rather than altering anything (e.g. fitting thicker anti-roll bars or torsion bars, or fitting up-rated bushes) as I think the original settings will be best for how I want to use the car (driving on normal roads). Once you start altering one thing, it has a knock-on effect with everything else and in trying to sort that out you can end up in a right mess. I also decided that I didn't want to fit power steering as the original steering is taut without being too heavy and it was an expensive option that I didn't need.

Next on the agenda was the steering rack. I think I made one of my biggest errors so far with this item. Having taken advice from various sources, I decided to buy a new rack rather than have my old one reconditioned.

5.8-4 *My new Greenstuff brake pads with their anti-squeal coating ready to be fitted (They probably can't wait to get off that horrendous floral tea towel!)*

My reconditioned calipers in **5.8-5** *place with the brake pads fitted. I always smear the backs and edges of the pads with Copper Ease to prevent them seizing or squealing*

(I had been informed that new racks were very good, cost not much more than a reconditioned one and that reconditioned ones were sometimes not done properly) My new rack duly arrived – looking like an extra from a cheap horror film. It was a mess: thick black messy paint all over it including where it should have been shining alloy, and generally slightly different and cheaper looking than my original. (See Photo 5.8-6) Unfortunately I decided to fit this abomination to my car and sold the old one, so I couldn't go back. I feel this was definitely not a good decision. The problem is knowing when to recondition an item and when to replace it with new old stock or with remanufactured ones or supposedly upgraded items. I have had bad experiences of all of the above with different components and there's no straight answer to this. Let's hope that my steering rack works a little better than it looks (it works very well, but the steering is definitely on the heavy side and I'm beginning to hanker after

5.8-6 *My replacement steering rack top and my original below. Finished to very different standards*

5.8-7 *The steering rack mountings fitted with safety bolts (with a large washer under the head). If the rack mountings fail, the rack won't come away completely*

power steering. The best laid plans...).

I fitted two safety bolts to the flanges on the rack (See Photo 5.8-7) so that if the rack-mounting rubbers should fail (it has been known), the rack won't fall off completely, but be held on by the large washers under the head of the safety bolt, which are in turn held in place by a collar (short piece of stainless steel tubing) on the bolt. I fitted two, one on either side, but some people fit four for total peace of mind. Finally, I removed the pathetic jubilee clips holding the rubber dust covers on the steering rack (you can tell I was not happy) and replaced them with stainless ones, and screwed on the new track rod ends - again slightly different to the originals (See Photo 5.8-8) The steering/suspension was now complete – apart from the camber/castor angles! (See Photos 5.8-9 and 10)

5.8-8 *The old and new track rod ends. The new ones are sealed for life and have no grease nipple*

The front suspension and **5.8-9**
steering assembly. Note: the stainless steel braided brake hoses – highly recommended

5.8-10 *The completed front suspension/ steering with all parts plated or powder-coated to prevent rust.*

Lessons learnt:

- Try to go on *E-type Club* CMC seminars, etc., *before* you rebuild the car, not afterwards.
- Camber and castor angles can be understood – and hopefully achieved.
- Buying new, New Old Stock (NOS), or having original items reconditioned, all have their pitfalls (wait for the story of the reconditioning of my windscreen wiper motor – in total it took four years to sort out - but I'm still mad about my steering rack!)

5.9   The Brake Master Cylinder And Pedal Box

So, time to recondition the brake master cylinder. I'd left the pedal box, brake and clutch master cylinders assembled as a unit since dismantling the car seven years before. See Photo 5.9-1. I decided to recondition both the brake and clutch master cylinders myself rather than buy new as I wanted to know how they worked and because replacements are very expensive in relation to the servicing kits.

On stripping down the brake master cylinder, the first thing I discovered was just how much horrible gunge there was inside. The whole piston assembly was covered in thick sticky goo and looked terrible. I was pleased with myself to discover this muck as I thought how much better the brakes would now work, free of this restraining mess (see Photo 5.9-2). What I didn't realise at the time was that most of this gunge was created *after* I'd removed the assembly from the car all those years ago and what a catastrophic effect this was going to have. I hadn't cleaned the old brake fluid out and it must have been this, combined with indifferent and sometimes very damp storage conditions, that had created the mess in the first place.

Blissfully unaware of this (and of the consequences this would have), I began to clean and recondition the master cylinder. Dismantling was quite straightforward, although some good quality circlip pliers were required to remove the circlip from the end of the unit. (Good quality tools are generally a must and, in areas such as circlip pliers, essential. As my father used to say, "Buying cheap is the most expensive option" as whatever you buy will turn out to be useless and you then have to spend even more money buying the proper item that you should have bought in the first place) The only other problem of note was the removal and refitting of the retaining ring on the piston (see annotations on Photo 5.9-3), as this strange little retaining ring is very fiddly and has to be removed and refitted with the main spring (no 16 in Photo 5.9-3) under tension – and this is by no means easy. All you require is a third hand and you're away!

Photo 5.9-4 shows how to remove the small piston activated by the reaction valve by inserting a screwdriver or similar into the outlet port and *pushing* it out – trying to pull it out with pliers, etc., may cause damage (it is this

5.9-1 *Left: A rather sorry looking pedal box with brake and clutch master cylinders attached, as removed from the car. (There's that damned floral tea-towel again!)*

The brake master cylinder piston **5.9-2** *assembly covered in thick sticky gunge*

piston that sometimes jams on, locking the brakes). Having cleaned everything up, I fitted new rubbers and seals, etc., as supplied in the refurbishment kit and began reassembly. When divided into its component parts, the main piston assembly is quite complex with many small washers and spacers, etc., so I didn't want to make an error in the order of reassembly. I therefore studied the workshop manuals and the instructions supplied with the kit very carefully. To my amazement, I discovered that there was a discrepancy between them. The order the manuals stipulated for assembly of one part was in reverse to that of the instructions.

If you look at Photo 5.9-3 where the exploded diagrams from the instructions (left) and the manuals (right) are shown, you will notice that the order of assembly for the secondary seal is reversed to those in the instructions. So, which is right? Luckily, I had my photos from the dismantling phase and, by looking at these, I was able to establish that in my case the instructions were right and not the manuals (see Photo 5.9-2 again and note the position of the bearing). I don't know if the manuals are for slightly different (earlier?) models, but be aware that, whatever the reason, there are variations as well as the usual Jaguar anomalies in such cases.

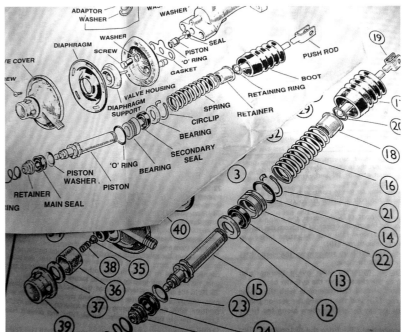

5.9-3 *The instructions and the manuals differ as to the order of reassembly of the piston unit, with the manual assembly being in reverse order. The instructions proved to be correct in this case*

Meanwhile I'd thoroughly cleaned, polished, plated and lacquered the cylinder body, the pipe unions, reaction valve and pedal box as appropriate. With the piston assembly fitted into the cylinder bore (after a long struggle with the circlip!), I got ready to bolt the valve housing (labelled on the instructions in Photo 5.9-3) to the cylinder body. I checked the manual to discover that the two bolts holding the valve housing to the body needed to be torqued down, to between 160 and 180 lbs f ins (1.8. to 2 kg f m). I duly reached for my trusty torque wrench only to discover that it only went up to 90 lb f ft and there was no scale showing kg f m on it. Hmmm. The torque setting seemed rather high (bear in mind that cylinder head nuts are tightened to 54 lb f ft). I checked my other manual which confirmed the setting. I looked for, but could not at that moment find, the instructions that came with the kit. I was in a rush (*never* do anything, especially anything mechanical in a rush) and I really wanted to get everything assembled. I started to tighten the first bolt up and got to about 50 lb f ft when I began

to think that maybe this was a bit too tight. I stopped and checked the manuals again which confirmed the high torque setting and, in my state of haste, decided to continue. At about 75 lb f ft the spring washer underneath the bolt head began to disintegrate – but I continued to tighten. At about 80 lb f ft, the inevitable happened and the thread in the cylinder body gave way – I'd stripped the thread completely.

I left the garage in a state of severe self-recrimination for being so stupid and left the investigation of what had gone wrong to the next day. When I eventually did return, I found the instructions that came with the kit and they stipulated a torque of about 28 lb f ft (can't remember the figure exactly now) not the 160 to 180 lbs f ins quoted in the manuals. So how on earth could they be so different? Then it hit me – the figures quoted in the manuals were for **lbs f ins** not **lb f ft**! The former was a scale I had never heard of before and was not listed on my torque wrench so in my haste I had misread the setting, thinking it had to be lb f ft. I still have no real idea of the difference between

Pushing the small piston out *from the end of the master cylinder to avoid damaging it*

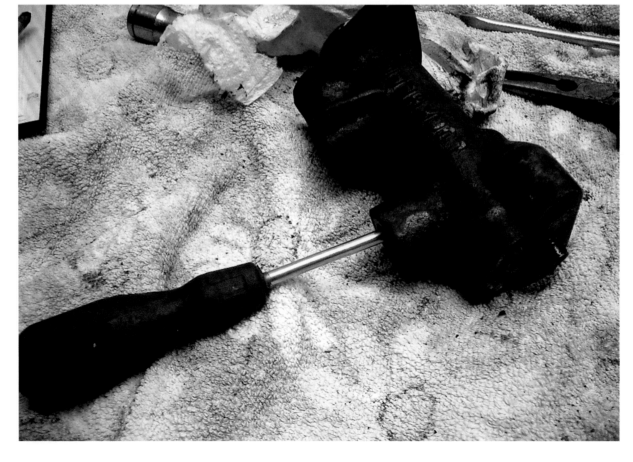

the two and why they are used for a certain application, except that one is a lot lower than the other one!

Still kicking and admonishing myself for allowing myself to continue tightening a bolt clearly way beyond its limit, just because I'd been in a rush, I bought a helicoil kit and inserted a new thread into the cylinder body, found a new gasket, as the previous one was completely crushed, and finished the assembly. At the same time, I replaced the rubbers in the clutch master cylinder (a much more straightforward operation) and I was nearly finished. I checked the two springs that hold the brake and clutch pedals in position, as these are known to break easily, but both of mine were in good condition and didn't require replacement (see Photo 5.9-5). I therefore reassembled the whole unit ready for fitting to the bulkhead (see Photo 5.9-6) – quite a nice comparison with how it looked before!

At the same time, I cleaned and refurbished the accelerator pedal and housing. Note that the pedal is different to Series I cars in that the tensioning spring is in the pedal housing, similar to that of the brake and clutch pedal, and not attached to the arm of the pedal (see Photo 5.9-7). Using new sealing rubbers, I then mounted both pedal boxes to the bulkhead (see

5.9-5 *The underside of the pedal box showing the two springs on the clutch and brake pedals. These are often found to be broken*

The refurbished pedal box **5.9-6** *cleaned, polished and chromed – quite a transformation*

Photo 5.9-8) and the job was complete ... or was it?

Later on, having reconditioned the servo, I filled the braking system with fluid. The brakes worked – but the master cylinder leaked! When I shone a torch up into the pedal box from the driver's footwell, there was a small amount of fluid leaking out of the back of the cylinder – only a little, but a leak is a leak no matter how small. I therefore had to completely remove the master cylinder again, having first drained the system, to inspect it. It is worth noting that you can remove the master cylinder without disconnecting the push rod from the brake pedal as this is separate to the cylinder unit. On inspection, I realised what I had missed previously – the gunge inside the bore of the cylinder referred to earlier had rusted, and therefore pitted, the bore rendering it US. Fitting new seals, etc., will make no difference if the bore is pitted; it will still leak past the seals. I therefore had no alternative but to purchase a brand new item and fit that in place of my original one. This now works perfectly, without leaks. So a lot of work and heartache for little result. However, at least I know how the thing works now and, with every such episode, you gain some understanding and learn a little more about yourself. Anyway, my existing clutch master cylinder seems to be OK!

Lessons learnt:

- When removing such parts as master cylinders at the start of a rebuild, ensure they are cleaned and stored properly until required.
- Manuals (especially for Series II cars) are for guidance and cannot be completely relied upon.
- If you are in a rush, you will fail.
- There is a torque scale lbs f in as well as lb f ft.
- Making a mistake is a sobering experience that you can learn from.
- There's nothing more expensive than buying cheap.

5.9-7 *The refurbished accelerator pedal and housing. The spring is different to this on Series I cars*

The reconditioned pedal boxes **5.9-8** *mounted on the bulkhead with new gaskets underneath*

5.10 The Brake Servo

Continuing with the restoration of my braking system, I turned my attention to the Lockheed servo unit as fitted to later Series I and Series II cars (and Series III?). I had taken the decision at the outset of the restoration that this was to be a complete 'nut and bolt' restoration and rebuilding the servo unit was part of this. Also, as I'd found so much gunge inside my master cylinder, I thought that the same was possibly the case with the servo, despite the fact that the servo had been replaced shortly before I purchased the car and appeared to be in generally good condition, if a little tarnished (See Photo 5.10-1).

I was lucky in that my servo is of the type that can be dismantled easily. It has a strap around the large circular vacuum cylinder shell that's held on with a nut and bolt and it's therefore easy to take apart. However, there are many servos that are screwed together without a removable collar and these require a special tool to separate the two halves, and so cannot be dismantled without the requisite tool.

Having separated the two halves of the vacuum cylinder shell, the large rubber diaphragm and the plastic support it sits on then comes free of the push rod by removing the little clip (called a key in the manual) that holds it on. The other half of the vacuum cylinder shell can then be removed from the cylinder body by removing the three bolts that hold the two together. This now allows access to the inner workings. If you look at Photo 5.10-2, you can see the

push rod and the plastic blue bearing which sits at the end of the cylinder. Mine appeared to be slightly damaged around the flange, but I didn't think this would affect its operation. In the background of this photo, you can also see the plastic diaphragm support and the box containing the rebuild kit which is quite large as it contains a new diaphragm.

The first thing I encountered on removing the push rod and piston assembly was a mass of horrid gunge that, if anything, was even worse than that found in the master cylinder. As I mentioned earlier, it was only later that I realised that this gunge was created *after* I'd dismantled the car, due to poor storage and can signal the end of the unit's life as it corrodes the inside of the cylinder. I therefore

5.10-1 *Left: The servo unit prior to reconditioning – still in quite good condition*

Removing the push-rod assembly **5.10-2**
from the servo body

The push rod assembly as **5.10-3**
removed

The piston assembly as removed **5.10-4**
(with gunge!)

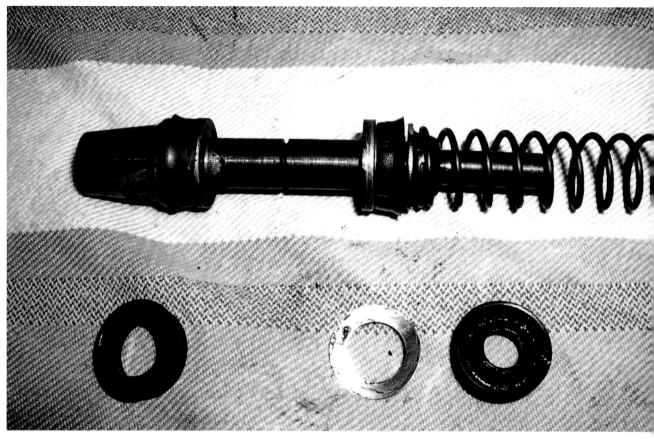

5.10-5 *New seals fitted to the piston assembly. Old seals below*

continued with my refurbishment in blissful ignorance.

I cleaned-up the push rod and piston assembly and fitted the new seals, etc., as in the rebuild kit. You can see how corrosive the gunge in the cylinder was as it has completely removed the paint from one side of the piston end (see Photo 5.10-5). Having completely cleaned the slave cylinder, it was quite straightforward to reassemble (lubricating the new seals with new brake fluid – as should be done with the master cylinder). With the vacuum cylinder shell and outlet ports plated (I couldn't find anywhere to get the shells anodised – I did buy some special spray paint that was supposed to create that look, but this produced a horrendous finish - so I had them nickel plated instead, although I would have preferred to have had them anodised – nice warm colour). Having reassembled the unit, I cleaned and refitted the trap valve under the outlet pipe connection and fitted the completed unit to the car. See Photo 5.10-6.

Another item of note (and

The rebuilt servo unit in place **5.10-6**
with nickel-plated vacuum
cylinder shell

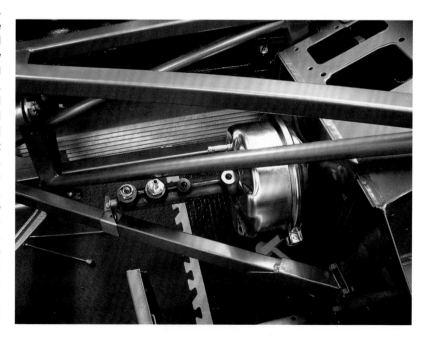

confusion) here is the difference in the order the brake pipes are connected to the servo between Series II cars and later Series I cars fitted with this unit. If you look at diagrams of the braking systems in the manuals (page 178 in the Haynes manual), they are identical, except that the pipes to the front and rear brakes are reversed – so on Series I cars the front outlet goes to the front brakes and the rear outlet to the rear – but the other way round on Series II cars. How can this be? I always thought that the brakes were slightly biased towards the front so one outlet would provide more pressure than the other. Even if this is not the case and the outlet pressure is the same for both outlets, why reverse them? The only difference I can think of is that I believe I'm right in saying that the brake pressure warning switch is not in the same place on the different models (on the front engine frame for Series I cars and on the bulkhead next to the servo on Series II cars) and possibly accounts for the different connections. (Or are the switches in different places *because* of the different connections and there's another reason for swapping the pipes round?)

Anyway, leaving aside such perplexities, the big question is, does the rebuilt servo work? Well, now that I've got the engine running I've been able to test it and the answer is a qualified, "Yes".

Starting the engine with my foot on the brake pedal, the pedal creeps towards the floor indicating that a vacuum is being created. However, there are two things I'm unsure about. Firstly, the brake pedal doesn't seem to go down very far on this test so I'm worried that although the servo is working, it may not be working properly. And secondly, does it leak? As you know, the corrosion caused by the gunge in the master cylinder led to it leaking irrevocably. The similar gunge in the servo slave cylinder would therefore suggest that it should leak as well. But how could I know that? Apparently, big leaks will show up as white smoke from the exhaust as the fluid is drawn into the engine and burnt. But what about small leaks? I think that the only way to check this is by monitoring the fluid levels in the reservoirs once the car is on the road. (3000 miles on and all seems

5.10-7 *The fluid reservoirs before cleaning*

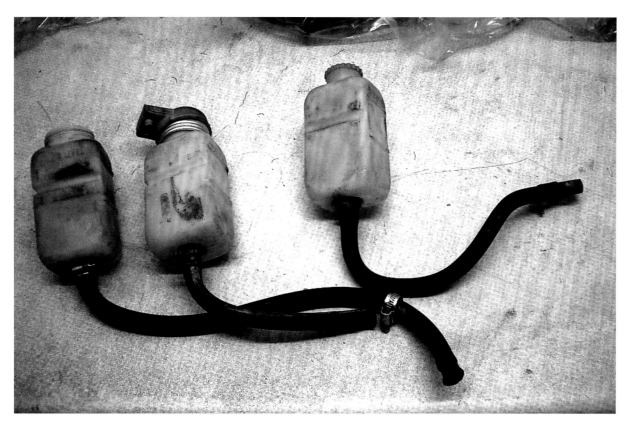

5.10-8 *A sweating brake fluid hose from the reservoir has stripped the paintwork*

well. However, although the brakes are good, they still require more pedal pressure than on a modern car which is tiring on a long journey. I'm now considering/investigating the fitment of a larger servo unit than standard if I can find one that will work and that doesn't look too different to the original)

With the servo finished, I cleaned-up the fluid reservoirs (see Photo 5-10.7 of the reservoirs before cleaning), had the single rear fluid mounting bracket on the nearside chrome plated – along with the corresponding bulkhead blanking plate – and replaced the other with a stainless steel item, and the braking system was coming along nicely. See Photo 5-10.10 of the reservoir on the bulkhead with temporary cap in place. Items of note are that the rubber pipes from the reservoirs must be of the proper type specifically for use with brake fluid otherwise they will 'sweat' brake fluid and very quickly ruin your lovely paintwork. I have seen several cars with just such a defect. See Photo 5-10.8 where the incorrect grade of rubber pipe has indeed sweated fluid and begun to strip the paint from the engine frames. Secondly, the short copper brake pipe between the clutch master cylinder and the rubber pipe (as seen on my car, Photo 5-10.9 shows the reservoirs with temporary brake cap in place) should have a flared end to ensure a good seal where the two pipes join. Replacement pipes are often not flared and so great care should be taken to prevent leaks here. Thirdly, ensure that the jubilee clips securing the rubber pipes onto the spigots at the bottom of the fluid reservoirs are not over tightened as the spigots are easily crushed.

5.10-9 *The fluid reservoirs attached to the bulkhead using a stainless steel bracket. All hoses and connections carefully checked*

The third reservoir in place **5.10-10** *together with chromed bulkhead blanking plates*

Lessons learnt:

- The more you learn about E-types, the more you realise your ignorance.
- In the land of E-types, nothing is ever straightforward.
- I might have rebuilt the servo, but I still don't fully understand how it works.
- I don't know where to get anodising done!

5.11 Finishing The Braking System

I completed rebuilding the braking system by refitting the vacuum reservoir tank and the check valve that together maintain some power to work the servo, after the engine has been turned off, in case of emergency. I had the tank powder-coated and then bolted it to the bulkhead (see Photo 5.11-1). I replaced the check valve as I knew my old one wasn't working (see Photo 5.11-4). One point of note is that on earlier cars the check valve is screwed directly onto the vacuum tank (see Photo 5.11-2), whereas on later cars the check valve is separate to the tank and attached to it via a short hose (see Photo 5.11-3). On later cars there is a little spigot that screws to the end of the valve and enables it to be connected to the vacuum hoses. This little spigot is apparently virtually

unobtainable so, if you ever replace your check valve, ensure you remove the spigot before binning the old one.

With the braking system finished, I filled it with brake fluid. I had considered using silicone brake fluid as it's not hydroscopic so doesn't require changing every few years and, if spilt, it won't damage paintwork. However, I've heard of stories of calipers seizing with silicone fluid so stuck to what I was familiar with even though the stories may well be false. With the system filled, I bled the brakes, the bleeding of the rear brakes being much eased by the remote bleed nipples I'd fitted earlier. The good news was that there was a nice firm brake pedal. The bad news was that the rear calipers were leaking where the pipe unions were screwed into the caliper bodies – all

eight of them (two of the holes should have had bleed nipples in, but had been replaced by pipes for the remote bleed nipples).

I realised that when I'd fitted the brake pipes I'd been worried about over tightening the unions and stripping the threads in the calipers and had therefore erred on the side of caution - but I'd clearly erred too much on the side of caution and all of the unions were leaking to some degree. Now, access isn't too good to the top of the rear calipers, nicely tucked away as they are up inside the cage at the top of the axle tunnel next to the handbrake mechanism and the UJs on the drive shafts. In order to reach and tighten all the unions, I had to remove one of the rear shock absorbers from either side, buy a variety of brake pipe spanners

5.11-1 *Left: The vacuum reservoir tank powder-coated and fitted to the bulkhead*

The check valve on earlier cars screws directly into the the vac. tank 5.11-2

I used a replacement check valve as I'm sure my old one wasn't working – the vacuum was lost as soon as the engine was turned off 5.11-3

5.11-4 *On later cars, the check valve is attached to the vac. tank via a short hose*

I cut holes in the ends of two ring **5.11-5** *spanners to allow them to fit over brake pipes*

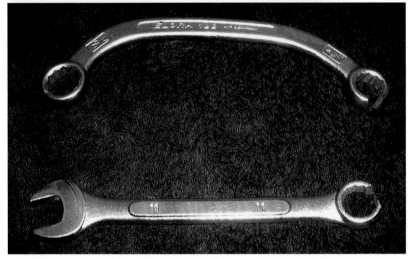

and cannibalise an offset ring spanner and an old metric 11mm ring spanner (a fitting end for a dreaded metric spanner! – 11mm is the same size as 7/16 AF by the way) by grinding slots to allow them to get past the brake pipes (see Photo 5.11-5).

This whole unnecessary episode took several days of particularly uncomfortable and knuckle-scraping contortionism, but somehow I eventually managed to properly tighten all eight unions without removing the whole rear suspension – which I came very close to doing on more than one occasion during this little diversion. With my reconditioned master cylinder replaced by a brand new one (as chronicled previously), the brakes now worked! Another major milestone.

Lessons learnt:

- Fully tighten the brake unions on the rear calipers before refitting the rear axle – or pay the price!
- Replacement parts don't always fit and are often poor substitutes for the real thing.
- Don't lose the spigot on the bottom of the vacuum check valve.

5.12 The Radiator Saga

Next up was the cooling system. I took the radiator cooling fan motors apart to check them and get the bodies and three-legged mounting arms plated. The motors seemed to be in good condition and, although the brushes were quite worn, I deemed them to be good enough so I simply lubricated the bearings and reassembled them. At the same time, I had the radiator cowling polished and this came up really nicely (see Photo 5.12-1). I then tried to bolt the cowling to my new radiator. My old radiator had been in a sorry state, leaking in various places and in need of a re-core. As a result, I'd bought a new radiator from one of the specialist suppliers and sold my original on e-Bay. I'd always wondered why there was a market for such dilapidated original items,

and now I know why. When I tried to attach the cowling to the radiator, it wouldn't fit, by a long way. The captive nuts welded to the sides of the radiator didn't line up with the holes in the cowling and, not only that, they had the wrong threads in them. I therefore had to remove them (most of them broke off when I tried to screw a bolt into them anyway) and replace them with the correct nuts in the right place.

Not only this, but on Series IIs there is a small pipe coming from the neck of the radiator that goes to the expansion tank. This pipe was much shorter and weaker than the original item and the end wasn't fluted. Some time later, when I actually got the engine started, the hose blew off this pipe and liberally sprayed my shining engine bay with highly corrosive anti-freeze.

As a result, I had to drain the entire system, remove the radiator and take it to my local repairers who replaced the pathetic pipe with a proper, long, fluted and substantial one. You shouldn't have to do this with a brand new unit (see Photos 5.12-2 and 5.12-3).

I replaced the original mounting brackets with stainless steel ones, although these too were different from the originals as they weren't fitted with the flat-head captive bolts of the originals. I had to grind down the head from an ordinary bolt to make it fit as otherwise the head fouls the bottom of the radiator.

I then fitted a Kevlar hose kit. I've heard mixed reports of these, but couldn't really find a better alternative so that's what I stayed with. It all seemed to fit OK apart from the short

Left: The polished radiator cowl in place (eventually!) with refurbished fan motors and mounting brackets

The pathetic pipe supplied with the reconditioned radiator, crushed by over-tightening the jubilee clip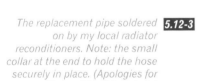

The replacement pipe soldered on by my local radiator reconditioners. Note: the small collar at the end to hold the hose securely in place. (Apologies for the quality of the photo) 5.12-3

The hose connecting the manifold to the bulkhead is one size. The union on the manifold is a larger diameter than the one on the bulkhead 5.12-4

A replacement fan blade. The blade on the right is clearly considerably longer than the others **5.12-5**

5.12-6 *The completed radiator assembly fitted to the car with new Kevlar hoses*

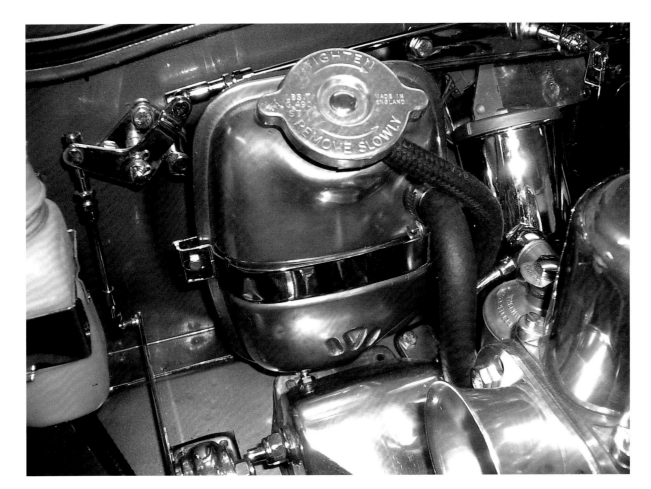

hose from the manifold to the bulkhead. The problem with this is that the two nipples are of a different diameter, but the hose isn't. This means that the hose is never going to fit properly (see Photo 5.12-4). Having said this, as far as I know, this was always the case, even on original cars: a hose with different diameters at either end was never fitted.

I decided to replace the blades on the cooling fans, despite being relatively expensive, as they were both discoloured and one was badly chipped. However, when they arrived, they were both out of line, one by a substantial amount (see Photo 5.12-5) and, as the clearance between the blade and the cowling is quite small, it took quite a bit of cutting and shaping to get them fitted and balanced. Again, you shouldn't have to do this with new items. The radiator was then fitted to the car (see Photo 5.12-6 – the radiator cap was later replaced with a chromed item).

I then stripped the paint from the radiator expansion tank as I realised it was brass underneath all the muck. I gave it a good polishing and it came up really nicely so I decided to leave it like that and simply gave it a coat of lacquer to try and maintain the finish (see Photo 5.12-7). I also fitted a new otter switch to the radiator and a temperature sensor to the inlet manifold, both of which are repro items that seem to work OK although the temperature sensor from a later car has a different connector to the original (a spade terminal as opposed to a circular screw down one). It's only a small

5.12-7 *The brass radiator expansion tank stripped, polished and mounted on the bulkhead*

detail but it's little things like this that can really alter the feel and look of a car from period to contemporary and personally I don't like it – in retrospect I should have sent it back and found an original style replacement. Anyway, the cooling system was complete apart from the heater, which proved to be a whole bundle of fun all by itself.

Lessons learnt:

- The expansion tank/bottle is brass and polishes up nicely.
- There is no special hose from the manifold to the bulkhead.
- Happiness is a firm brake pedal.

5.13 The Heater Box

The final job to be done on the cooling system was the reconditioning and refitting of the heater unit. I knew that my heater wasn't in the best of shape, but I didn't realise just how bad it was until I took it apart. I was presented with a rusty pile of bits that had once been a heater unit (see Photo 5.13-1). It soon became clear that, at some point in the car's life, the heater matrix had been leaking (see Photo 5.13-2) and caused all the corrosion. In my experience, many cars have a heater box that appears to be OK on the outside but is in fact very rusty inside due to slight water leaks over the years.

It was only after completely stripping the whole unit down that I realised the damage was even worse than I first thought. The corrosion had been so severe that it had actually rusted right through the underneath of the heater box, creating a large hole, and that a patch had been fabricated to cover it (see Photo 5.13-3).

I looked at prices of replacement heater boxes and decided that I just simply couldn't afford a new one (the rebuild had already nearly bankrupted me as it was!) so I took the pragmatic decision to re-use the old one, fitting a new plate to the large hole in the bottom. I didn't think this would matter too much as the underside of the heater box is virtually invisible when fitted to the car. My thinking was that this will be a relatively easy item to replace in the future so the existing one will do fine for now.

I decided to take the heater motor apart to check it and have the body powder-coated (see Photo 5.13-4). I found it quite difficult to get the motor apart as the bearings had seized on the shaft and came out of their housings when I separated the two halves. They proved very difficult to refit. Also, on their return from being powder-coated, the two halves wouldn't fit back together as they had been painted on the sleeves where they slide together and so were too tight. I did get the whole thing back together eventually but the result was a mess – the motor worked rather haphazardly and occasionally jammed solid as the bearings weren't working properly. I therefore took the decision to buy a new motor - but these aren't easy to find. I eventually tracked down a supplier and ordered one (expensive) - back came a heater motor for a Series III. The body of these

5.13-1 *Left: The dismantled heater box showing just how bad a state it was in. This was probably caused by a leaking heater matrix*

The sorry looking heater matrix and felt fitting pads. This was a replacement for one that had leaked previously – wonder what that one looked like! **5.13-2**

5.13-3 *The heater box had rusted right through, leaving a very large matrix-shaped hole that had been covered with tin plate pop-riveted in position*

motors are slightly different and the main shaft is a little larger in diameter. I decided to fit it anyway as I thought that maybe Series II motors weren't available and the Series III unit looked more powerful. In order to do this, I had to enlarge the hole in the fan to fit the larger drive shaft, but it seems to work OK.

I bought a new heater matrix, a foam seal/fitting kit and had all the parts plated and painted as applicable. The finished item doesn't look too bad (see Photo 5.13-5) although there is still some pitting from previous corrosion evident on the top of the heater box. I also fitted a new heater valve to the bulkhead as a matter of course and fitted new operating cables to the valve and the heater box (to try and ease the heater operation as my existing cables were either kinked or rusty). Despite being of completely different lengths, they are apparently the same part number (and the same again as the choke cable) and I had to shorten one of the cables in order to fit it to the heater valve.

Trying to adjust the various levers, etc., to get the heater working properly was a bit of a nightmare. The flap that opens and closes inside the box controlling the air flow is assisted by a rather bizarre spring-loaded affair on the operating lever. The lever has to be set in exactly the right place to enable the spring to both open and close the flap. Too far one way and it'll open but not close, and vice-versa. I think I've just about sorted it now – and the heater works. The irony is - who needs a heater in an E-type!

5.13-4 *The dismantled fan motor. I have to admit that I never got it back together again!*

The reconditioned heater unit **5.13-5** *back on the car with a new matrix and fan motor fitted*

Lessons learnt:

- Heater boxes are often rusty inside and are expensive to replace.
- A Series III motor can be fitted to the earlier system with a bit of fiddling.
- Trying to get the heater valve and heater flap properly adjusted is not easy.

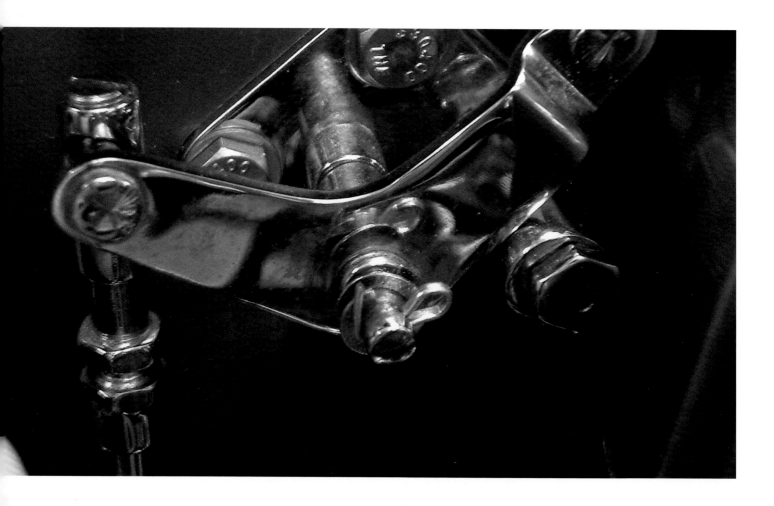

5.14 The Carburettor Linkages

Having finished the cooling system, I fitted the carburettor linkages. I am pretty certain that, prior to rebuilding the car, I could never achieve full power because the carburettors never opened fully due to the linkages not being set properly. With the accelerator pedal to the floor, the butterfly valves still weren't fully open. As I wanted to ensure this wouldn't happen again, I spent a lot of time trying to get the accelerator linkages set correctly. I really wanted to fit a stainless steel linkage set, but they were simply too expensive so I had my original set chromed and they look pretty good.

The first thing to realise is that the linkage rods themselves are adjustable and can be lengthened or shortened by undoing the lock nuts on the rods

(see the linkage on the left of Photo 5.14-1). There is also a bracket bolted to the bulkhead that the slave shaft sits in that can be adjusted up or down to suit. There is a rubber bush which fits in this bracket and holds the slave shafts for the carbs – but the correct bushes are unobtainable so you have to fit one from a Series III which is a loose fit in the bracket but this play can be adjusted out to some extent on the linkages (see Photo 5.14-2). I know that some restorers weld a smaller diameter washer to the bracket so the bush fits properly. One other item of note is that, in typical Jaguar fashion, the bracket over the windscreen wiper motor on Series II cars - rather than being adapted to clear the slightly larger wiper motor - is simply one from a Series I mounted on spacers (often

oval washers from the bonnet! See Photo 5.14-3).

The slave shafts running underneath the carburettors are in two pieces, joining under the rear carburettor and this joint is difficult to tighten without causing the shafts to bind on their bearings. It is important to fit the requisite number of washers/spacers and use a good nut and bolt to ensure smooth operation (see Photo 5.14-4).

I then discovered an error in what I have written above, regarding the throttle linkages. It came to light as I was relaxing by the pool on my summer holidays in the Tuscan hills of Italy (beautiful). Christine was intrigued to know what book had me so engrossed as I must admit that in recent years my reading has dwindled to virtually non-existent. She was disappointed

Left: The linkage mechanism on the bulkhead with adjustable linkages either side

Bracket on the bulkhead for the carburettor slave shaft with a new rubber bush inserted from a Series III. Still quite a loose fit **5.14-2**

The bracket over the wiper motor **5.14-3** *needs spacers behind it to clear the motor housing. I used large rubber grommets. These were placed under the bracket behind the bolt on the right in the picture (and on the corresponding bolt at the other end of the bracket)*

to discover the object of my undivided attention was not in fact anything by Tolstoy or Hardy but was actually an E-type parts catalogue I just happened to have with me. (Why let a small thing like a foreign holiday get in the way of enjoying all things E-type?) It was during my examination of this fascinating and informative tome that I discovered part of the throttle linkage I didn't know existed. It transpires that there's actually a special connector to join the two slave shafts under the carburettors rather than the bolt and spacers I referred to previously. See Photo 5.14-5 of the missing connector. When I bought my car, it had a bolt fitted and so I assumed that that was the correct part. No wonder it took several spacers to get it to work properly. One wonders how many other parts there are like that: parts incorrectly fitted in the past before we bought the car which we assume are original.

The links on the carburettor spindles are designed to be loose which I think is to ensure that there is a little play in the system to allow for engine movement (see Photo 5.14-6) and these can be rocked slightly when fitted. Finally, there is a cam on the bracket on the bulkhead that can be rotated to remove any remaining play in the system (the cam can be seen on the right of Photo 5.14-1). It's also important to check that the return springs on the carburettor shafts and the accelerator pedal are in place and tensioned properly to ensure full closure of the carburettor butterflies.

Having made a series of adjustments to a combination of the above, I eventually achieved what appears to be a nicely sorted linkage system, providing immediate throttle response and fully opening butterflies - but it did take quite a lot of time and patience to get right. At first I over-adjusted the whole system and then wondered why the engine revs wouldn't fall below 1200rpm and spent ages fiddling with the carburettors before I realised what the problem was – don't forget to leave at least a little play in the linkages. Now that it is done it's so much better than it was before and it was well worth the time invested in getting it sorted.

5.14-4 *The nut, bolt and assorted washers I used to join the two slave shafts together...*

...and the correct bespoke item **5.14-5** *that should be used to join the two spindles together*

5.14-6 *The links on the carb. spindles should have some play in them to absorb movement from the engine*

Lessons learnt:

- Throttle linkages can be chromed and are fully adjustable.
- Adjusting the play in the throttle linkage isn't easy but it's worth it in the end.
- Money isn't everything, but it sure helps.

5.15 Electrics: A Dark Art

My restoration turned inexorably towards that which I had been dreading for so long – the electrics. Now, as a mechanically-minded sort of person, the electrics are one of those areas that are a bit of a mystery: nothing moves or can be seen to move apart from magical things that happen when wires are connected to a battery - it's a Dark Art. Not only this but it's one of those areas that's not really in the manuals, apart from indecipherable wiring diagrams that are only a pictorial representation and even when followed don't relate to 'real life' and fail to show where anything actually is on the car.

The first thing to realise is that when you buy your wonderful new wiring loom, you get exactly that – a wiring loom: no instructions, no guidance, just a confusing array of wires. My first

problem was trying to work out where the various different looms actually went on the car - and which way round! There are four main looms: engine bay, dashboard, and left and right body shell, but which was which and where did they go? I turned for help to Ken Verity of Series I Spares in Rotherham. I arrived at his garage with my wiring looms in tow, whereupon he proceeded to go through them one at a time, and from memory (!) told me exactly which loom was which and what wire was what. I'd taken some tape with me and I quickly labelled each wire or group of wires in turn until virtually every single wire for the whole car was identified and marked (as ever, Ken was used to working on Series I cars so some of the wiring on my Series II was foreign to him – most restorers and available information

tends to be for Series I cars and often has to be amended accordingly). The whole job took a couple of hours and I'm eternally grateful to Ken for all his help so freely given. I really wouldn't have had a clue where to start otherwise. See Photo 5.15-1 of one of the looms now appropriately labelled.

Back at the ranch, I hesitantly began the slow process of fitting the looms to the car after fixing the fuse boxes to the bulkhead. I still wasn't exactly sure where the looms ran, especially on the bulkhead behind the dashboard. Did the wires go through the dashboard mounting plates or under them? Did the wires go through the steering column mounting or under it? See Photo 5.15-2 of the start of the wiring process. (I hadn't any reference photos from any other cars as the wiring was always hidden on cars I took photos

5.15-1 *Left: One of the main wiring looms on the car labelled up ready to be fitted to the car*

To begin with, one of the major **5.15-2** *problems I encountered was ascertaining where each loom actually ran*

The completed dashboard wiring. **5.15-3** *Note the replacement hazard flasher unit screwed to the bulkhead*

of - that is, complete ones) The answers to many of these questions only became clear much later when I thought I had completed a fairly tidy wiring job – and then tried to fit the windscreen demister tubes which invariably ran where I had put most of the wiring necessitating much untidy rewiring. (No, the wiring doesn't run through the steering column mounting – that's where the demister tube goes!) As a result of the above, I am forced to admit that the finished wiring behind the dashboard on my car isn't anything like as tidy as I would have hoped – but at least it's all hidden. See Photo 5.15-3 of the nearly-completed wiring.

Apart from Ken's invaluable advice, the one essential help to rewiring the car was a complete, easy to understand, clear and detailed Series II wiring booklet from Coventry Auto Components (0044 [0]2476 471217). With this booklet in hand, even I was able to follow and understand the basic wiring of the car – now that must mean it's good! These are available for all E-type models I believe and are an absolute must for anyone contemplating rewiring a car or who just wants a wiring diagram they can actually understand. I found one or two minor errors in the edition I used but it's still an invaluable aid.

I slowly progressed through the car, routing and re-routing cables as necessary with the wiring booklet in one hand and the original wiring diagram and magnifying glass in the other. See Photo 5.15-4 of the engine bay wiring loom. You slowly begin to realise that there is a method to all this wiring madness with different coloured wiring actually being the same throughout the car! For example, red for tail and side lights, red/white and red/green for indicators, brown for permanent live and green for switched live and so on. There were one or two occasions when the colour of certain wires on the loom was different to that in the manual (which I had been expecting, given the varied wiring used by Jaguar over the years) but on the whole it all went OK. I even managed to get the more visible wiring looking a bit tidier - see Photo 5.15-5 of the alternator wiring held in place with stainless steel clips.

One item to note is that the loom I bought was slightly unoriginal in that some of the connectors were modern and some wires that were originally braided were plastic. If you look at Photo 5.15-6, you can see that the plastic connectors to the bottom of the alternator regulator unit, next to the battery (mounted on a stainless steel bracket) aren't original and nor is the multi-pin connector for the hazard warning unit on the bulkhead (see Photo 5.15-3) which should be mounted on a bar across the aperture in the bulkhead rather than screwed to the side of it as mine is. Because the connector is different, it has to be mounted differently (I found it virtually impossible to reuse the old connector which is soldered internally). You need to be aware that there are different quality looms available, some with original fittings, some without.

I bought an old style black battery as I think they are more in keeping with the age of the car than modern ones – expensive but well worth it in my book. We had now reached the time to connect the wiring loom to electricity! With the ignition off, I connected the battery – and thankfully there was no massive spark or wires burning or fuses burning out, etc. So far, so good.

I then very gingerly turned on the ignition – all Hell broke loose! There was a screaming whine, a whirring sound and a mad clicking sound.

With my heart pounding, I quickly turned the ignition off again, calmed down and investigated. Thankfully, it was all very simple and no harm was done. It turned out that one of the inaccuracies of the wiring booklet was that some of the switches are wired the wrong way round in the diagrams, so when they were off, they were actually on and vice-versa. This included the windscreen washer switch and the screaming whine I'd heard was the washer motor going full pelt – thankfully without water (no windscreen yet!). Many thanks again to CMC who subsequently sent me a wiring diagram showing the correct connections for the dashboard switches and dip switch.

The mad clicking was of course the fuel pump, clicking wildly in a vain effort to deliver non-existent fuel (I'd opted to fit a pump with points rather than the

new electronic ones for two reasons: 1. I love that clicking sound when you switch on the ignition, and 2. As someone had pointed out at the previous year's *E-type Club* Weekend, if you have a slight petrol leak, the occasional 'click' from the pump with the ignition on will alert you to the fact, which may otherwise go all-too-easily unnoticed. Having said this, someone told me that the new electronic ones still click like the old ones so my concerns may be unfounded). The whirring sound was the windscreen wiper motor. I thought that it, too, had a wrongly wired switch, but after checking

5.15-4 *Beginning to sort out the engine bay electrics with wiring diagram, wiring booklet and magnifying glass to hand*

I finally managed to get the **5.15-5** *alternator wiring appear a bit neater by using stainless steel 'p' clips*

it I found that it was wired correctly but the motor decided to run continuously anyway. I disconnected it and left further investigation until later.

Apart from that, everything seemed to work OK, much to my relief. The only real problem (apart from the damned wiper motor – I'm going to give you the whole unbelievable story on that later) was the brake warning light. It wouldn't work. The problem is that it is multifunctional, being connected to four different items: the brake pressure switch, the two brake fluid reservoirs and the handbrake. So, trying to find the source of the problem wasn't easy. Eventually it turned out to be twofold and relatively simple: the handbrake switch had decided that seven years in storage was enough and had given up the ghost, the other problem being the bulb holder itself. Whoever designed the brake light warning bulb holder wants shooting. It is the most complicated set of little springs and contacts I've ever come across and it was quite simply this that was the main problem: the bulb wasn't making proper contact. Why not just use a straightforward screw-in holder like all the other warning lights?

My last major problem was with the relays. The problem here is that they are all referred to as being the same relay: Lucas LR6A - but there are at least three different types! If you look at Photo 5.15-7, you can see that there are three different styles of relay. So, which one goes where? To be quite honest, despite various investigations and enquiries, including getting my hands on the original Lucas relay workshop manual, I can't answer this question. The thing is they all seem to work wherever they are in the car, e.g. the same relay will work the horn and the radiator fans and the starter solenoid. Different part numbers are referred to, but the part numbers aren't on the relays – so which is which and which one goes where? (Even now some 3000 miles later I am still not sure if I have the correct relay in the correct circuit. The only good news being that [miraculously] the electrics all still work and there's been no sign of overheating wiring, etc.).

Anyway, I now had a car that had electrical power! The good news was that I was able to do things like crank the engine over and get oil pressure; the bad news was that I realised that in order to complete the wiring I had to have my time clock reconditioned, which had never worked since I bought the car. The problem here is that late Series II clocks are a particular breed apart and are very complex to repair and I knew it would cost a packet. In the end it was a mere £120 - what had I been worrying about!

5.15-6 *Below: I fitted an original style black battery to which I later added a LUCAS transfer. Note the modern style spade connectors going to the alternator regulator unit to the right of the battery instead of the original one piece item*

Bottom: There are three different **5.15-7** *styles of relay used on an E-type - although they are all referred to as LR6A. Which one goes where?*

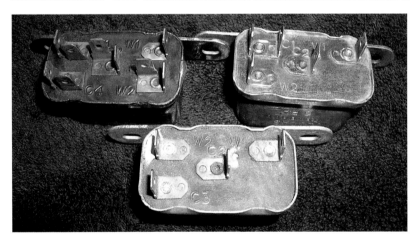

Lessons learnt:

- Vehicle electrics are a Dark Art.
- Having help on hand is a great help – one advantage of being a club member!
- Wiring looms vary in their degree of originality (and accuracy).
- Lucas (and their relays) remain as much a pain in the backside to me now as they did in the '70s and '80s!
- Happiness is a flashing indicator.
- Time is money.

5.16 The Saga Of The Windscreen Wiper Motor

So, the saga of the windscreen wiper motor: a cautionary and almost unbelievable tale of how *not* to recondition a wiper motor. As part of the total restoration of the car, I decided to have the wiper motor reconditioned as a matter of course. The main part of any such reconditioning is the replacement of the brushes. I have for a long time been annoyed that brush kits for Series II wiper motors are not currently available - so how can those who recondition motors source them? I think they *are* available for 2+2 and Series III cars, but the brush sets are slightly different and won't fit two-seater cars.

Anyway, I took the motor to one of my local Jaguar specialists to be sent off to the, "Reliable company we've used for years" to be reconditioned.

I wasn't sure how much of the motor would be required so I took the whole assembly – the motor and its mounting plates. This was May 2005. I knew I wouldn't require it for some time, so I wasn't too concerned when I was told it may take several weeks before it was ready. However, the weeks soon turned into months and there was still no sign of the motor. I complained to the company who chased it up and a few weeks later, in about November 2005, the reconditioned motor duly arrived – looking nice and shiny and new. Everything was great apart from one small problem – not only was it not my original unit, but it was a completely different model of windscreen wiper motor altogether - from a Series One E-type! I began to have concerns.

Things weren't looking good.

Any specialist who could actually manage to supply the completely wrong motor obviously wasn't too reliable. I emphasised to the company that not only did I want my original motor returned but I also wanted the associated mounting plates. With Series II cars you are trying to bolt a totally different type of wiper motor to what is essentially still a Series I bulkhead - and they won't fit. To get them to fit, there is an adaptor plate that bolts onto the mounting plate and allows the later motor to be bolted to the earlier bulkhead – and these are virtually unobtainable. Mine were now apparently with a "specialist reconditioning company" who obviously couldn't even tell the time of day let alone find my mounting plates. (See Photo 5.16-1 which shows the

5.16-1 *Left: My Series II wiper motor with the standard mounting plate on the right and the adaptor plate on the left - hard to replace*

standard mounting plate on the right and the adaptor plate peculiar to Series IIs on the left. Photo 5.16-2 shows them assembled)

The incorrect wiper motor was sent back, but there was still no sign of mine. I was then informed that the man in question was hard to reach as he was busy touring Europe, "Trading in electrical components". Further enquiry revealed that this in fact meant that he had probably sold my unit to someone along the way and was now in the process of finding a new one to replace mine. I was informed that this was, "usual practice"! Personally, I didn't think this sounded like the best practice I'd ever heard of. I began to have serious concerns.

Eventually in May 2006, a year after I'd taken my motor in, a reconditioned Series II motor arrived. It clearly wasn't my original item, but it was a Series II motor and it was reconditioned. It was of no surprise to me, however, that there were no mounting plates. The company I was dealing with accepted liability but said they were unable to supply me with any plates themselves, but that they would refund me if I bought them myself. Hardly the best customer service in the world. I sourced the standard mounting plate (as used on Series Is and Series IIs) without too much difficulty, but the adaptor plate was a different matter.

I tried all my usual suppliers with little success and a large telephone bill. One supplier told me to try RM & J Smith as they specialise in hard to find parts. They proved to be extremely helpful. They did have several such adaptor plates in stock but they were unfortunately attached to brand new original wiper motors and so, naturally, they did not want to split such valuable parts. Instead, they very kindly made a

diagram of the plate and sent it to me with a view to having one made up if all else failed.

I eventually rang CMC to seek further advice and to my amazement they told me that they not only stocked adaptor plates but could supply me with one straight away! (They use them to upgrade the wiper system on Series I cars by fitting a Series II motor and therefore get them made) So my 'totally unobtainable' adaptor plate duly arrived, brand spanking new. This only goes to show that you need to ring round suppliers for that elusive part which some may claim to be unobtainable. (N.B. I have since learned that RM & J Smith have also begun manufacture of the adaptor plate)

I now had a reconditioned wiper motor and the necessary mounting/adaptor plates! I sent the plates and motor body off for plating and made a gasket to fit between the mounting plate and the bulkhead as I couldn't find anyone to supply an original one (I now hesitate to say 'unobtainable' – see Photo 5.16-3 of my home-made gasket and the wiper mechanism). On return from the electro-platers, I refitted the

wiper motor body which is a bit tricky as the strong magnets in the body keep pulling the armature out of position as you lower the body on. The best way to avoid this happening is to fit the gear wheel and stop it rotating by putting the end of the drive shaft in a vice. This effectively stops the armature from moving as it is held in position by the worm gear and the motor body can then be replaced without the magnets unseating everything. See Photo 5.16-4 of the armature and gear wheel in place.

At long last, in November 2006, I fitted the motor to the bulkhead and the job was finished! (Or so I thought) Joyfully turning on the ignition for the first time, the motor started to run of its own accord and wouldn't stop. Actually switching it 'on' with the switch led to the appropriate fuse on the bulkhead

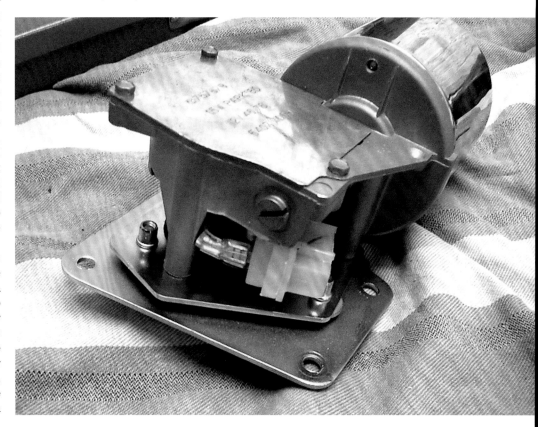

The assembled wiper motor, **5.16-2** *mounting plate and adaptor plate ready to be installed*

The worm gear attached to the armature

Self tapping screws

The white resin gear wheel attached to the metal drive shaft

burning out immediately. I spent ages trying to find the source of the problem, but to no avail. I duly enlisted the help of Chris next door (MKII Jaguar) and, with the help of the wiring on his car as a reference and a multi meter, we finally cracked it. It wasn't the wiper motor; it was the new wiring harness - they had accidentally wired the multi-pin connector the wrong way round and this was the cause of all the problems. (This was the second incorrect bit of wiring on the new loom, the other being to the rev. counter – see Photo 5.16-7 - more on this later) By swapping the wires round in the connector, the wiper motor worked properly at last! (Or so I thought) It was now December 2006.

At this point, I must reiterate that the one really essential tool required for rewiring a car is a multi meter. Mine has a bewildering array of functions, but all you really need are two or three. You require one which bleeps if a circuit is made and one to check voltage. The first function is used initially to work out which wire is which. For instance if you have a bundle of green wires going into a loom at one end you can easily work out which is which coming out of the loom at the other end by checking

5.16-3 *The wiper motor with operating arm attached and home-made bulkhead gasket*

5.16-4 *The drive gear inside the wiper motor after I had tried to correct the parking position by moving the drive shaft round and securing it to the resin gear wheel with self-tapping screws*

5.16-5 *If you're trying to sort the wiring out on your car, one essential tool is a multi-meter. I can now use at least three of its 700 functions!*

The wiper motor finally fitted **5.16-6**
to the car and working - after a
fashion. I later had the whole unit
fully reconditioned again

for a circuit. You can then also check for a good earth, check fuses are working, check connections, etc., etc. The second function is great as you can actually read the voltage being delivered to a component – to one such as I who knows nothing about such things, it's fantastic! (I'm easily pleased) I even managed to check the resistance of my new coil as part of the investigations into my malfunctioning rev. counter (more on this later). See Photo 5.16-5.

With the wiper unit now working at both high and low speeds, there was one last check – the wiper blade parking position. I checked – it was a mile out. The wheel boxes stopped about half way through a cycle when the wiper blades would be virtually vertical. Oh, joy. I then spent an awful lot of time removing and refitting the wiper motor trying many different permutations of setting the position of the wiper mechanism to remedy the situation. This wasn't fun as the wiper motor is not designed to be repeatedly removed and refitted and is a fiddly, awkward

job that led to some of my wonderful new paintwork on the bulkhead being damaged. I wasn't happy. Also trying to bolt the assembly to the bulkhead is really tricky as the washers keep falling off the mounting bolts which have to be fitted pointing downwards. I got round this by Super Gluing the washers to the mounting bolts – and it worked!

I took the motor back to the garage and they sent it off to their new electrical man – for some reason they'd stopped using the previous chap who had now apparently gone out of business – can't think why! The new electrical chap said the motor had the correct gear wheel in it and that the park function was working correctly. I went home, re-fitted the motor (for about the 20th time) and begged to differ. I returned it again, but with the same result.

By this time, it was February 2007 and time for my second *E-type Club* CMC technical seminar so I took my much-loved motor down with me and left it with them for checking. They returned it several days later, confirming that the wipers were indeed parking in the

wrong place and included a diagram of where the gear wheel should stop for the wipers to park correctly. It confirmed the obvious in that this wasn't my own original item that had been reconditioned but a replacement unit, and one from a different type of car with a different gear wheel.

I once again returned the unit to my supplier together with the diagram and instructions from CMC and they once again sent it to their repair man. He said that a replacement gear wheel was unobtainable and that he'd

adapt mine (This later proved to be completely false as I now finally have the correct gear wheel in the unit - four years later!). The motor eventually came back with the mounting lugs on the gear wheel removed and the gear wheel Super Glued in a new position! I thought that there was no way this was going to work but, to give him the benefit of the doubt, I refitted the unit and turned it on. It lasted three wipes before the Super Glue let go (two more than I'd expected anyway). Just to add insult to injury, the repair man did not return the instructions and diagram supplied by CMC so I didn't know the correct gear wheel positioning.

By this time it was April 2007 and my patience was at an end. I now had little choice but to do the job myself. I'd had enough of complaining and waiting, and being let down. The problem was that this was a garage who had given me considerable help during the rebuild and, as a result, I felt I couldn't really make a stronger complaint. It was an awkward situation. So I wearily took the motor off again and began to think how I could make it work properly.

I spent a long time ensuring the correct positioning of the gear wheel and then considered how to lock the plastic gear wheel to the metal shaft permanently. In the end I came up with this solution: I used two self-tapping screws to hold the two together. (See Photo 5.16-4) This worked well although I had to cut the tips off the screws to stop them fouling the park switch (which is under the gear wheel) and at long last I now had a working windscreen wiper motor. Hurrah! It was now May 2007. So, the reconditioning of my windscreen wiper motor had taken almost exactly **two years** and even then I'd ended up doing half the work myself! See Photo 5.16-6 of the wiper motor finally installed.

I'm not really sure what lessons are to be learnt from this story. All I can say is that I took the unit to a reputable specialist who subcontracted to a reputable electrician and all I got was a lot of grief. I suppose it goes to show that, no matter how careful you are, things still go wrong. Perhaps I should have asked to see samples of completed work or sought an assurance that

5.16-7 *The blue box for my intermittent wiper switch mounted to the dashboard under the rev. counter aperture*

my own unit would be reconditioned and returned or just been more hard-headed when dealing with the garage. I suppose the moral of the story is that age old adage: "If you want a job doing properly, do it yourself".

A postscript to the above is that I've also fitted an intermittent wipe facility and it works really well. I always wanted to have intermittent wipers and I saw a good system at the CMC seminar so I bought one. I had also got an extra hole in the dashboard that someone drilled in the distant past to fit an electric aerial switch and I needed something to put there anyway.

The intermittent switch comes with all the necessary wiring instructions and is quite straightforward to fit as the new wiring connects with the existing wiper switch. However, the wiring is different for earlier and later cars so you need to ensure you get the right one. As it was, mine was wired for an earlier car and I had to swap it all round. The electrics for the system are all contained in a plastic box behind the control knob, the problem with this being that this is quite big and you need a good space to fit it – often on a separate plate below the dashboard. As luck would have it, the hole in my dashboard was in almost exactly the right position to allow room to fit the unit – there is a God after all! (See Photos 5.16-7 and 5.16-8)

Now I have infinitely variable intermittent wipe from something like once every 30 seconds through to virtually continuous, simply by turning the knob on the dashboard. It really does appear to be a good system.

(3000 miles on and, despite my best efforts, the motor still wasn't right. Occasionally it wouldn't turn off – problem with the self park switch – and the wipers wouldn't stop in exactly the right place – problem with the positioning of the self park switch on the gear wheel. Note that, this being a Series II car, you can't adjust the park position as you can on Series I cars. (As a result I later had my motor re-reconditioned by CMC who replaced the gear wheel with a new 'unobtainable' one and the whole thing finally works - four years on!)

5.16-8 *The intermittent wiper switch mounted on the dashboard - simply turn it to vary the time between wipes*

Lessons learnt:

- New brush kits aren't available for Series II wiper motors – but you can get the motor reconditioned.
- Parts that some suppliers claim to be unobtainable are obtainable elsewhere.
- Series II wiper motors require an adaptor plate to fit them to the bulkhead.
- Electrics are a Dark Art – but an Art that can be mastered.
- New wiring harnesses aren't always wired correctly.
- To stop washers falling off bolts held vertically downwards you can Super Glue the washer to the head of the bolt.
- Don't Super Glue your wiper motor together.
- Patience is a virtue – but two years is really pushing it!

5.17 The Water Pump And Steering Column

My next job on the car was a backwards step and one completely of my own making. At the outset of the restoration, I had decided to completely refurbish and recondition all components regardless of condition, which I scrupulously followed, with one exception – the water pump. As the pump had been working fine previously, I saw little reason to replace/recondition it and, as such, refitted it to the engine. However, as soon as I filled the engine with coolant, even before I started the engine, the pump started leaking quite badly. I now realise that the main seal must have dried out during storage and lost its elasticity. So the one part I didn't recondition breaks down before the car is even finished – no comment. How come all my dry parts went rusty

in storage and my wet parts dried out!

I therefore set about removing the old water pump and fitting a replacement unit. All I can say is that it's far, far easier to fit the water pump with the engine out of the car than when it's in situ. The first thing I did was to remove the radiator (again) to improve access. I'd already needed to remove the radiator previously as I discovered that I couldn't fit the lower steering column with the radiator in place, because you can't fit the column from inside the car (as I'd planned to do) as it won't fit through the hole in the bulkhead. I refitted the upper steering column at the same time. I'd had a look at reconditioning the upper steering column bushes, but failed to actually get it apart. I undid the various nuts, etc., and removed

the indicator switch mechanism, but couldn't actually get the column itself to come apart. All I managed to do was break the pin holding the two halves of the collapsible column together (which is designed to snap in the event of an accident and allow the column to collapse). I tried several times but simply couldn't work out how to dismantle it. As there's nothing in the manuals to tell you how to tackle such a job and as I thought that the bearings were OK anyway, I decided not to risk any further damage and reassembled the column as it was.

I replaced the shear pin in the column with a small self tapping screw, snapping the head off when it was fully home and this seems to have worked OK. I replaced the two universal joints on the steering column as a matter of

5.17-1 *Left: The universal joint at the bottom of the steering column in the engine bay*

course. On inspecting them, I found that they were both quite worn – possibly due to the relatively heavy steering on an E-type? See Photo 5.17-1 from later in the restoration of the new UJ at the lower end of the steering column. One 'upgrade' I made here was to fit an alloy steering column housing to the bulkhead to replace the original composite/plastic (?) one. See Photo 5.17-2 of the old and new housing without the circular rubber seal that goes over the end.

Continuing with the removal of the water pump, I encountered various problems. To begin with, I couldn't get the crankshaft drive belt off the water pump pulley. The belt was simply too tight so I unbolted the pulley from the water pump in an effort to remove both it and the belt. However, with the pulley unbolted, the picture frame was in the way, stopping the pulley from coming off its spigot – there simply wasn't enough clearance. Much jiggling and levering later (with cloths over the picture frame to protect the paintwork), I finally got the pulley off and the drive belt with it.

Removing the old pump and replacing the new one was relatively straightforward, the main problem being the removal of the various hoses in such a restricted space. Eventually the replacement pump was fitted and the job completed. Only after I'd fitted the replacement unit did I consider that I could have reconditioned my old pump for a lot less money – but it simply never occurred to me. One item of note here is that the gasket for the water pump is different for Series I and II cars (along with many other gaskets on the engine, e.g. the oil filter body to engine block gasket) and you have to ensure you get the correct gasket – and the correct pump! Engine and chassis numbers are important when ordering some parts, as E-types were constantly being updated and revised throughout their production and even the same model can have very different specifications.

5.17-2 *I replaced the original composite steering column housing with an alloy one*

Lessons learnt:

• The one item you don't recondition is the one that lets you down.

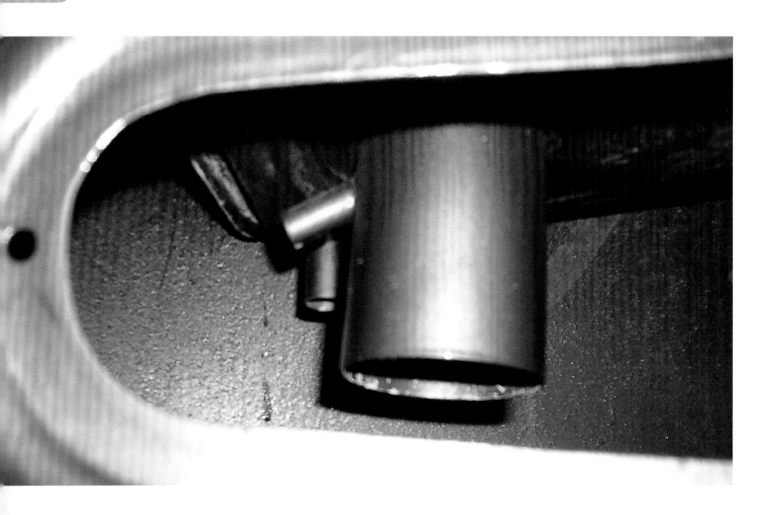

5.18 Petrol Tank And Fuel Pump

My next task was to fit the petrol tank, fuel pump and associated parts. Again this was a job I'd not really been looking forward to as I knew how tight a fit the petrol tank was. I remembered advice tendered earlier and bought some mounting rubbers for a MkII Jaguar that are apparently slightly smaller than the E-type ones. I had the outside of the tank powder-coated and then I painted/coated the inside of the tank with a proprietary sealant because, although the tank was quite sound, I decided to err on the side of caution. This involved pouring an evil smelling blue concoction into the tank, swilling it around a bit and then leaving it to dry (and drip from various openings in the tank). I then copiously rust proofed the nearside inner wheel arch as it's hard to get to with the tank

in situ and then fitted the separate breather tank (peculiar to Series IIs, I believe) and associated pipe work on top of the nearside wheel arch. It was then time to fit the tank.

One problem is that you have a newly-painted petrol tank and a newly-painted boot area, and you don't want to scratch them. The other problem is that you've got to try and fit the tank *and* the filler hose at the same time – you can't fit the filler hose after the tank's fitted as it's too hard and inflexible. On Series II cars you can't slide the hose right up the filler pipe either to gain clearance as there's a breather pipe in the way. See Photo 5.18-1 showing the take-off for one of the breather pipes half way up the filler pipe.

I bolted the one removable mounting bracket to the rear axle tunnel and tried

to fit the tank – absolutely no way. I therefore removed the bracket with a view to fitting it when the tank was in place. The tank now had some chance of going in, but it was by no means easy. I managed to get the tank in a couple of times, but not the filler hose – all you need is five hands and you might be able to do it. I was at an impasse. In the end, the only way forward I could see was to slightly shorten the fuel filler hose – something the books tell you never to do. It worked! After many choice words, grazed wrists, climbing in and out of the rear hatch and the inevitable scratching of paint and skin, the tank went in. The fuel filler hose still seems to seal OK even though it's shortened and there's less hose to slide over the flanges. I then tried to refit the removable rear central

mounting bracket, but of course now the tank was in place it wouldn't go in. After much head scratching and consideration, I decided to use brute force and, using various levers, I eventually persuaded it to go in, but at the expense of my paintwork. See Photo 5.18-2 with visible scratches to the rear of the tank and the boot floor near the bracket – but it is in place!

I later repainted the scratched areas and they now look OK. How you fit the tank without scratching the paint or shortening the fuel filler hose is beyond me. The final job was to insert the mounting bolts through the rubber mountings which was another nightmare but, with more 'gentle persuasion', they eventually went in. One tip is to use a small torch to look down through the bushes and see if they line up with the captive nuts and, if not, which way the tank needs to be moved.

The tank was now in and I proceeded to fit the pick-up pipe and fuel gauge to the top of the tank and connected the fuel pipes to the fuel pump. All these need to be sealed carefully as otherwise they can allow fumes into the car (a very small amount of petrol makes a very strong smell in an enclosed space). I replaced the fuel pump with a new unit as the points were badly worn on my old unit and I couldn't find anyone who could supply replacement points. See Photo 5.18-3 of my old petrol pump points with hardly any metal left on them.

5.18-2 *The petrol tank is fitted! Note the scratches to the rear bulkhead and tank that required touching-up*

The very worn points on my original petrol pump called for a replacement unit **5.18-3**

Lessons learnt:

- The petrol tank is every bit as hard to fit as people say it is.
- Use the slightly smaller rubbers from a MKII to fit the tank.
- I still don't know how to dismantle the upper steering column.

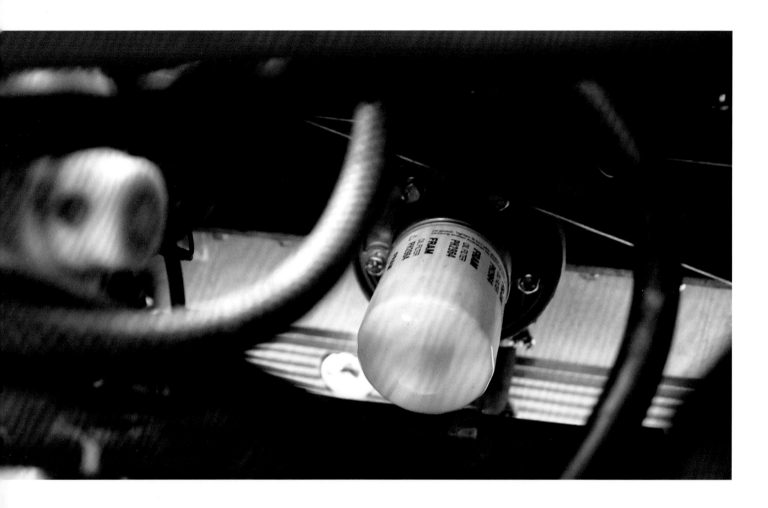

5.19 Spin-on Oil Filter Conversion

With electrical power now available I cranked the engine over with the ignition (and fuel pump) disconnected. The first thing of note was a dreadful knocking sound from somewhere near the rear of the engine. My heart sank. It was clearly happening with every revolution of the engine. Had I done something stupid as part of the engine rebuild? I investigated further and realised that it was coming from the ring gear on the flywheel. I suspected that one of the teeth may be damaged but hadn't noticed it during the rebuild. Every time the damaged tooth came into contact with the starter motor, it gave a resounding clunk. The proof would be when the engine started – if I was right the clunk would disappear with the engine running and the starter

disengaged. If I was wrong... (Thankfully this clunk has totally disappeared now that the car is running)

The good news was that after about 30 seconds I obtained good oil pressure. The bad news was that I then checked for oil leaks only to discover a huge pool of oil under the engine. It was immediately clear that there was a massive leak from my much-heralded spin-on oil filter conversion. It appeared that the leak was coming from the oil seal around the spin-on oil filter itself. My first thought was that the oil seal wasn't the right one as it seemed to be loose in its groove. Replacement of the oil seal made no difference and I investigated further. I finally realised the problem: the body of the conversion bolts on to a central spigot on the block and the body of the filter was

tightening on this central spigot and not on the oil seal. Machining down the body of the conversion where it made contact with the central spigot to allow it to seat properly on the oil seal cured the problem. One unfortunate postscript to this is that I rang the well known suppliers to inform them of an apparent generic defect with their spin-on oil filter upgrade so they could change the design in future – but they weren't interested (I wasn't buying anything and my oil filter conversion was working now so what was I worried about - "Get off the phone, there are customers out there waiting to get through"). I have a nagging doubt that perhaps they're still making them like this.

Lessons learnt:

• Those wonderful upgrades aren't always quite what they seem.

5.20 Some Thoughts On Parts Suppliers

I also have to report that recently another parts supplier blatantly lied to me on two separate occasions in an effort to get a sale. I have a strong suspicion that their salesmen are on commission and will do anything for a sale. I ordered some parts which failed to arrive. I rang the company to see what was happening and they told me that the parts had been despatched that morning and not to worry. The parts still didn't arrive. I rang again and they assured me the parts had been sent and that they were probably, "held up in the post". When the parts finally arrived a week or so later, I checked the credit card receipt they sent, only to discover that it had only been processed two days previously, long after they claimed to have sent the parts. They were obviously worried that I would cancel the order and so lied to me saying that the parts had already been sent when they hadn't in an effort to keep the sale.

As well as lying to me, one salesman recently told me that some chrome trim I was unsure about ordering, "looks really good when fitted to E-types". He obviously had no idea what the part was and thought it was some accessory I was ordering. I won't be using this company again. I don't want to complain about parts suppliers generally – on the whole, they do a great job in difficult circumstances and without them where would we be?

I might suggest that a good measure of a parts supplier is how involved they are in supporting the classic car scene and, of course, E-types in particular. Over the years, I've used many suppliers and found myself naturally gravitating to one or two companies who provided good parts and good service. (As I get older, good service becomes more and more important) I've found that different people have had different experiences with different parts' suppliers, some recommending the very supplier I've castigated above and others pouring vitriolic scorn on suppliers I rate highly. You pays your money and you takes your choice. My experience is that one supplier isn't good for all parts. They may have supplied a wonderful part 'A' but their part 'B' may be poor. It's always worth checking different suppliers.

Lessons learnt:

• Parts suppliers: can't live with them; can't live without them.

5.20-1 *Parts' suppliers - some are better than others - but which is which? This is one of the best*

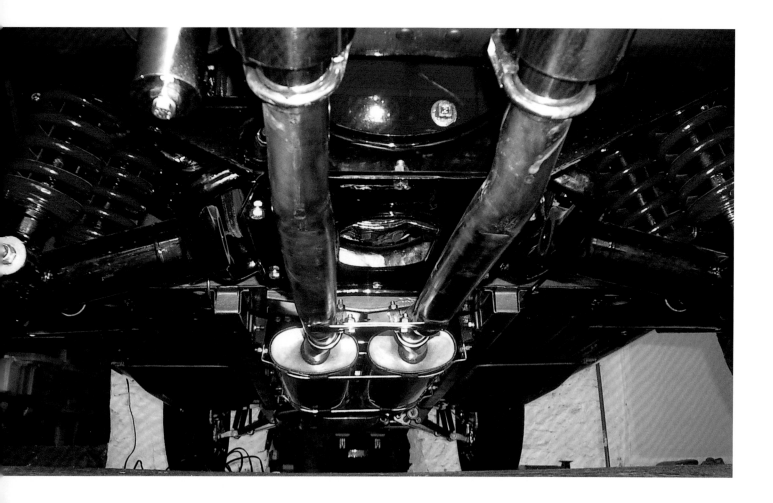

5.21 Refitting The Exhaust System

So, nearly time to start the engine! Just a couple more jobs: clean-up the old stainless steel exhaust system and assemble it on the car, and complete a basic adjustment on the carburettors, fettling them properly when the engine is running.

Now, despite my love of the wonders of digital photography, I have to report that a whole set of my photos of the restoration have disappeared into the ether, namely all those photos of refitting the exhaust system. I have tried to take a few pictures retrospectively but with very limited success - so I'm afraid you'll have to use your imaginations a bit to visualise the work.

The first thing to note was that the stainless steel system had rusted. Not badly, but the down pipes in particular

and the connecting pipes under the rear suspension were badly tarnished. How come if they're stainless steel? By using a magnet, I established that the various parts of the system are made from different grades of stainless steel with the silencer boxes and tailpipes being of a high grade and the pipes of a lower grade. This means that whilst I'm sure the pipes would never rust through, they do go rather rusty (the silencer boxes and tailpipes, on the other hand, were almost like new). One of my down pipes was also very dented where it ran underneath the engine, obviously having sustained damage from heavy grounding at some point. The dent was quite severe and undoubtedly restricted the flow of exhaust gases. Because of these factors, I elected to buy two new down

pipes to replace my old ones.

I also spent quite some time cleaning up the rest of the system because, before I rebuilt the car, it suffered from very heavy oil leaks from the (warped) cylinder head and the (completely worn out) rear differential and the oil had welded itself to all parts of the exhaust system very effectively. Having cleaned the system, I had the tail pipe mounting, the manifold brackets and the U-bolt clamps plated as well – why fit a stainless system with mild steel clamps that will rust and seize completely solid?

Fitting the system on the car wasn't too bad although there are a few items to note:

Trial-fit the various pipes before re-fitting to the car as if it's been used before (like mine) the flanges will all

be bent and crushed.

Ensure that the two asbestos (?) heat shields are in place under the gearbox and the transmission tunnel. See Photo 5.21-3 of one of the heat shields under the gearbox.

Preferably use a new rubber mounting kit as old ones can be weak.

Although my exhaust manifold studs weren't in bad condition, I replaced them anyway as the threads break down quite quickly due to the extreme heat they are subjected to.

Special brass manifold nuts are used to attach the manifold to the down pipes and these are available in two lengths: standard and long. If the threads of the manifold studs appear slightly worn, then use the longer nuts.

Tightening the exhaust manifold nuts isn't easy as access is poor but most can be reached by socket extensions from underneath the car (but a couple are real swines!).

There are two special circular seals that fit over the ends of the down pipes and are essential to ensure a leak free joint.

Use jointing paste on all the joints. See Photo 5.21-2.

In my case I fitted the exhaust system without using assembly paste and had to take the whole thing off again as it leaked from virtually every joint. See Photo 5.21-1 of my newly fitted exhaust system with tell-tale drips around the tailpipe joint revealing one of the many leaks.

Use proprietary exhaust sealant, **5.21-2** *or silicon, on all the joints to ensure a proper leak-free seal*

The exhaust heat shield under **5.21-3** *the gearbox - make sure they are fitted first*

on chamber

Slow running volume screws

5.22 Tuning The Carburettors

With the exhaust finally in place the last job before trying to fire up the engine was to roughly set the carburettors and then fettle them properly with the engine running. There are three adjustment screws on SU HD8 carbs: the slow running volume screw, the mixture adjusting screw and the fast idle screw as seen in pictures 5.22-1, 5.22-2 and 5.22-3. The fast idle screw is simply set with a small gap between it and the choke operating lever beneath it and left. The mixture adjusting screw alters the level of the jet inside the carb and is set as follows:

Remove the dash pot (suction chambers) by undoing the four screws that hold them on – the dash pot will only fit back on one way so don't worry - and the carb piston and damper

spring inside the dash pot. This reveals the jet, see Photo 5.22-3.

The jet is the inner of the two brass circles shown and can be adjusted up or down. The carb needle sits in the hole in the middle of the jet. By lowering the jet more fuel can get past the needle and the mixture is made richer and vice-versa.

Start by setting the jet level with the outer brass circle by turning the mixture adjusting screws up or down.

When the jet is level with the carb body, turn the mixture adjusting screw down two-and-a-half turns and that is the basic setting.

Next, turn the slow running volume screw down until it stops and then unscrew it two turns. That is the basic setting.

(N.B. Ensure you know the difference

between a whole turn and half a turn – we've all got it wrong at some time or other!)

Refit the carb piston with jet needle attached – it will only fit one way round (ensure the needle is neither bent nor scratched) - then refit the damper spring and dash pot.

Fill the dash pot with the correct grade of oil: SAE 20 which took me some time to track down. See Photo 5.22-4.

Basic setting accomplished!

I finally fitted my new camshaft oil feed pipe, which wasn't too easy with the engine in situ, but this was a deliberate decision. I'd discovered that my old pipe was rather crushed at the top, where it runs behind the engine, and I thought that the pipe could only have been damaged in such a way

5.22-1 *Left: The slow running adjustment screw on the SU HD8 carburettor*

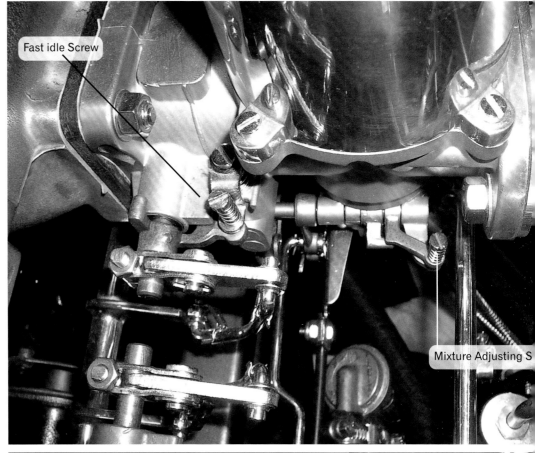

Fast idle Screw

Mixture Adjusting S

The fast idle screw and the **5.22-2** *mixture adjusting screw*

during engine refitting and so decided to fit my replacement pipe after the engine was in to avoid this happening again. See Photos 5.22-5 and 5.22-6 of my old crushed oil pipe. The copper sealing washers have a flat side and a contoured side. I believe that the correct way to fit these washers is with the flat side facing the pipe union.

I then set the static ignition timing at 10° Before Top Dead Centre (BTDC). The correct timing is 11° BTDC but I set it a little retarded to be on the safe side. To achieve this, I set the pointer on the crankshaft pulley at 10° BTDC and then turned the distributor until I was just getting a spark on number six cylinder from my electronic ignition system.

Main Jet

The main jet which can be **5.22-3** *adjusted up or down allowing more or less fuel to pass*

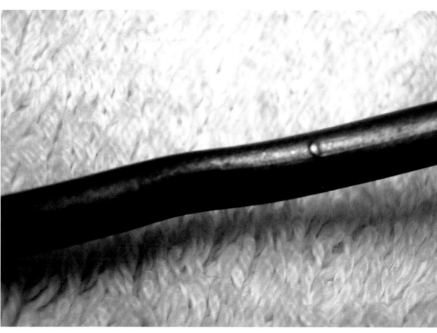

A close-up view of the crushed **5.22-5** section of my camshaft oil feed pipe

5.22-4 To ensure optimum performance use the correct grade of oil in the carburettor dash pots

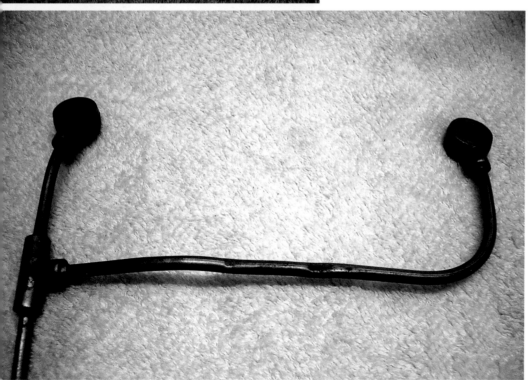

5.22-6 My crushed oil feed pipe was almost certainly caused by poor engine re-fitting in the past

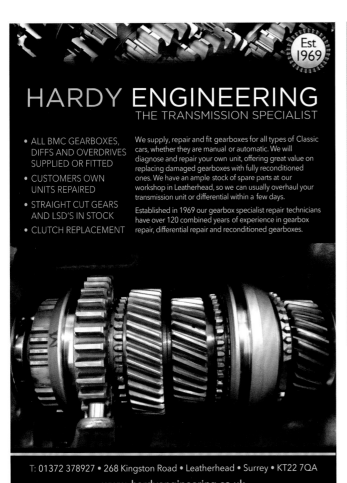

5.23 Starting The Engine!

With all this done, it was finally time to start the engine! With no small degree of hesitation and trepidation, I checked everything about nine times and then took the plunge and went for it. It was the biggest moment so far in the restoration. Would this odd pile of bits that I'd bolted together actually work, actually start? To be honest it seemed improbable. Turning the key (Series II) with the choke out a little resulted in a few coughs and splutters and then to my complete amazement the whole thing simply erupted into life with a thunderous roar. It was fantastic!

I immediately did a visual check of the engine bay to find to my relief that everything seemed to be OK with no obvious oil leaks (especially from the rear crankshaft seal!) and that the knocking noise from the flywheel I mentioned previously had indeed disappeared. I checked the gauges to find them all apparently functioning properly, which was so satisfying. The only problem was the rev. counter which wasn't registering at all. The engine was now officially running! It was a real milestone for me and great motivation to get the car completed.

The next step was to see if the car would actually drive. With my heart in my mouth, I depressed the clutch, engaged reverse and let off the hand brake. Gingerly I engaged the clutch and the car moved under its own steam for the first time in over seven years! It really was a wonderful feeling driving the car out of the garage and seeing it in daylight for the first time. See Photo 5.23-1 of the car on the driveway enjoying the sun for the first time in a long while. The neighbours came round to congratulate me as well – you couldn't really miss the noise! It was an indescribable moment.

With the engine now running, it was time to try and tune the carburettors using a balancing gauge (see Photo 5.23-2). This involved running the engine up to temperature (when the electric fans switched in!) and then fitting the gauge to each carb in turn and adjusting the slow running volume screws until the reading was the same for each carb. Sounds simple but, six months down the line, I'm still not sure if they're tuned correctly. For a start, I'd fitted different carb needles as I'm running the car without the air filter. These needles make the car run richer and I'm unsure if the

This is a balancing gauge for **5.23-2** *setting the carburettors. The head is pushed against the carb intakes to gain a reading*

One of the carburettor butterfly **5.23-3** *valves I suspected of not seating properly causing fast idling*

recommended settings are correct as a result. Consequently, I've been messing around with the jet screws and air screws ever since trying to get the carbs balanced.

I still felt that one of my exhaust pipes got hotter than the other one indicating that some cylinders were working harder than others. The other problem was getting it to idle smoothly at tickover. The manual says this should be 700rpm (Series II). It idled fine at 850rpm but started coughing at 750 and really didn't like 700. At least it seemed to run fairly smoothly so I decided to get the car tuned properly when it was on the road.

Teething problems so far, most of which have been chronicled previously:

On reaching temperature, a pipe blew off a poorly made union on the brand new radiator spraying the engine bay with coolant under pressure. This necessitated removing the radiator (yes, again) to have it modified – and thoroughly cleaning the engine bay!

Although the engine ran my rev. counter wouldn't work. In trying to get it to work, I shorted the electronic ignition and have now gone back to points. The wiring loom was to blame for the non-functioning rev. counter (two white wires going to the unit were the wrong way round at the plug) which now works perfectly.

Initially I couldn't get the engine to idle below 1100 rpm and thought that I'd not fitted the butterfly valves correctly in the carbs, causing an air

leak and resultant fast idling. (The butterflies should fit snugly in the body of the carburettor to prevent air leaking round the edges – to achieve this the butterflies should be tightened in situ but the screws can only be reached from the engine side of the carb hence requiring their removal to realign them). I therefore laboriously removed all the carbs I'd spent ages fitting and reset the butterflies (see Photo 5.23-3) only to find this made no difference. I finally realised that I'd over-adjusted the throttle linkages and slackening these off solved the problem.

N.B. The two screws holding the butterfly in place on the spindle are cut down the middle (like an old style clothes peg) and when the screws have been properly tightened the two ends are opened out thus preventing them from coming loose – allegedly – see below.

Before I rebuilt the car, I had a mystery problem: occasionally the engine would idle at about 1500 revs after a run and would only settle to a lower idle when you blipped the throttle. On dismantling the engine much, much later I discovered that one of the butterflies had come loose and sometimes it would unseat itself so jamming the throttle open – blipping the throttle would allow the butterfly to slip back into place. Mystery solved.

Lessons learnt:

- Starting the engine for the first time suddenly makes the whole restoration thing worthwhile.

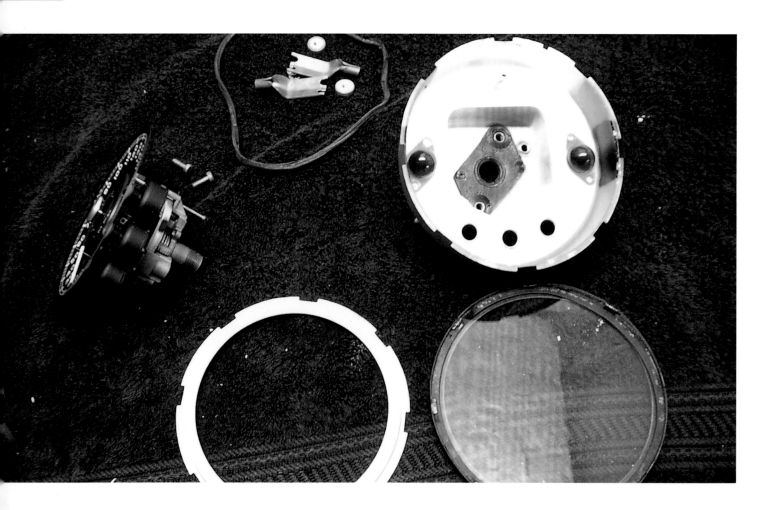

6.1 The Speedometer

Now the engine was running I turned my attention to other matters. One job I'd been considering and decided to take on was zeroing the speedometer. When I was young, I was intrigued by unscrupulous car dealers 'clocking' cars by taking the speedos apart and removing the odd 30,000 miles or so. (I'm sure they still do, now made easier by digital speedos that can be wound back with a laptop and the right software) I thought it was about time I learnt how to take a speedo apart so the car could be 'reborn' with zero mileage instead of the meaningless figure on the mileometer before – something like 60,000 miles. How many times it had been round the clock is open to question.

Removing the speedo from its case was relatively straightforward. I unscrewed the bezel holding the glass in place and then removed the two screws holding the mechanism in its housing. See Photo 6.1-1. Dismantling the speedo mechanism itself was more complicated than I'd imagined. Obviously there's nothing in the manuals on how to do this and you're dealing with a very delicate instrument that is easily damaged. I slowly and carefully dismantled the unit bit by bit and eventually withdrew the central barrel and set the tumblers back at zero. See Photo 6.1 2. However, to get this far wasn't easy and it's not a job for the faint-hearted. As can be seen from the photo, it's a very complicated instrument with a plethora of tiny washers and springs that could easily be lost, damaged or incorrectly

reassembled. Having put the whole lot back in what I hoped was the correct order, I was rewarded with a speedo showing zero miles. See Photo 6.1-3.

On refitting the speedo to the car, I was more than a little nervous as to whether it was still working. I ran the engine with the rear of the car securely jacked up with the wheels off the ground and engaged first gear. I was relieved to see the needle steadily climbing up the dial and the mileometer numbers slowly beginning to turn – and not all at the same time! (How many older cars have I owned where the individual mileometer barrels begin to turn long before they're due and sit irritatingly half way between two numbers!) Of course, mine might not have been working properly but the

6.1-1 *Left: The speedo removed from its housing before being fully dismantled*

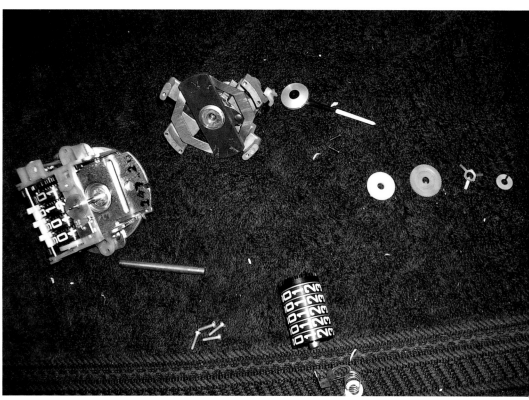

initial signs were good. (3000 miles on and I'm really proud of the speedo. It is accurate to within two miles an hour at all speeds – as checked against my Sat Nav – the needle doesn't wobble and the numbers on the odometer remain (relatively) in line with each other. Result!)

Lessons learnt:

- I now know how to 'clock' a car.

The speedo fully dismantled and the numbers set to zero **6.1-2**

6.1-3 *My reassembled speedo showing many zeros – and all in line!*

6.1-4 *3000 miles on and the speedo's working perfectly with digits still in line – well, sort of*

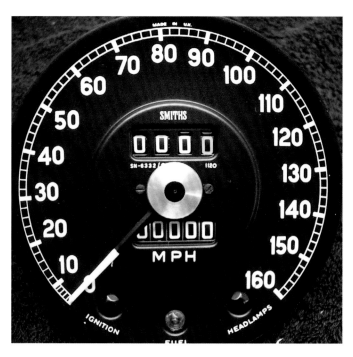

6.2 The Rev. Counter, Rear Lights And Reversing Lights

At about the same time, I dismantled the rev. counter as part of my investigations into why it wasn't working. (This later turned out to be because the two white wires going to the unit were wired the wrong way round on the plug on the wiring harness) Having removed the rev. counter from its housing, it was clear that there were no mechanical parts to work on, just a mass of electrical gizmos that meant nothing to me (see Photo 6.2-1) so I simply reassembled it and left it well alone. The only item of note is that there is a lever on the back (not visible in the photo) that allows you to finely adjust the rev. counter reading.

(I unwisely fiddled with this lever which meant that when I finally did get the rev. counter working it gave completely false readings and I ended up having to send it off to have it recalibrated by Speedograph Richfield at considerable expense – a very costly mistake!)

I finally fitted the gauges into the dashboard that I'd already fitted to the car. I hadn't done much to the dashboard itself apart from thoroughly clean it and glue down some of the edges that had come adrift using contact adhesive supplied by Mick Turley that seems to have done the job. (Mick has helped me enormously with the interior trim – much more on this later)

My next job was to fit the rear bumper and lights. To begin with, I found I had to buy two new reversing lights as mine were simply too far gone to repair. These are screwed to the underside of the rear bodywork using some plastic plugs that fit into square holes on the body. I found it very difficult to find anyone who could supply these plastic plugs but eventually tracked them down. They are the same for Series III cars and I think they are also used in the doors to secure the interior door handle mechanism to the door frame. See Photo 6.2-2. I believe the part no. is C31973/11 if anyone requires them.

I refitted the rear lights to the body, which was quite straightforward although I struggled to fit the strange rubber seals that fit between the chrome base of the light and the metal housing, as they just kept squeezing out of their groove when they were tightened up. They were pattern parts and possibly this was the problem. Eventually I gave up on them and refitted my old seals

6.2-1 *Left: The rev. counter removed from its housing. Not much to mess with here*

The square plastic plugs for **6.2-2** *attaching the reversing lights to the body – it's parts like these that are often the hardest to track down*

that fitted well even if they weren't in the best of condition.

I decided to fit halogen bulbs to the rear lights. Lighting on older cars isn't anything like as good as that on modern cars and I feel it can be slightly dangerous driving at night. So, I thought I'd try to get the brightest lights I could. Having seen halogen stop and tail bulbs advertised somewhere, I finally tracked some down (not easy) and ordered them in the hope that they

would increase the brightness of both my brake and tail lights. When they arrived, I quickly fitted them and was eager to see the difference in intensity. I have to say I was rather disappointed, especially with the tail lights which seemed to be no brighter than the standard bulb. As a test, I fitted one halogen and one standard bulb and asked Christine, my long-suffering wife, to tell me which was the brighter. She couldn't spot any difference either.

I think the stop lights were a little brighter, but only very slightly. So, for the money, I wasn't too impressed.

Lessons learnt:

- Different parts are available from different suppliers.
- Halogen stop/tail bulbs. Are they worth it?

The new reversing lights screwed **6.2-3** *to the bodywork underneath the bumper*

6.3 No. Plate Plinth And Rear Bumper

I polished and then screwed the stainless steel plinth that goes between the rear lights to the body. My plinth has two extra holes in it next to the number plate that I don't think should be there. This is because when I purchased the car, some numpty *[idiot or fool, believed to have been a Scottish expression originally. Ed]* had fitted a Series I exhaust system. The Series I exhaust has tail pipes close together in the centre of the car, unlike the Series II which has splayed pipes to clear the square number plate. (N.B. 3.8 and 4.2 tail pipes are slightly different to each other) As a result of having a Series I exhaust system, they had been forced to fit an oblong number plate instead of the standard square one. To do this, they'd drilled another couple of holes in the plinth that are now visible with

the proper square number plate in place.

I really couldn't justify the expense of a new plinth for such a minor defect and so refitted it as I had previously – with a couple of stainless steel self-tapping screws to fill the holes. It looks OK. I refitted my old number plate as it's still in good condition. I'd had a new acrylic plate with 'Silverline' numbers made before the restoration and it was still as good as new. (Definitely not standard but I just love it!) It was at this point, however, that I realised that my lovely new body shell had one problem I hadn't previously spotted. One of the mountings for the rear lights was slightly closer to the upper bodywork than the other. See Photo 6.3-1 showing the nearside light visibly higher than the offside). Fitting the rear

bumper and getting it to look straight wasn't going to be easy.

I took my re-chromed rear bumpers out of storage (see Photo 6.3-2) and started to refit them. I had spent some time trial-fitting them before having them chromed to ensure a good fit to the body (sadly not with the rear lights in situ so I had no idea about the problem with the lights). I now realise that when people tell you to trial-fit the chrome before re-spraying the car, they mean trial-fit **all** the chrome work (I've also had problems with the bonnet eyebrows – more on this later). It is worth noting that Series II cars have more generous mounting rubbers between the edge of the bumper blade and the body than Series I cars (I think they'd spent long enough in the preceding seven years trying to get

6.3-1 *Left: With the rear lights in place, it was clear that the left hand lamp unit was closer to the upper body than the right one*

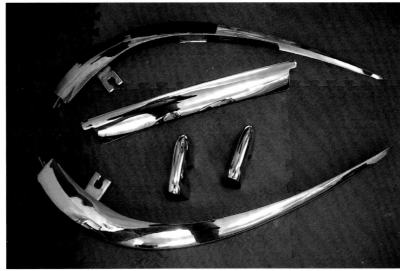

My re-chromed rear bumper **6.3-2** *blades, centre section and over-riders awaiting fitment*

6.3-3 *The rear end beginning to take shape with lights, plinth, bumper and number plate all in place*

the bumpers to fit snugly and took the easy way out). As a result, the bumpers on my car lined up nice and snugly against the body. (There are some advantages to owning a Series II you know) The main problem I had was that every time I tightened the bumpers up, the aforementioned rubber seals worked themselves out of place. Eventually I elected to Super Glue the seals to the bumper blades to stop this happening, and it worked. I don't think it's recommended practice, but it worked for me and I now have bumpers with a very nice fit to the body. After an awful lot of messing around with spacers and bolts of varying lengths, I managed to get the bumper looking fairly horizontal and in line with the lights. See Photo 6.3-3. Suddenly the rear of the car looked like the rear of a car again!

A couple of items to note are that, before I fitted the petrol tank, I loosely fitted the mounting bolt to the wing behind the petrol tank. You can just about get to the bolt to tighten it, but I wouldn't like to actually try to fit it with the tank in place. Secondly, I realised I didn't know how to end the rubber seals where they meet the rear wheel arches. I cut mine off flush with the end of the bumper blade, but I have since learnt that the seal should actually curl round the end of the bumper and be cut off underneath. Still, mine looks OK.

Another problem I encountered was to do with the stainless steel nuts and bolts I used to mount the bumpers to the body, and indeed throughout the car wherever possible. I was talking to someone recently who is some kind of metallurgist and he told me that the stainless steel will react with the mild steel and may cause it to corrode in some way or other. Although this would take quite some time, it would eventually happen. Agh! The whole reason for fitting stainless steel fasteners was to try and avoid corrosion, but I seem to have built the corrosion in as standard. Perhaps I should have got a job with British Leyland! (Subsequent investigations have found that, although this is the case, the corrosion will take a considerable time and is less aggressive than the normal rust on standard steel fittings)

Lessons learnt:

- Different Series cars have different exhaust tail pipes.
- Trial-fit *all* exterior chrome before re-spraying the body.
- Stainless steel reacts with mild steel. Oh, joy!

6.4 Refitting The Bonnet

And so to the bonnet. Since the body was painted, I'd been fortunate enough to store the bonnet at the paint shop (albeit on the first floor up a staircase with a right-angled bend in it!). This had helped me enormously as space is at a premium in my garage and having the bonnet sitting around would have meant such jobs as fitting the rear suspension and engine would have been twice as difficult.

Getting the bonnet back down from storage took four of us and was by far the scariest moment of the entire restoration. If I hadn't actually carried it up there myself, I would never have believed it could get down those stairs again. Somehow we managed it, with about ½ inch clearance and without any damage, just various cuts and bruises where people had sacrificed themselves

to save the bonnet. (There's a picture of the staircase and door in the background of photo 2.5-7) I'd borrowed a Transit van and, having miraculously manoeuvred the bonnet downstairs, we loaded it into that without too much trouble. My neighbour Chris, who I'd drafted in again to help, and one of the lads from the paint shop (also called Chris, of course!) sat in the back and held the bonnet safe while I drove home. See Photo 6.4-1 of the bonnet finally arriving back home - relief for everyone (it's amazing what you can find in the back of a Transit van these days!)

Before refitting the bonnet, I made a radical change to my plans. Many years ago, I saw an absolutely breathtaking V12 E-type at Roger Brotton's garage in Barnsley which had stainless steel nuts, bolts and oval washers holding the

bonnet together and I remember thinking how stunning it looked. At the last minute I decided to do the same and replace all my bonnet fixings with stainless steel ones. This was rather a rash decision as I'd already had the bonnet painted and I didn't know how much damage would be done to the paintwork by removing the nuts, bolts and washers, plus it was a rather expensive idea. In the end, I think it was worth it.

Undoing the nuts I discovered that most of the washers simply fell off without disturbing the paintwork and were not a problem. To my slight consternation, I also discovered just how little paint (if any) was on the various panels where they bolted together. Removing the mud shields at the rear of the wings revealed panels with minimal amounts of primer on the mating surfaces and indeed bare

6.4-1 *Left: Triumphal Entry! The bonnet is brought home from storage in the back of a Transit van. Great to have it back!*

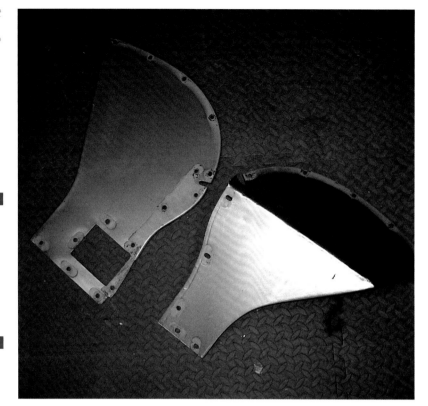

To my amazement, I found the **6.4-2** *hidden edges of the bonnet were just bare metal*

With my Preval sprayer, I used **6.4-3** *some of the paint left over from the re-spray to cover the exposed metal*

metal in places – which had already started to rust! The various bolts and screws themselves were all rusty to some degree. I was shocked to discover how little attention had been paid by the manufacturers to rust-proofing a brand new and incredibly expensive bonnet. See Photo 6.4-2 showing the thinly-painted edges of the mud shields.

I had half a can of paint left over from spraying the car and, using a small 'Preval' sprayer that effectively turns your tin of paint into an aerosol, I touched up the various edges of the bonnet and mud shields until they were well covered. See Photo 6.4-3 of the underside of one of the wings. I then sent off the various bonnet catches and brackets to be nickel-plated and the large Phillips screws, that hold much of the bonnet together, for chroming. I was a little surprised to discover that, while I could replace the oval washers with stainless steel ones, I couldn't replace the screws, and the only alternative was to get them plated. Having collected them from the platers' and having bought a large quantity of stainless steel nuts, bolts and spring washers, I began to reassemble the bonnet using stainless oval washers – all 157 of them!

I'm really pleased with the result

The bonnet back on the car with **6.4-4** *stainless steel fittings, original heater intake and plated radiator shield*

although there is one slight problem: because I've sprayed the car Opalescent silver grey metallic, it's a similar colour to the stainless washers and so after all that work and expense you don't really notice them anyway! At least they're stainless steel and that's the main point. I also had the radiator stone guard nickel-plated and fitted that in the Series II position, nearer the front of the bonnet than on Series Is. (When they redesigned the cooling system for Series II cars, they had to move the radiator forwards slightly and this meant that the stone guard couldn't be fitted in its correct place. In typical Jaguar fashion, they simply made the guard slightly smaller and fixed it nearer the nose of the bonnet using some of the aforementioned 157 nuts and bolts to hold it in place. It's worth noting that all bonnets purchased today – and originally – have the various redundant features still in place from the early Series I onwards, e.g. the stone guard mountings and the mountings for the spring loaded bonnet opening mechanism are still there despite being no longer required)

I also painted the heater intake and refitted it with a new seal and it looks good, despite having one of its vanes missing (I think the vanes are only fitted to Series II and III cars), but after the amount I'd spent on the washers I couldn't really afford a new one – easy to replace another time if I wish. See Photo 6.4-4 of the finished bonnet in place, complete with stainless steel fixings.

Then came the moment of truth – refitting the bonnet to the car. There had been quite a bit of discussion in the *E-type Club* magazine just prior to this about whether or not a bonnet would still fit perfectly once the engine was in the car if the bonnet was originally fitted without the engine in place (as mine was) due to the weight of the engine flexing the body slightly and causing bonnet gaps to open/close. Unfortunately I can't shed too much light on this argument due to gross idiocy on my part.

Some months previously, after the car was sprayed, I'd arranged to remove the bonnet at the paint shop and store it there, bringing only the body shell home for reasons of space. The last and only time I'd removed a bonnet previously was eight years ago (when I embarked on what was then an 18 month project!) and basically, in the intervening years, I'd forgotten how to take one off! I knew they were really simple and so didn't bother to check the manual first. Imagine the scene then at the paint shop, when, with the whole of the garage watching, together with one of my other neighbours (Jenny, who'd volunteered to help in Chris's absence), I undid the two mounting bolts to remove the bonnet and nothing happened…

Embarrassment quickly followed by panic, fuelled by imminent humiliation, kicked in. Here's an E-type 'expert' and he can't even undo the bonnet! I therefore rushed headlong into Plan B – remove the hinges from the bonnet by undoing the four bolts on either hinge. This worked, of course, and the bonnet was lifted away with great ceremony – leaving a trail of different bonnet hinge shims behind it on the garage floor. I had absolutely no idea which shim went where. So, now much later on when refitting the bonnet, I had to start from scratch. Hence I can't say if the bonnet would have fitted perfectly or not with

the engine now in place. Incidentally, the bonnet does come away very easily without undoing the hinges if you undo the two mounting bolts *and then simply slide out the 'top hat' bushes behind them!*

I then discovered that there are in fact *three* sizes of bonnet shim available (from various suppliers) in thicknesses of 36 thou, 64 thou, and 128 thousands of an inch. (See Photo 6.4-5 of the three different thicknesses and the two different types of shim – some with two vertical slots and some with a horizontal slot like a tuning fork. I was surprised to find that I could actually fit both types of spacer to either face of the hinge with the hinge in situ. Why then are there two types of shim?) Using various combinations of shims of different thicknesses led eventually to a perfect bonnet fit, even better than it had been previously!

The only real mistake I made was in loosely fitting the various bonnet catches to the bulkhead first. Refitting the bonnet for the first time with shims fitted in an order I thought looked right led, in fact, to the bonnet being slightly askew and, with the first trial-shutting, the left hand wing caught on the catches and chipped a bit of my precious paintwork from the rear edge of the wing. Note that even when properly fitted, the bonnet only clears the catches by a fraction of an inch and so with the bonnet even slightly out of line it fouls on the catches. Thankfully I can report that the bonnet is now repaired and the blemish virtually unnoticeable, but a salutary lesson – bodywork is not like a mechanical part: it doesn't allow you a second chance if you make a mistake. I'd paid a high price for my panic. See Photo 6.4-6 of the bonnet on the car at last.

One item of note is the seal on the rods that clamp the bonnet shut. See Photo 6.4-7. This seal stops fumes from the engine bay entering the car through the oval hole the rods go through. My original seals were old and squashed and not really serviceable and so I determined to replace them. Unfortunately, however, I think these seals are unobtainable and so improvised, making them from foam. They're not pretty but are hopefully effective and are hidden inside the bulkhead so they're not really seen. It's only a small thing but it can make all the difference to the driving pleasure of a finished car. Fumes inside the cockpit are really unpleasant.

The three different thicknesses **6.4-5** *of steel bonnet shim on the left, going up from 36 thou. to 64thou. to 128 thou. On the right is an alloy 'tuning fork' spacer. Why they are different and which ones go where I'm still unsure*

The bonnet on the car and **6.4-6** *adjusted for a perfect fit by using different size shims*

Fitting a new foam seal to the **6.4-7** *bonnet locking rods where they go through the bulkhead in an effort to minimise fumes inside the car*

Lessons learnt:

- Even brand new bonnets aren't properly rust proofed.
- There are no less than 157 oval washers holding the bonnet together.
- Bonnets are still made (and always were) with redundant features from earlier models still in place.
- Never work on your car in front of a garage load of mechanics and neighbours.
- Don't fit the bonnet catches to the bulkhead before fitting the bonnet.
- The bonnet comes off easily by removing the bolts *and then the top hat bushes.*
- Bodywork doesn't give you a second chance if you make a mistake.
- Ensure the seals on your bonnet catch rods are in good order to avoid engine fumes entering the car.

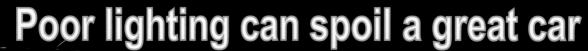

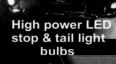

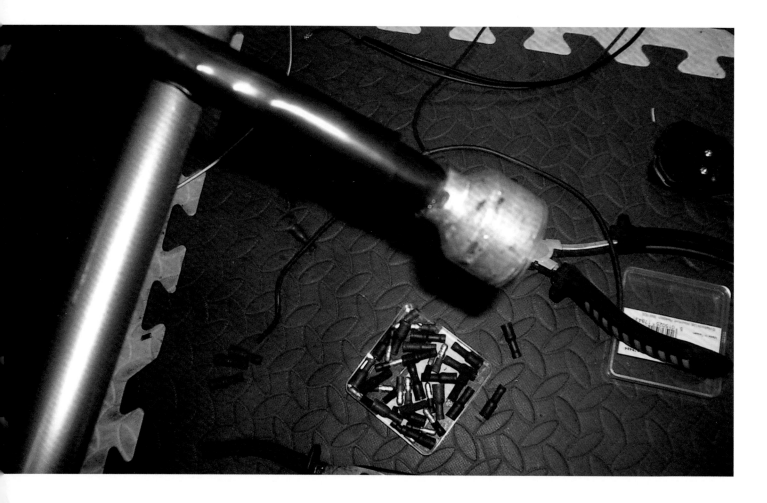

6.5 Refitting The Bonnet Electrics

So, time to fit-up the bonnet. This proved a harder task than I had bargained for (as usual!). The first job was to insert the wiring loom in the nose of the bonnet and wire it up. New wiring looms arrive minus the multi-pin connector for the bonnet and simply terminate in a bundle of cut wires. I think if you are going to do things totally properly you need to buy a new connector and solder it all up as I can't see any way of easily re-soldering the existing plug (or socket). However, these are very expensive so I elected to connect the new loom to the old plug and socket by joining the new loom to the old wiring a few inches either side of the plug and socket and hide/protect the connections inside the plastic sleeve that leads to fit connector. This I did and you can't really tell there are

any connections in the sleeve. I'm not sure how weather proof or generally reliable this will prove to be, but it's working OK at present. (All well so far!) See Photo 6.5-1 of the bonnet plug with the connections made, just before I slid the protective rubber grommet over it. The connections to the socket are inside the bonnet so are unseen.

Yes, I am rather embarrassed about the naff looking connectors I used for this, but the thinking was that they're completely hidden, so why not? I have to admit at this point that I didn't solder any of the connections on the wiring of the car but just used a very good crimping tool and (usually) the proper bullet connectors. I hope my lack of ability with a soldering iron doesn't come back to haunt me. I have to say that I've tried many times to solder

connectors in the past using a variety of solders, flux and soldering irons/torches and the result was always way, way worse than a good crimp - so I keep on crimping!

With the bonnet loom in place (serving the headlights, sidelights and indicators), it was an ideal time to very thoroughly rust-proof the valance area. With the headlights not yet fitted, there is excellent access inside the front of the bonnet and I used several cans of *Dinitrol* rust preventative, paying particular attention to all the joints (remember how poorly similar joints were rust-proofed on the rear of the bonnet – I'm sure the same would be true of these joints but, as I couldn't take them apart, I made sure they were heavily sprayed with rust inhibitor). See Photo 6.5-2 of the inside of the bonnet

6.5-1 *Left: The original bonnet plug connected to the new loom by bullet connectors under the plastic sleeve (and it works!)*

Before the headlamps are fitted, *6.5-2* *it's an ideal opportunity to give the hidden recesses of the bonnet a really good spray with rust inhibitor !*

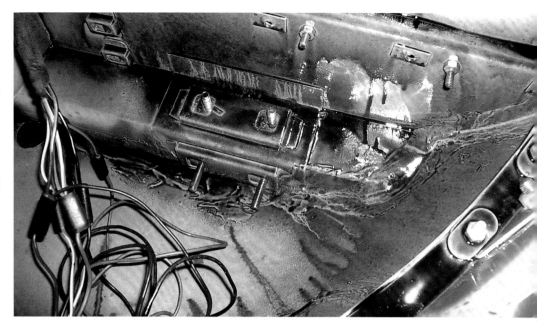

The re-chromed front bumpers, *6.5-3* *etc. Note: the rear light chromes for the side of the rear lights on the top right of the picture. It took me a while to realise what these were and where they went!*

with the wiring going to the multi-pin socket. One word of warning, however, it did make the remaining work very messy!

I fitted the sidelights/indicators and the re-chromed front bumper without too much difficulty. Both items proved easier to fit than their counterparts at the rear of the car and I didn't encounter any real problems. See Photo 6.5-3 of all the re-plated bonnet chrome and Photo 6.5-4 of the bumpers in place. (If you look closely at Photo 6.5-3, you can see that I've actually included the covers for the rear lights – Series II – by mistake and it took a while for me to work out why they wouldn't fit at the front!) The only other thing to note was that I had the sidelights (and rear lights) re-chromed but was unable to dismantle them completely to do so and this meant that the inside of the lights around the bulb holders came out of the chroming process rather discoloured and tarnished. As a result of this, the lights are now slightly dimmer than they should be. All bumpers and over-riders were liberally rust-proofed on the inside before and after fitting - having spent a fortune on new chrome, etc., you don't want it to rust! Also, there are small rubber seals that fit round the over-riders and prevent them from scratching the bumpers.

The front bumpers and sidelights *6.5-4* *in place on a strangely 'blind' looking E-type*

6.6 Fitting The Chrome To The Bonnet

I moved on to the wing beading which was marvellously easy to fit as you simply slide the head of the little brass clips into the beading and then feed the ends of the clips down the gap between the top of the wing and the centre bonnet section folding the clips over underneath: Finished! See Photo 6.6-1 of the beads being inserted. The only note of caution is that you have to ensure you don't scratch the paint on the top of the bonnet with the little brass clips as they are pushed down. In retrospect, I should have run some masking tape down either side of the gap before inserting the clips to prevent this from happening. You have to be so careful putting all this chrome onto your new paintwork; one slip and you'd never forgive yourself. I think it's worth stating the fairly obvious at this point – when the car's finished,

all that most people will ever see will be the outside of the car, i.e. the bodywork and the chrome. It doesn't matter how long you spent on the rear suspension or rebuilding the engine, what people *see* is paint and chrome.

With this in mind, it was on to fitting the headlamp eyebrows (yes, those rather ugly but very necessary items for open headlight cars) and the beading below them. The first thing I realised was why headlamp eyebrows in good condition are so sought after. I'd originally thought that my eyebrows were in good condition and had then re-chromed. It was only when I came to fit them that I realised the problem: it's not the eyebrows that get broken, it's the clips that hold them to the bonnet that snap off, rendering the eyebrow useless. Needless-to-say, the clips on both my eyebrows were broken.

Replacements don't come cheap.

I therefore took the pragmatic decision to fit the eyebrows by means of screwing them to the bonnet! In effect, this meant putting a stainless steel self tapping screw through the flange on the bonnet and what was left of the eyebrow clips. See Photo 6.6-2 showing the underside of the wing with the screw through the flange and clip. I was very aware that this was a permanent and not-at-all-desirable modification to the car but, with my budget spiralling out of control, I had to try and make some savings, and this was one of them. It's invisible from the outside of the car and only just visible on the underside, so I think it's acceptable. The eyebrows were later pop-riveted to the headlamp nacelles after the headlamp beading was in place.

6.6-1 *Left: The chrome wing beading is inserted in the gap between the wing and the bonnet centre section using special brass clips which fold over underneath to hold the beading in place (just below the oval washer)*

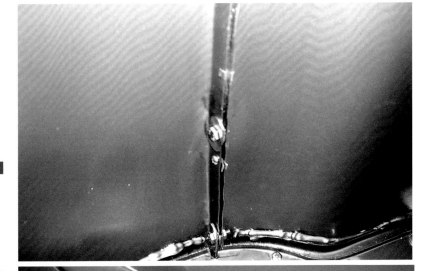

With the clips to hold the **6.6-2** *headlamp eyebrows in place broken, I secured the eyebrows to the wing by means of a self-tapping screw through the remains of the clip*

Fitting the beading around the headlamp nacelles proved to be a nightmare. The nacelles are held in place by special rivets with rounded heads that the chrome beading then clips onto. See Photo 6.6-3 of the nacelles held in place by the rivets and Photo 6.6-4 the rivets themselves. A special washer goes under the head of each rivet to give sufficient clearance for the beading to clip onto the rivets above the bodywork and the rubber strip that the chrome beading sits on. See Photo 6.6-5 of my re-chromed beading. The rubber strip goes under the beading and the edges of the eyebrows. If you look at Photo 6.6-6, you can see that I got this wrong to begin with, cutting the rubber where it meets the eyebrow instead of running it under the eyebrow as well.

Fitting the pop rivets was a stressful job because of the recoil of the rivet gun which meant it was always in danger of jumping onto the paintwork. Having successfully fitted the rivets, I cut the rubber strip in two and joined it at the

The headlamp nacelles being **6.6-3** *riveted in place*

The special rivets and washers **6.6-4** *that the chrome beading then clips onto (supposedly!)*

front. I'm not sure whether or not it should be cut, but I couldn't get it to go round such a sharp bend otherwise. Apparently the original rubber had holes pre cut in it to go over the rivets but, because they're reproduction parts, you have to cut the holes in the rubber strip yourself. With this achieved, all that remained to be done was to clip the headlamp beading onto the rivets. Simple? Of course not! No matter how I tried, the beading simply would not clip onto the rivets. Sometimes they clipped on only to pop off again and frequently they refused to clip on at all.

Having taken advice, I decided that the only thing to do was to remove the rivets and replace them with new rivets with more washers under the heads to allow greater clearance (the chrome trim generally clipped on OK without the rubber strip in place, suggesting that more clearance would solve the problem). In order to do this, I had to drill out the rivets that I'd just fitted. This meant wielding a large electric drill around my sparkling new bonnet. Not only this but some of the rivets started spinning in their holes so making drilling impossible. I had to struggle with various small cutting and grinding bits in my *Dremel* mini-drill (a virtually indispensable tool) until I finally got them out – with the paintwork intact. (This sentence doesn't really do justice

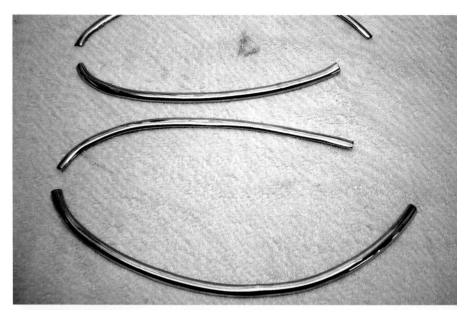

6.6-5 *My original chrome beading which later proved too damaged to re-fit and was replaced with new items*

My first efforts at fitting the **6.6-6** *rubber seal under the beading. It should go under the eyebrows and ideally not be cut at the front*

Altering the wiring to allow a **6.6-7** *sidelight bulb to be fitted inside the headlamps*

to the amount of really stressful work involved)

Replacing the rivets this time with two washers underneath made little difference: the beading still wouldn't fit. Not only this but after trying to persuade the beading to fit for some hours using ever-increasing amounts of force, my re-chromed beading was looking a bit tired and I'd actually almost flattened one in a furious attempt to force it onto a rivet. I realised that the edges of the trim were damaged where they were supposed to clip onto the rivets and trying to force them to fit had damaged them so much they were never going to fit securely. I, therefore, tried a new tactic and replaced my original beading with costly new repro items. This worked and after much, much jiggling and fiddling, I eventually got all the beading to fit, but it was a devil of a job (and an expensive one). See Photo 6.6-8 of the bonnet with all chrome finally in place.

I then fitted the headlamps. I decided to fit halogen units to replace the originals and ones with integral sidelights as I don't think the existing sidelights are bright enough on their own. (Yes, I do have a bit of a thing about lights on classic cars) In order to facilitate this, I had to run a wire from the existing sidelights into the headlamp nacelle and add another earth wire, which was a bit fiddly but fairly straightforward. See Photo 6.6-7 of the headlight being fitted. Switching the sidelights on now illuminates both the original lights under the bumper and the sidelights in the headlamps at the same time.

The final job was to stick the adhesive number plate onto the front of the bonnet. This was a job I'd really been looking forward to as it's such an iconic part of an E-type and it gives the car its identity back. But where on the bonnet did it go? I studied various photos of where the number plate was fitted on various cars. It quickly became clear that there were as many different positions for the number plate as there were cars. I decided that the plate looked its best about five to five-and-a-half inches up from the lip of the bonnet (Series II) and prepared the soapy water to fit it. I put marks on the bonnet to help me line up the self-adhesive plate. As soon as I wet the bonnet, however, the marks washed

off and I was left to fit the plate without them. After much sliding and smoothing I eventually got it nice and straight and only later realised that I'd fitted it an inch higher than I'd planned, but it still looks OK. I spent ages trying to smooth out the inevitable air bubbles and did the best I could but it wasn't perfect. I later found to my relief that after a few days the remaining bubbles slowly disappeared and left a nice smooth number plate. See Photo 6.6-8 of the finished bonnet with the number plate in place. It was really beginning to look like a car again now!

As a footnote to any number plate buffs out there, my registration is not original but is an age-related number supplied by DVLC after a variety of private plates had been put on the car in the past, including, wait for it … GAY II. I very nearly didn't admit to that one. I have noticed that there are a number of cars around with similar replacement registrations to mine that DVLA clearly issue to replace a private plate. I have discovered that the original registration for my car is, in fact, PBH 543H but decided to keep LWR 207H for various reasons. (I later reversed this decision and now have the original reg. no. on the car)

6.6-8 *The finished bonnet with all chrome, lighting and number plate in place*

Lessons learnt:

- Rustproof everything as fully as possible before reassembly.
- Refitting chrome work is the most stressful job I have yet encountered.
- Examine the clips on second-hand headlamp eyebrows as it's these that are the problem.
- Refitting the headlamp beading is a complete nightmare.
- Refitting the beading on top of the wing is very easy and very satisfying!
- Putting the registration number back on gives a car its identity.
- Sometimes it's hard to live with a E-type, but it's even harder living with an E-type that was once registered as GAY II!

6.7 Fitting The Windscreen

With the bonnet finally finished, it was time to fit the windscreen. (There's no rest for the wicked) I had already decided that I would buy a replacement windscreen and get someone else to fit it for me. I had heard and read so much about the problems of fitting a new windscreen and, without the necessary tools, help or experience in such work, it was an easy decision to make. My old windscreen had cracked *taking it out*. If I had managed to crack the old one trying to remove it, what would I do to a new one? It was one of the best decisions I've ever made.

I had gone to a Jaguar Spares Day at Stoneleigh a few months previously and collected the new screen (managing to catch one of the edges as I exited the turnstiles!) and bought

a new windscreen seal, which comes in two pieces: the main seal and the round insert that goes inside it. On arriving home, I offered up the screen to the aperture to ensure an even ¼ inch gap all round the windscreen as recommended by various specialists (notably CMC). I had my original chrome trim re-plated rather than use pattern parts to try and ensure a good fit.

All that remained to be done was to find someone who knew what they were doing to fit the screen for me. I had heard that large companies wouldn't touch such work and I was wondering who to approach (although I recently contacted *Autoglass* and they seemed happy to fit a windscreen). I simply couldn't afford to have the work done by professional restorers

and I was just beginning to despair when I chanced upon Paul and James who are bodywork specialists and had fitted many E-type windscreens between them. They agreed to come round and fit the screen one Saturday. "It should only take a couple of hours," they said, but wanted to be paid by the hour - "Just in case it's 'one of those' and takes much longer than normal." (I bet you can guess what's coming).

I believe the problems of fitting an E-type screen are caused by three main factors:

- As the cars were basically hand-built, each one is slightly different.
- The screen is very curved, not flat like the majority of car windscreens.
- You are inevitably using reproduction screens which may vary slightly from the original.

6.7-1 *Left: The rubber seal fitted to the windscreen surround ready to fit the windscreen. Note: I fitted the dashboard top first*

Paul and James lubricated the seal and encouraged the windscreen to bed down as deeply as possible **6.7-2**

James injects special non-hardening adhesive under the exterior edge of the seal **6.7-3**

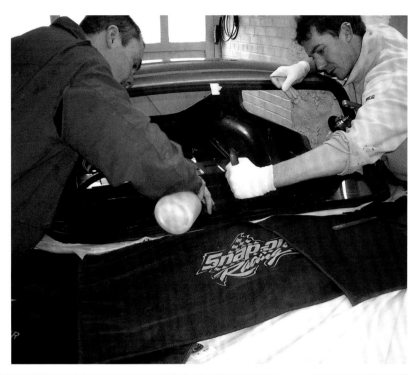

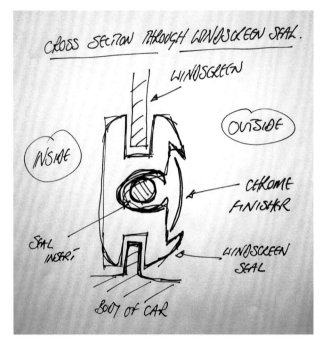

So, the day duly arrived and so did Paul and James, bright and early as promised. They wasted no time and got stuck straight in. To begin with, they took the main seal out of its packaging and left it a while to fall to shape whilst they thoroughly covered the bonnet in an assortment of protective sheeting and prepared their tools. The seal was then fitted to the windscreen aperture on the body. See Photo 6.7-1.

Using two special suction clamps (completely essential for this job), the screen was then lifted into position and slotted into the seal at the bottom. Paul and James then used small plastic spatulas (as for clay modelling) and soapy water to seat the windscreen as deep in the groove as possible so that the top edge of the screen could be inserted. See Photo 6.7-2. This is where the fun started.

After about half an hour of persuasion and fiddling, the top of the screen was no closer to going in. Paul and James struggled on manfully, using increasing amounts of brute force and soapy water, but the screen steadfastly refused to go in. At this point, we really should have stopped and called it a day. It was clear that the screen was basically too big for the aperture and did not want to go in. The problem is that it's only at this point that you really find out if

6.7-4 *A sketch showing a cross-section through the 'H'-shaped windscreen seal*

6.7-5 *Paul and James used a special tool to fit the insert into the seal – and even then it wouldn't go in!*

Fitting the top and bottom **6.7-6** *chrome trim into the seal*

6.7-7 *Fitting one of the side trims which also proved to be a very tricky operation*

the screen will fit, regardless of how much trial-fitting and measuring you have done previously.

Unfortunately, however, stopping work at this point and trying to fit a different screen wasn't quite so easy as it sounds. Various factors were involved. James and Paul had travelled 25 miles to be there and wanted to get the job done. I obviously didn't have another screen lying about to try instead and this meant I would have to take the original one back to the shop in the UK Midlands, swap it for another one, drive all the way back home and get the guys out again on another day. And even then what guarantee would there be that that the new one would fit? So we persisted. Needless to say that, with hindsight, this was probably the wrong decision.

After no less than 2½ hours, we finally forced the top of the screen into the seal. The windscreen was in place at last! James then injected special non-hardening windscreen sealant under the seal. See Photo 6.7-3. At last I thought that the hard work was done and all that remained were the easy bits (fit the circular-ish seal insert and then the chrome trim). **Wrong!** In fact, our troubles were just beginning. By forcing the windscreen home, we had squashed the seal right down and this, in turn, created major new problems. The screen seal is in an 'H' shape with a hole in the side. See Photo 6.7-4 of a particularly bad sketch of the seal and the seal insert – sorry, I'm no artist. The seal was so squashed that the seal insert wouldn't go in, despite using the proper special tool for the job. See Photo 6.7-5 of the guys trying to fit the insert.

Once again we persisted and, after 3½ hours, the seal insert was finally in (just) and it was time to fit the chrome surround. The first thing we discovered was that the screen pillar finishers on the sides of the screen

were too small to fit. The screen was obviously oversize and so the distance between the top and bottom of the windscreen was larger than that of the chrome trims which follow the curve of the seal and fit under the outer lip of the seal. Trial-fitting showed the 'ears' of the trims to be almost ¼ inch too close together. Disaster! We spent another frustrating hour fiddling with the trim in an effort to get it to fit but to no avail. We were also in danger of damaging the lip of the seal beyond repair. There were now two options: take the windscreen back out again and fit another one or grind the trim down to get it to fit.

By then we'd been toiling for 4½

hours and I took the pragmatic decision to grind the chrome trims down. A radical step but at the time it seemed a natural decision – after 4½ hours you're ready to try anything. As a general rule when you get to the point of being tired, frustrated and 'ready to try anything', you should put tools down, walk away and come back tomorrow. Decisions and work completed at this time are almost always bad ones. However, as usual, I ignored my own advice and got the grinder out.

Grinding the trims down wasn't easy as the edge of the trim is curved inwards so grinding it down is difficult as this edge can be lost. It is this curved edge that fits under the lip of the seal.

6.7-8 *The windscreen now finally fitted with the chrome trim held in place with suction clamps whilst the adhesive dried*

Right: The completed bonnet and **6.7-9** *windscreen – bring it on!*

However, this radical solution seemed to work and the side trim was offered up and judged to be OK – it can't be properly fitted until the top and bottom trims are in place. How this will work in the long term remains to be seen. Will the chrome rust or begin peeling where the edges were ground down? Only time will tell. In retrospect, I should have stopped work there and not fitted the trims. The windscreen was now in place and I could have fitted the trims myself at a later date or Paul could have helped when he came back to fit the rear screen – there was no way I was doing that one either!

The next job was to fit the top and bottom chrome trims. These fit under the lips of the seal (see Photo 6.7-3 again). I didn't realise that these trims aren't just decorative but have a function. The trims serve to open the seal and push the edges tight up against the windscreen and bodywork. Needless-to-say, this proved harder than anticipated as the windscreen was wider than normal as well as deeper. This meant that the holes at the end of each chrome strip (no-one

seems to be sure as to why they are there) were in danger of being visible as they are usually covered by the ears on the side trim,. After a lot of fiddling, we got them seated. See Photo 6.7-6 showing the fitting of the top and bottom trims. Note the extra protection to the bodywork using masking tape.

The final job was to fit the side trims over the top and bottom strips. These were glued on using a special black adhesive under the back edges by the gutter and then tucked into the seal lip at the front edge. See Photo 6.7-7 of Paul and James trying to fit one of the side trims. The final, final job was to run a skim of adhesive between the top of the side trims and the roof to make a smooth join. The side trims were then

held in place with special clamps stuck to the windscreen whilst the glue dried. See Photo 6.7-8 of the windscreen in post-operative surgery.

So a mere 6½ hours later the screen was finally fitted. It had taken three of us, two of whom were experienced E-type windscreen fitters, no less than 6½ hours to fit the screen, and even then we'd had to resort to grinding down the chrome trims. Anything you've ever read about how difficult it can be to fit a windscreen to an E-type is true. I was just so relieved it was finally in. It was one job that had been hanging over me for several months and now it was done (just). See Photo 6.7-9 of the completed bonnet and windscreen. Never again.

Lessons learnt:

- Fitting E-type windscreens is every bit as difficult as they say it is.
- Giving advice is easy; taking it is a bit more difficult.
- Easy jobs always turn out to be the hardest.
- Difficult jobs are virtually impossible.
- Keep the faith.

6.8 Fitting The Gutter Trims

With the windscreen fitted, there were a few odd jobs that needed to be done before beginning the interior trim. These final jobs were ones that I'd not been looking forward to, but they had to be done: fitting the chrome gutter trims, fitting the seal retainers around the door/quarterlight apertures and fitting the radio aerial.

I'd had both my gutter chromes re-chromed as they were in good condition and I'd heard that reproduction ones didn't fit that well. My main problem (as with all the bodywork) was that I was using a different body shell and so wasn't completely sure that they'd fit. The right hand trim went on perfectly, clipping onto the edge of the roof securely and cleanly. It was such a good fit that it didn't matter that the little tab

at the end of the trim was missing; it was securely fastened already. I used some of James and Paul's glue (left over from fitting the windscreen) under the trim to ensure it stayed in place and that was it.

The left hand trim was a different matter. It just didn't want to fit. It didn't seem to follow the curve of the roof and, despite numerous efforts, it just wouldn't go on. I ended up putting a slight kink in it as I tried to force it to fit. I now had one ex-gutter trim! I therefore bought a reproduction item to see if that would fit. When it arrived, I was surprised to find it was nearly identical to the original one. So, replacement parts can be as good as the originals. However, this didn't help me as it was just as far out as the previous one.

After much head scratching and

pondering, I realised the problem. It wasn't the curve of the trim that was wrong; it was the lip on the roof. The metal lip on the roof had somehow been bent inwards towards the roof and it was this that was preventing the trim from clipping on. This had almost certainly happened before I bought the body and I hadn't noticed it before. The lip needed to be bent outwards so the trim could clip over it. So, all I had to do was bend the lip on my perfectly-painted body shell outwards without cracking the paint! To a greater extent, and to my surprise, I did actually manage to do this, but there were inevitably cracks and chips at certain points. I covered these by simply touching up the cracks and chips and applying liberal quantities of rust-proofing wax. The trim now fitted.

I only really had myself to blame.

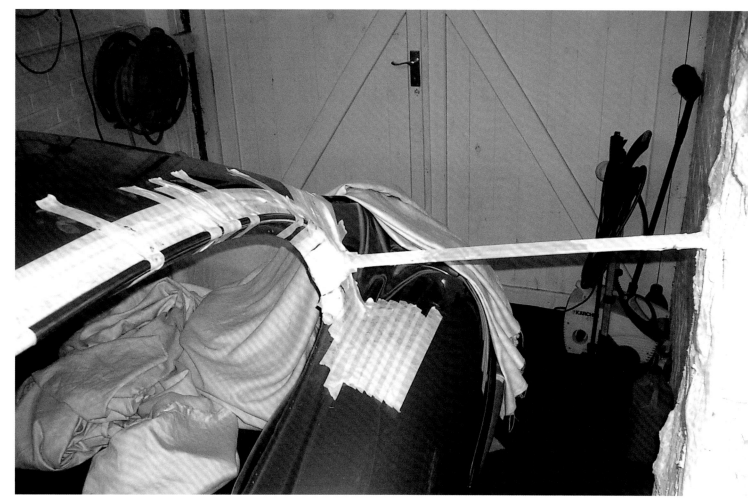

Firstly, I should have checked the gutters were OK when I bought the body shell as I just assumed they were right – after all, why shouldn't they be? Secondly, and more reprehensibly, I should have trial-fitted **all** the chrome trim on the car before sending it to the paint shop. If I had done this, the problem would have come to light prior to painting when bending the lip wouldn't have been a problem. Anyway, the repro gutter now clipped on well. The only difference was that it was slightly too long (better than being too short!) and- required cutting down. See Photo 6.8-1 (Note extensive protective tape!) I had already fitted the gutter on the offside and it fitted so well it didn't require the little tab on the end which bends under the lip to hold the trim secure. I therefore cut the trim to size flush with the bodywork without the tab. I immediately discovered I needed the tab as, although the trim now fitted OK, the end of the trim round the rear quarterlight kept lifting away from the

body. Oh, dear.

I then involved myself in several days of serious bodging where I tried to glue the trim to the gutter with copious amounts of masking tape, applying more and more adhesive and masking tape each time my previous effort failed. I even resorted to wedging a piece of wood between the trim and the garage wall in an effort to glue the trim down. See Photo 6.8-2. All to no avail as, no matter what I tried, after a day or so the glue slowly let go and the trim inexorably pinged off. Finally, I thought I'd better stop bodging and do the job properly. After much pondering, I eventually realised that the trim wasn't clipping on the lip properly on this final sharp curve as the gutter needed to be bent further outwards. After bending the lip out a little more the trim clipped on with a satisfying snap. A little adhesive underneath and it was job done. I just hope my roof doesn't start rusting where I've had to adjust the lip. Time will tell. (So far, so good)

6.8-1 *Opposite page: On fitting the new left hand chrome gutter trim, it proved to be slightly too long and required cutting down*

6.8-2 *Above: Attempting to persuade the gutter trim to remain in place using a piece of wood jammed against the garage wall – all to no avail!*

Lessons learnt:

- Trial-fit *all* chrome to the body before painting (this is the second time this lesson has popped up – 'nough said).
- Bodging jobs just isn't worth it – you'll only have to do the job again properly at a later date.

6.9   Electric Aerial And Radio

Another little job was to fit my electric radio aerial. Don't ask me why but I've a thing about automatic radio aerials and was determined to fit one to my car. Where to site the aerial? Some cars have them in the scuttle just in front of the windscreen but I think that can be rather unsightly so I opted to put mine in the rear offside wing. The problem with this is getting it in the right position so it doesn't foul the fuel pump or get in the way of the spare wheel. The electric aerial I bought was quite a large item, larger than I'd hoped, but there was still room to fit it. I worked out where the aerial should go and with fear and trepidation I drilled a large hole in my brand new bodywork. See Photo 6.9-1. Why I didn't do this a long time ago, before I had the body shell painted, I

don't really know. It was a job that I'd always done previously with the car painted (back in the '70s and '80s) so I think I just thought that I'd do the same again. Poor planning.

I then fitted the electric aerial under the wheel arch with the metal fitting strip supplied (see Photo 6.9-2) and screwed the universal fitting escutcheon on top of the wing. See Photo 6.9-3. I also needed to run two wires from the dashboard to operate the aerial; one permanent live and one switched live from the radio. I now had a working fully automatic electric aerial! See Photo 6.9-4.

I'm generally pleased with the result, but there are one or two niggles. The aerial is a pretty meaty affair and more suited to large corporate saloons than delicately sculpted E-types.

The escutcheon on top of the wing is consequently rather larger and clumsier than I'd like. Also the body of the aerial is large and as such needs very careful positioning to get right as otherwise it'll foul the boot floor or the spare wheel. I've found that I've sited mine just too close to the spare wheel so that it's difficult to tilt it to get the aerial so it comes out of the body at a nice rakish angle – too late to change it now.

I also sent my radio off to the *Vintage Wireless Company* to have it modernised and updated. One of my pet hates on older cars is to have a brand new anachronistic stereo sitting in the dash. It's just as difficult to live with an original radio that simply pumps out static and barely discernible music in the background. Not only that

6.9-1 *Left: The large hole drilled in the rear wing to take the electric aerial*

The electric aerial held in place inside the rear wing **6.9-2**

The chromed escutcheon holding the aerial in place on top of the wing **6.9-3**

Just enough headroom in my 'garage' to try out my new automatic aerial **6.9-4**

but I was very aware that one essential item to make Christine, my lovely wife, happy with the car (which at that time simply represented a waste of time, money and space to her) was to have a decent stereo in place. Anyway, I sent my original *Radiomobile* unit off to have it converted to FM, enable it to play MP3s and have a take-off for the electric aerial fitted. It cost me an arm and a leg and took far longer to do than the three weeks quoted (more like three months) but I think it'll be worth it. More on this later.

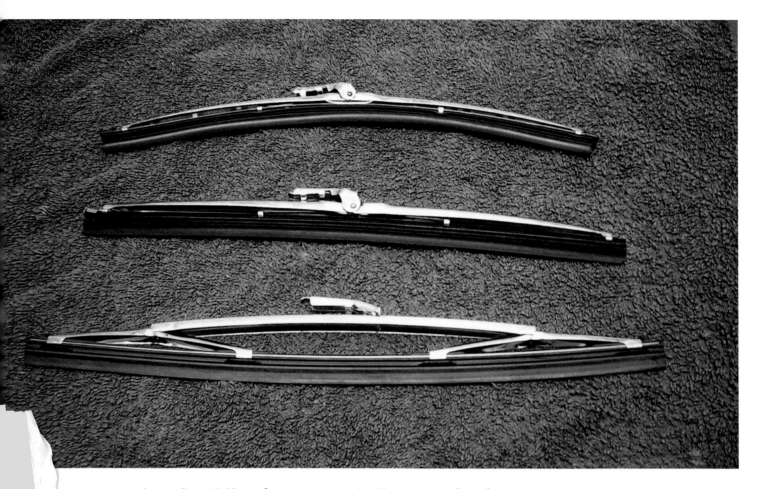

6.10 Windscreen Wiper Blades and Door Seal Retainers

Other minor items of note were the fitting of the windscreen wiper blades: small items but of immense importance. When I had the car on the road (eight years previously), the wipers drove me mad as they simply wouldn't clear the windscreen but left a horrible smear and in places didn't even touch the screen at all. I have subsequently discovered three types of wiper blade on sale: Tex, standard and SNG ones. Of these three, I think the SNG Barratt blade seems to be the best as they are specially made to follow the quite acute curve of the E-type windscreen. See Photo 6.10-1 Also note that the Tex ones are 12 inch, not 11 inch. However, I've not had the opportunity to try the new wipers out so I'll have to reserve judgement for the time being. (3000 miles on and

the wiper blades work OK, but still not perfectly. Perhaps this is just one of the little foibles of a classic car and should be celebrated rather than cursed?)

The final job to be done before starting the interior trimming was to fit the seal retainers around the doors and quarterlights. (They hold the rubber seals for the doors and rear quarterlights in place) I had inadvertently left my original ones on my old body shell when I sold it and so had to buy new. One problem was that many suppliers simply denied that they existed let alone try and supply them. I eventually tracked them down at Martin Robey's and paid the hefty price tag (another expensive mistake on my part). Fitting them was a really horrible job and again one that should be done before painting the car.

The seal retainers are held on by pop rivets and the cant rails (trim) on the inside of the car are later screwed on through the groove of the retainers. As my parts were new, I had to drill new holes all around the aperture and through the retainers - not an easy job drilling through bodywork edges full of welding spots, etc. To do this, I held the retainers in place with clamps. See Photo 6.10-2. (N.B. Pairs of holes are drilled, one used to attach the retainers to the body, the other to later screw the cant rails on through the retainers) I then tried to pop rivet the retainers to the body. Unfortunately the nozzle of my rivet gun was relatively wide and sat on the edges of the retainers, not in the base of the groove. This meant that when I tried to put in the rivets, the nozzle of the gun simply crushed the

edges of the seal. Not only that but the pop rivets snapped off only half way in and had to be drilled out. I subsequently discovered that professional restorers use an especially thin nozzle for this job that fits inside the edges of the groove and seats properly in the bottom of the seal retainer. Not having such a nozzle and being totally fed up with pop rivets in general, I elected to screw the retainers to the body, using countersunk screws, and then saw the threads off where they protruded into the car. A really horrible job that took several days and I hated every minute; the only good bit of the job was when it was finished. (This later proved to be a mistake as, even though the heads of the screws I used were countersunk, they still protruded into the seal retainer and, when I came to fit the rubber seals in the retainers, the screw heads were very much in the way)

6.10-1 *Opposite page: The three types of blade I found on sale. From top to bottom: SNG Barratt modified blades, original style and the longer Tex blades*

I held the seal retainers in place whilst I drilled pairs of holes through them and the bodywork in preparation for riveting them to the body **6.10-2**

Lessons learnt:

- Getting windscreen wipers to work properly on an E-type is not easy.
- It's the small fiddly jobs like fitting gutter trims and seal retainers that are the worst.
- Flowers and chocolates may sound old-fashioned, but they work (at least temporarily!).

7.1 Beginning The Interior Trimming

And so onto fitting the interior trim. I had rather mixed feelings about this. On the one hand, I was very happy as I knew it was the last big job and then the car would be finished; on the other hand, I was worried as I knew I wasn't a trimmer. I'm a self-confessed trim dunce. I've never been any good at anything like this. At school I once deliberately dropped a 'vase' I'd made in pottery as it was so bad I was too embarrassed to let anyone see it. When I built Airfix model planes as a child, I'd always end up with more glue on my fingers and the pilot's canopy than on the model itself.

Another consideration was that I knew trimming the car was going to be a big job, but not *that* big a job! It took far longer than I anticipated and was very difficult to complete. My advice is if you can find someone to trim your car for you at a reasonable price, then go for it, but don't underestimate how big a job it is and therefore how much it will cost. I did have a secret weapon though – Mick and Chris Turley from M.C.T. Trimming. Mick used to work at Jaguar as a trimmer and trimmed E-types for several years. Both he and his son Chris helped me immeasurably throughout the re-trim and their assistance proved invaluable.

I started by buying a trim kit from them. If you're really serious about trimming, you could just buy the rolls of material, but it's hard enough even with a trim kit which basically consists of all the trim you need cut to size and shape and the leather for the seats ready made to cover the frames. A few weeks after placing the order, I went down and collected the beautifully-made kit from their premises in Nuneaton and Mick spent several hours explaining how to trim an E-type and in what order, etc.

I learnt the following basic, essential information:

There are six different visible types of trim on an E-type:

Vinyl for the sills, boot boards, doors and wheel arches, etc.

Leather for the seat fronts and sides, the centre arm rest and the top of the gearbox cover.

Hardura for the outer sides of the footwells and under the dashboard and seats.

Ambla (slightly elasticated) for the seat backs and the gear lever gaiter.

Printed Millboard for the under-dash panels.

7.1-1 *Left: The six different types of trim on an E-type, clockwise from top left: carpet, vinyl and Ambla (on the gear lever cover and gaiter respectively), Hardura, printed millboard and leather*

Carpet for the floors and gearbox tunnel. See Photo 7.1-1 respectively.

Use the proper glue: 1358 contact adhesive, coat both surfaces to be glued*, allow the glue to go off (about 10 - 20 mins) and then stick them together.

Don't forget that it's a contact adhesive so, as soon as it touches, it sticks – you can't reposition it.

Many pieces of vinyl trim have foam underneath them to make them soft and give them a smoother profile, e.g. the sills and boot boards. In these cases, coat only the metal or wood (not the foam) with glue; then *gently* stick the foam on straight away and leave to go off. (Push too hard and the foam will 'dent' and never be flat again) The foam should be ½ inch smaller than the vinyl all the way round. The vinyl then glues

over the top of the foam by sticking it only around the outside of the foam, - never glue directly onto the foam. Your sills, etc., are therefore only glued at the edges, not all over. Don't believe me? Run your hand over your sills – it's true!

There doesn't seem to be any kind of solvent/cleaner available for the contact adhesive (and I've tried most things!) so it's not easy to remove if you get it wrong.

*Except when gluing foam to the body in which case just glue the body not the foam.

7.2 Fitting The Headlining

Unfortunately the first job to be undertaken is one of the most feared – fitting the headlining to the underside of the roof. This actually turned out to be one of the easiest jobs. One problem that had been at the back of my mind was the condition of the underside of my roof. I'd filled the hole where a Webasto sunroof had been and had sacrificed the finish on the underside of the roof for the sake of a perfect finish on the outside. I was very worried what the headlining would end up looking like. My fears proved groundless, however, as Mick supplied me with a foam-based headlining that was about ¼ inch thick. This effectively hid any unevenness of the roof surface and produced a nice smooth finish.

Not only that but fitting this type of headlining was far easier than fitting the original thin cloth type as the foam holds its shape and can be manoeuvred without too much difficulty. My great neighbour Chris was once again on hand to help as this is definitely a two-person operation (four or five with the original cloth covering). Having liberally sprayed Dinitrol into the edges of the roof, under the guttering, it was time to fit the lining. Be careful with the rust proofer as you don't want to get it on the headlining. We initially

7.2-1 *The new, thicker headlining covered in glue waiting to be offered up to the inside of the roof*

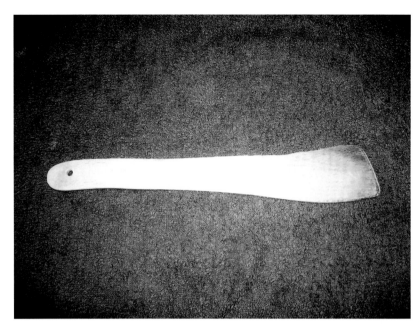

7.2-2 *My bespoke headlining fitting tool – a wooden kitchen spatula*

offered the lining up to the roof and cut it roughly to size and made clear marks (on the underside!) so we could line them up when ready to be glued. The next thing was to coat the underside of the roof and the headlining with glue and leave to go off. We then placed the lining on the bonnet, ready to feed it through the windscreen aperture. See Photo 7.2-1 (Note that the headlining was actually fitted before the windscreen, but I thought it made more sense to chronicle it this way round) It was then a fairly simple task to feed the lining into the cockpit, with me lying underneath it and then, when it was in line, to simply push it up in the middle of the roof and then smooth it out towards the edges. Being thick, it didn't ripple or crease and went on nicely.

The headlining is then pushed under the inner lip of the roof, but I found that the gap was too small and the headlining wouldn't go under it. There were two reasons for this. Firstly, when the E-types were built, the trimmers apparently put the headlining in place and then simply hammered the lip up tight and, secondly, I was using a much thicker headlining than normal. This combination of factors meant that the headlining wouldn't go under the lip. I therefore had to carefully (very carefully!) bend the lip downwards sufficiently to allow the headlining to fit under it. This was particularly difficult at the corners as they wouldn't bend. Eventually, using my new special tool – the thin end of a wooden kitchen spatula (perfect – see Photo 7.2-2) – I was able to push the edges of the lining underneath the lip. (Being careful not to get rust proofer or glue on the headlining – rust proofer is bad but glue is even worse) I then hammered the lip back up again where necessary. Job finished! See Photo 7.2-3.

When the headlining was in **7.2-3** *place, I carefully hammered the lip round the edge of the roof up tight against it*

7.3 Fitting Vinyl To Rear Hatch Aperture

The next job was to fit the trim to the lip of the rear hatch. Originally Series I and II cars had a sort of plastic retainer here but these aren't available now so I trimmed it as for Series III cars with vinyl. This meant initially gluing a thin strip of foam to the inside edge (see Photo 7.3-1) and then gluing a slightly wider piece of trim over the top of it (see Photo 7.3-2) which was then stuck down and trimmed to fit. See Photos 7.3-3 and 7.3-4. But slight disaster! If you look again at Photo 7.3-2, you might be able to see that I put glue *all over* the back of the vinyl and stuck it directly onto the foam, not just round it (just not concentrating). As a result, the foam twisted slightly out of shape and caused a couple of ripples that shouldn't be there. Never mind, it still looked OK and I now had the first piece of red vinyl trim on the car!

Another problem that I came across several times was simply not knowing what can be seen and what can't. For instance, how far did the vinyl have to go under the roof so it wouldn't leave a gap when other pieces of trim were fitted? I had no idea and trusted to the trim kit to ensure that I had been given enough material. Again, the more reference photos you have the better; you simply can't have enough.

A thin piece of foam in place **7.3-1**
round the rear hatch lip ready to accept the vinyl

Beginning to glue the vinyl down **7.3-2**
over the foam

7.3-3 *The vinyl in place around the outside of the rear hatch aperture*

Lessons learnt:

- Trim adhesive is a contact adhesive – it sticks as soon as it touches.
- Leave the glue to go off before sticking together.
- Glue foam to the body by only gluing the body and not the foam.
- Don't glue vinyl directly onto foam; glue the vinyl round the edge of the foam.
- There are at least six different types of trim on an E-type.
- Trimming an E-type is a very big job.
- With the right help and support, you can trim an E-type (if I can, anyone can).
- Keep going – you're on the home straight!

The vinyl viewed from inside the car **7.3-4**

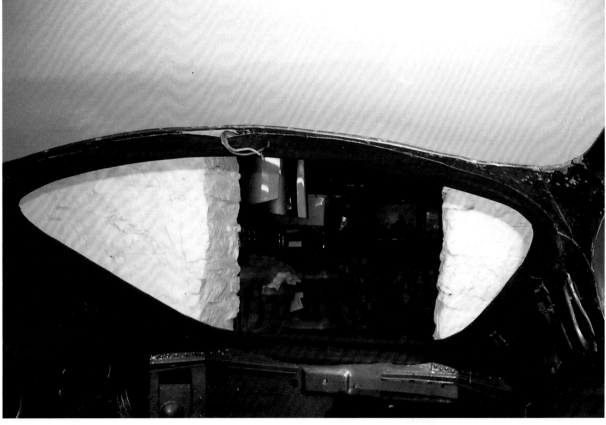

7.4 Trimming The Lips At The Side Of The Roof

My final job at this stage was to fit headlining strips over the lip at the edge of the roof. In order to facilitate this, I needed to fit trim retainers to the rear of the roof, see Photo 7.4-1. These are just basically toothed pieces of metal that grab the pieces of headlining that cover the lip of the roof. These were another part that I had left on my old body shell when I'd sold it without realising they were actually a separate part (like the seal retainers) and had to buy new. Not only this but I also discovered that they're generally unobtainable. I finally tracked some down at RM & J Smith's (how many times he's been able to supply 'unobtainable' parts I can't tell you) paid the money (whilst kicking myself) and fitted them to the roof ready to receive the headlining trim strips. See Photo 7.4-2 of the trim retainers. The headlining trim strips have a rolled edge and this is tucked under the roof lip (using my trusty spatula) and the other edge is hooked under the trim retainers at the rear of the roof and glued down at the sides - see Photo 7.4-3. Slowly but surely the trim was beginning to go on.

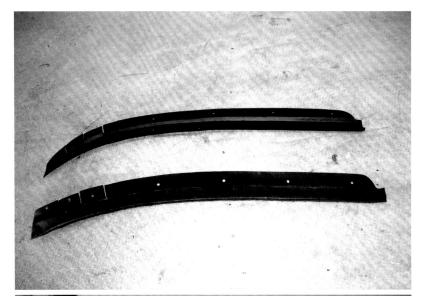

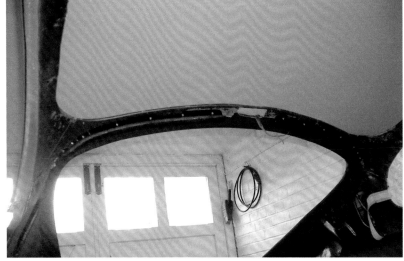

The rear trim retainers that I didn't even know were missing from my car until this point

The rear trim retainers screwed in place

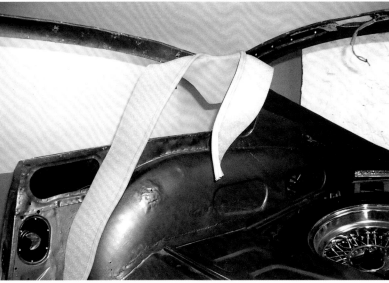

Fitting the headlining trim strips under the roof lip and over the seal retainers

7.5 Rear Wheel Arch Covers, Armrests And Sun Visors

I finished fitting the trim to the inside lip of the roof by tucking the rolled edge under the lip on the underside edge of the roof and then gluing the bottom edge onto the lip. I was then able to fit the interior light which was great as I finally got rid of the dangling wires that had driven me mad for ages. See Photo 7.5-1.

By now I was feeling bolstered by my trimming efforts to date and so, feeling increasingly confident, I tackled the next job on the list - the rear wheel arch covers. These were to be my nemesis. Armed with an increasing belief in my own ability, I tried to fit the foam - a seemingly simple job that I made a complete mess of. I just couldn't quite get the foam to fit the contours of the wheel arch and so began to hack it about with predictable results. See Photo 7.5-2.

To compound my mistakes, I pressed on and tried to fit the vinyl over the top of the foam. Basically I made a total pig's ear of it. *[Meaning a mess or a muddle, derived from C14th proverb: You can't make a silk purse out of a sow's ear. Ed]* See Photo 7.5-3. All I can say is, I tried to fit the vinyl without any creases but failed miserably. As soon as I pulled it one way to try and remove the creases, they simply appeared in other places. Not only this but I was dealing with contact adhesive. So every time I got it wrong, I had to rip off the adhesive and start again, making even more of a mess. In the end, I left it in a bit of a state and vowed to return to it later on. (When I did, I'm glad to report that I finally managed to get them looking 'something like' and not noticeably creased, but they're still not perfect)

My new-found self belief evaporated. I was forced to compare my efforts with those of Mick Turley who'd made the trim kit for me. He had already agreed to do the difficult bits for me and busied himself covering the radio fascia, the rear hinge covers, the 'B' post edges and the gear lever cowl and gaiter. See Photo 7.5-4 of Mick using his years of skill and experience to form complex curves in vinyl with no problem whatsoever. He also covered my header rail above the windscreen and sun visors in vinyl because I didn't want them in the original cloth as I think they look so much better in vinyl. See Photo 7.5-5. He also went on to cover my horrible plastic armrests (Series IIs have these horrible foam injected mouldings that are pretty vile) as I was changing the colour of the

7.5-1 *Left: With the interior light fitted, I finally got rid of those dangling wires that had driven me mad since I'd bought the body shell – a long time!*

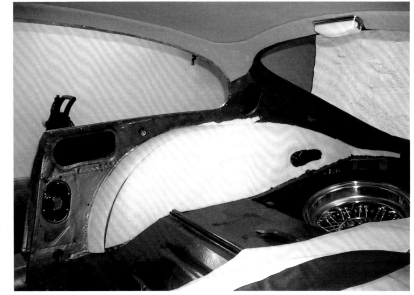

I just couldn't get the foam to fit the rear wheel arches properly. And if I couldn't get the foam to fit what about the vinyl...? **7.5-2**

interior from beige to red and armrests aren't readily available (once again I hesitate to say unobtainable) and I wanted to be rid of those nasty plastic things anyway. See Photos 7.5-6, 7.5-7 and 7.5-8. The armrests are a triumph of trimming – they look immeasurably superior to the originals and make all the difference to the feel of the interior. So Mick had done the 'difficult bits' for me, but I couldn't even manage the easy bits like the wheel arch covers.

My first woeful attempt at fitting the vinyl rear wheel arch covers **7.5-3**

Mick Turley at work creating beautifully trimmed parts for E-types **7.5-4**

My sun visors trimmed in vinyl rather than cloth – I think they look a lot better like this **7.5-5**

Mick makes new end caps for my old and crumbling armrests out of wood **7.5-6**

In a trice he's sewn new vinyl covers together and fits them over my horrible original items **7.5-7**

My finished armrests trimmed in red vinyl (Sorry about the photo, they look even better 'in the flesh') **7.5-8**

7.6 Footwell Carpets - 1

Ah, well. I decided to turn my attention to the rather more straightforward task of fitting the carpets to the footwells. The general rule of trimming being to start in the middle and work outwards so you don't damage the trim you've just fitted. So don't fit the sill trims first as you'll have to crawl all over them to get to the rest of the interior.

The carpets proved a more straightforward and achievable task. To begin with, I fitted the underfelt to the toe board and the gearbox tunnel. See Photo 7.6-1. Note that there is no felt on the triangular section of the tunnel. I then fitted the millboard to the outer sides of the footwell and then the underfelt and Hardura to the underside of the dashboard, followed by the air vents which were fairly straightforward. See Photos 7.6-2 and 7.6-3.The main thing that struck me about all this was how hidden and difficult to access all the parts of the car were becoming. You really need to ensure that all is well with the workings of the car before fitting the trim as getting to many parts means ripping the trim off and causing considerable damage. Something as simple as a loose connection takes on massive significance when under several layers of carefully glued trim. To remove the brake servo or the engine frames would require massive destruction/ removal of the trim, just to gain access to the nuts and bolts inside the car. Even the gearbox cover becomes inaccessible when the carpet is glued to the tunnel. See Photo 7.6-4. Note that the carpet isn't quite the lurid shade of red it appears in the photos; it just looks like that with flash photography for some reason.

The next job was to fit the wiring harness cover to the top left hand side of the left hand footwell. This is just a simple metal conduit that is then covered in vinyl and subsequently screwed to the body. The vinyl is then left in a big tail at the top so it can simply be tucked up under the dashboard in a fairly loose fashion to hide the wiring as it goes up under the dashboard. See Photo 7.6-5. Oh, how basic some bits of trimming can be! See Photo 7.6-2 again.

7.6-1 *The underfelt glued to the toe board and gearbox tunnel of the passenger footwell*

Plain millboard is glued to the **7.6-2** *outer sides of the footwell (as a base for the red Hardura to be fitted to later) and underfelt followed by black Hardura is glued underneath the dashboard*

My rejuvenated air vents waiting **7.6-3**
to be fitted

Beginning to glue the carpets in **7.6-4**
the footwell and over the gearbox
tunnel

The wiring harness cover **7.6-5**
trimmed in vinyl with a large 'tail'
that simply tucks up underneath
the dashboard to hide the wiring

Lessons learnt:

- Fitting the rear wheel arch covers is a really difficult job.
- Re-trimming the horrible plastic armrests in vinyl is a vast improvement.
- And the same goes for the sun visors.
- Ensure that all mechanical work is properly completed before trimming as access is difficult and it's easy to ruin/tear/ discolour your trim.
- Watching an expert at work always engenders a mixture of awe and humility.

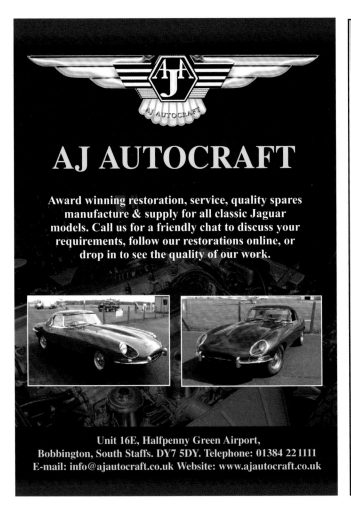

7.7 Fitting The Millboard

At this point let me just reiterate that trimming the car proved to be a far bigger job than I had anticipated. With the rest of the car completed, I thought that the trim would be a relative breeze. How wrong I was. One major factor in all of this is that there's absolutely no manual available for fitting the interior trim. You're on your own - 'off manual' (until now that is!). No amount of peering at your Haynes manual will do any good at all.

Thankfully, I had Mick Turley on hand to assist and I rang him on countless occasions when I needed help or clarification about some piece of trim or other. Without his help, I literally wouldn't have known where to start. Even with his advice and the excellent trim kit he provided, the

whole process was time-consuming and demanding of skills I didn't possess. However, I was spurred on by the knowledge that this was the home straight in terms of the restoration. It was time to crack on and learn new skills as I went along. (As ever with these things you only really learn how to do the job properly when you've finished it - by which time it's a bit late!)

Anyway, onwards and upwards. I decided to finish the footwell and under-dash area first. I repainted and refitted the air vents to the underside of the dash, and with these in place I fitted the printed millboard under the dashboard. These slot under the lip of the dashboard at the front and are secured by two self tapping screws at the rear edge which screw

into two spire nuts clipped onto two brackets under the dash. The problem being where to make the holes in the millboard for the screws? Since the millboard covers the whole area it's impossible to know where the brackets are when you offer the millboard up for trial-fitting. I came up with a cunning plan to get round this. I screwed the self tappers *down* through the top of the spire clips and then offered the millboard up and when it was in the right position pushed up hard against the point of the screws. This left clear marks on the underside of the board, showing exactly where the holes should be drilled. Clever, huh? (Well, I thought so anyway) See Photo 7.7-1 of the passenger footwell from later in the restoration with the under dash millboard fitted along with the

7.7-1 *Left: The finished footwell from later in the restoration showing the carpets, Hardura and wiring harness cover in place, plus the back edge of the printed millboard screwed under the dash*

Three of the four different styles and sizes of spire clip I used to assemble various parts of the car **7.7-2**

Hardura on the side of the footwell (fitted after the sill vinyl).

On the subject of spire clips, there are at least four different types/lengths/sizes of spire clip used on an E-type (see Photo 7.7-2 of three of them – I couldn't find a fourth one to photo!) and it's always a good idea to stock up on these prior to assembling the interior. Other items that proved invaluable are a large supply of different sized self-tapping screws (stainless in my case), plus a selection of trim screws. However, every supplier I ordered from sent me galvanized (?) trim screws instead of the original chrome-plated ones. I never found anyone to supply them in chrome. Another essential item is a very large supply of small drill bits for making holes for the trim screws. I'm afraid I got through a frightening amount of them – often using one drill per hole. I tried different drill speeds on my trusty Dremel, I tried tungsten-tipped and superior quality but it seemed to make little difference – they still burnt out. I used mainly 2mm, 2.5mm, 3mm drills (B & Q don't do Imperial).

Lessons learnt:

- There's no manual available to my knowledge on how to re-trim an E-type (apart from this one!).
- Seeking the advice of an expert is pretty essential where trimming is concerned – especially if you're as inept and inexperienced as me.
- When you've finished a job, you'll know how to do it.

7.8 Trimming The Rear Bulkhead And Up-stand

With the millboard in place, I turned my attention to the rear bulkhead. This is the only bit of vinyl that is fitted without foam underneath. The vinyl is glued straight onto the panel. See Photo 7.8-1. The only thing that should be under the vinyl is sound-deadening Flintkote. Unfortunately I looked for a supplier of *Flint Coat*, as I thought it was called, and used this name to search the internet and therefore drew a blank. If I had simply telephoned one of the main spares stockists, they would have been able to supply it immediately, as I have since learned. My car therefore has no sound deadening fitted, Flintkote or otherwise. (Now the car is on the road I can happily inform you that it is still very quiet and more refined than I'd anticipated)

With the rear bulkhead covered, I trimmed the up-stand which sits on top of the bulkhead. This was another of those 'straightforward' little jobs that proved to be particularly difficult. One upgrade I'd decided upon early on in the restoration was to fit inertia reel seat belts. When the car was on the road previously, the old static belts had driven me mad, getting stuck beneath us on the seats and jamming between the seats and the gearbox tunnel. I therefore bought a pair of inertia reel belts that I was told would fit. They are a three-point fitting with a stalk on the gearbox tunnel. I decided that the best place to site the main reel was against the base of the rear wheel arches. In order to facilitate this, I had to adapt the up-stand so that it fitted tightly against the wheel arch with no gap.

Normally, the up-stand sits about ½ inch in front of the wheel arch on either side of the car.

I therefore made a cut in the up-stand that allowed its outer edges to clamp against the arches whilst allowing the main centre section to remain in its usual position. See Photos 7.8-1 and 7.8-2. I then drilled holes through the up-stand and the wheel arches to accept the large bolts securing the inertia reels. Notice the use of masking tape on Photo 7.8-2 to protect the piping on the rear wheel arch trim whilst trial-fitting the up-stand. More on the fitment and use of the belts at a later date – but I can tell you that they work pretty well and are a vast improvement on the old static ones. I then covered the up-stand in foam and then vinyl. As with the rear

Jaguar E-type Club

The Jaguar E-type Club was formed by leading Jaguar author Philip Porter and his wife Julie in 2005.

At the Club's heart is the E-type magazine, our vibrant 52 page, full-colour, monthly magazine, which is dedicated to E-types and E-types only. Articles encompass everything from restoration stories and technical advice to originality, E-type racing, upgrading, E-type histories and event reports. It is no ordinary club magazine!

The E-type Club is truly international with members in over 50 countries who enjoy a variety of events worldwide focussed entirely on E-types and maximising enjoyment of the world's favourite sports car.

We produce a digital edition of our magazine, which includes videos, extra photos, live links to websites and much more.

Jaguar E-type Club
Tel: +44 (0)1584 781588   Email: info@e-typeclub.com
www.e-typeclub.com

7.8-1 *Left: The rear bulkhead vinyl, behind the seats, is glued straight onto the body without foam underneath. My new up-stand is loosely fitted above it*

I modified my up-stand rather **7.8-2** *crudely by making a cut either end which allowed the inertia reel seatbelts to be bolted up tight against the wheel arches*

wheel arches, I just couldn't get the vinyl to fit properly and neatly without creases but, as with the wheel arches, I persevered and did the best job I could - but it still isn't perfect. I then screwed the up-stand to the rear bulkhead and rear wheel arches. I think it was originally pop riveted to the wheel arches but I decided to use screws to

enable it to be removed more easily in future if necessary.

My philosophy behind this is simple: if you put something together in such a way that it can't be taken apart again easily, you will need to take it apart again. If you put it together in a way that enables you to dismantle it easily, you will never need to take it apart again.

(Well most of the time!) I therefore ensure that all parts can be dismantled easily, safe in the knowledge that they will therefore not require dismantling in the future. Sorted!

7.9 Footwell Carpets - 2

With the up-stand in place, I returned to the footwell carpets and fitted the carpets to the sides of the gearbox tunnel. It was at this point that I learned that the passenger side carpet isn't glued down all over but only at the top to allow the carpet to be hinged up to give access to the gearbox filler plug. This piece of carpet therefore has a pocket on the inside for the under felt so that it doesn't need gluing down either. See Photo 7.9-1.

The passenger side gearbox **7.9-1** *tunnel carpet – designed to hinge upwards to allow access to the gearbox – but I don't know why as the filler plug is on the other side!*

7.10 Trimming The Sills

It was time to have a go at the sills. I was worried about these as they are such a major piece of trim and they are so visible. I needed to get them right. I started with the relatively simple job of gluing the foam down. See Photo 7.10-1. The only real problem with the foam is to ensure that you leave enough of a gap at the outer edge to fit the chrome sill trims later, but not too much of a gap as will leave a dent in the vinyl behind the chrome trims.

I then glued the edges of the vinyl trim and the metal around the edges of the foam and, after allowing a few minutes for the glue to go off, I set to work. Although it wasn't easy trying to get them to fit without creases, etc., I'm quite pleased with the result. Note that the rear edge of the trim is folded over where it meets the 'B' post

to make a neat edge. See Photo 7.10-2. The front edge, the cross member on the floor and the lower rear edge of the trim are hidden by other panels and can therefore be glued without too much worry. However, it's worth noting that apparently on some cars the rear edges were never folded over from new – probably on cars made on a Friday afternoon!

With the vinyl in place, I was then able to fit the chrome sill finishers. I had bought the requisite clips for this but, when I came to fit the sill finishers, I discovered they were a perfect interference fit without the clips and so left them out. I'm not sure why this is, but is probably due to the way the new sills were welded onto the body making a thicker than standard joint. I was then able to fit the Hardura to the

outer side of the footwells and around the back of the 'A' post and then glue the carpet over the cross members. The footwell carpets and under felt were then simply laid in place, not glued down to enable easy removal for drying out, etc., if necessary. (What, an E-type leak? Never!) See Photo 7.10-3 of the nearside sill and footwell area with carpets, vinyl and Hardura all in place. Also see Photo 7.10-4 of the interior of the car from slightly later in the restoration showing the trim in place for both footwells. (I later fitted two plastic carpet lugs to the rear edge of both footwell carpets to hold them in place)

7.10-1 *Left: The first job when trimming the sills is to carefully glue the foam onto the sill – leave room round the edge to glue the vinyl down around it*

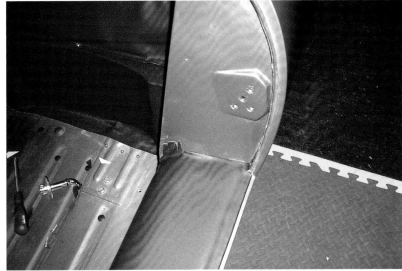

The rear edges of the vinyl folded over to make a nice edge against the 'B' post **7.10-2**

The nearside sill and footwell finished with vinyl, Hardura and carpet **7.10-3**

The nearly completed interior beginning to look really good **7.10-4**

Lessons learnt:

- It's Flintkote not Flint coat, you nana *[slang expression for a fool, probably from banana. This is also the only motoring manual to educate you in ancient slang! Ed]*.
- If you ensure a part can be easily dismantled in the future, then you should never have to dismantle it again (allegedly).
- Getting the footwells and sills trimmed makes you feel like you're making real progress at last!

7.11 Wheel Arch Hardboard Trim

The next job on my list was the fitting of the vinyl covered hardboard trim that goes over the top of, and in front of, the wheel arches. There are two pieces either side and they are attached to the car by means of little trim clips that fasten into small holes already in the car's bodywork. The rearmost trim is fitted first and the forward one goes on afterwards, overlapping where they meet at the top of the wheel arch.

In theory, clipping these trim pieces on is easy, but in reality they're total swines to fit. The clips often don't match up with the holes and, when they do, the clips don't want to snap home, either refusing to go into the hole or popping back out again afterwards. Also, as you fit the panel, it becomes harder to fit the later clips as

access becomes increasingly difficult with half the panel now clipped to the bodywork. All I can say is that it takes an inordinate amount of time, an awful lot of contortion to the upper body (as with virtually all aspects of trimming) and a high degree of patience to get them to fit. If you're not careful, you resort to trying to get them to snap home by hitting them with a hammer, which means hammering the trim, not best practice and not recommended – but, yes, I did resort to this method on occasion (with a cloth over the hammer to protect the trim) and just about got away with it.

You also need to have fitted the rear hatch locking mechanism and hinges before fitting the trim. I trial-fitted the hatch and added special spacers where required to the hinges to get

a perfect fit (even though I'd already done this prior to painting – more on this later). I also spent a considerable amount of time ensuring that the catch worked properly. There are various adjustments that can be made to the mechanism and the hook on the door as well as fitting spacers under the mechanism on the body if required. I'm very pleased to report that I managed to get mine working well – opening properly and more importantly shutting cleanly and securely.

With the hinges and locking mechanisms in place, I began to fit the trim. See Photo 7.11-1 of the trim beginning to go on, but with the inevitable creases. This is the real problem with trimming generally – it's fairly easy to fit the trim to an E-type, but getting it to fit *properly* so that

7.11-1 *Left: Starting to fit the vinyl-covered hardboard trim over the wheel arches. The real task is to get rid of those damn creases!*

it doesn't look a mess is a complete nightmare. Once again, I can now happily report that I did manage to remove most of the creases later on, but it was really difficult and incredibly time-consuming.

Lessons learnt:

- Trimming an E-type is relatively straightforward. Getting it to look right is another matter altogether.
- Being a contortionist is a definite advantage where trimming is concerned.

7.12 Fitting The Inertia Reel Seatbelts

With the trim around the wheel arches finally clipped in position and screwed to the sills where they meet the floor behind the seats, it was time to fit the inertia reel seatbelts.

With the up-stand panel on the rear bulkhead already altered to allow the reel to be bolted firmly to the wheel arch (as described earlier), I drilled holes through the wheel arches and mounted the reels using a spreader plate in the wheel arch to spread the load in the event of an accident (see Photo 7.12-1). I then utilised the existing seat belt mounting points above the wheel arches for the two remaining brackets (see Photo 7.12-2). The seat belts came with the appropriate brackets, bolts and spacers, etc., and I found these fitted OK after a little judicious manipulation of the brackets (which I then had chrome-plated). Later on, I fitted the stalks to the existing mounts on the prop shaft tunnel when the trim was in place (see Photo 7.12-3) and the job was complete.

The nearside wheelarch showing the inertia reels bolted through the body with a plate underneath the nut to spread the weight in the event of an accident. Also notice copious amounts of sealant **7.12-1**

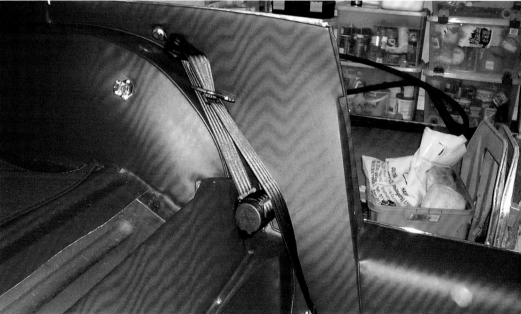

I was able to use the existing mounting points above the wheel arches for the new belts **7.12-2**

The stalks bolt straight onto **7.12-3** the existing mountings in the gearbox tunnel

(Having now driven the car some 3000 miles I can report that the inertia belts work well. The only downsides [apart from the obvious change from original spec.] are, firstly, that you can't pull the belts out on an uphill slope [and as our garage and driveway are on a quite steep slope this doesn't make life easy] and, secondly, that the belts seem to be a bit on the tight side so you have to keep pulling them loose every so often. I remember that they sold some rather naff after-market seatbelt tensioners at Halfords years ago and I thought I'd at least try them, but they no longer sell them - probably just as well!)

7.13 Trimming The Cant Rails

Next up were the cant rails that go up the sides of the windscreen, over the doors and round the rear quarterlights. These are basically a kind of hard foam backed with thin metal reinforcement and these are screwed to the car through the seal retainers (so you can't fit the door seals before the cant rails - which is why the doors still aren't on the car). See Photo 7.13-1 of the smaller cant rail that goes under the quarter light with the vinyl glued and waiting to be stuck down (after the glue had gone off). Again only glue the edges, don't glue over the foam. The cant rails are another seemingly simple job that are really tricky to get right. In particular, the sharp curve on the large cant rails near the bottom of the windscreen are really difficult to get a smooth finish on without creases. It took me about three attempts to fit the vinyl to the rails and even then mine are still creased. The long cant rails do have the normal thinner foam under the vinyl on the wide section at the

end which is why you'll find a sudden change in the profile of the cant rails near the top of the windscreen where the hard foam starts. See Photo 7.13-2 of the finished large cant rails with their chrome edging in place – this was

7.13-1 *One of the small cant rails which fits under the rear quarterlight being trimmed with vinyl*

the original edging simply polished up and hammered back in place.

The cant rails were then clamped in position and screwed to the bodywork by means of small screws through the seal retainers. See Photo 7.13-3. You have to be sure that the screws aren't too long as otherwise they can come out through trim, especially near the bottom where the foam backing is much thinner. The very bottom sections of the cant rails by the dashboard are held in place by quadrant-shaped chrome trims and the grab handle on the passenger side.

Now I have to say that fitting the cant rails was one of the most difficult jobs so far on the entire car. If I had been using the original body shell and cant rails with all the holes already drilled in the correct place and it was simply a matter of lining them up, it would have been a lot easier. As it was, I found it really hard to get them to fit neatly all the way round and especially around the quarterlight. It's worth noting that the lip of the quarterlight fits just inside the cant rails – fit the rails too close to the aperture and the quarterlight won't close, too far away and it'll look a mess. I managed to fit them fairly neatly eventually but only after several attempts.

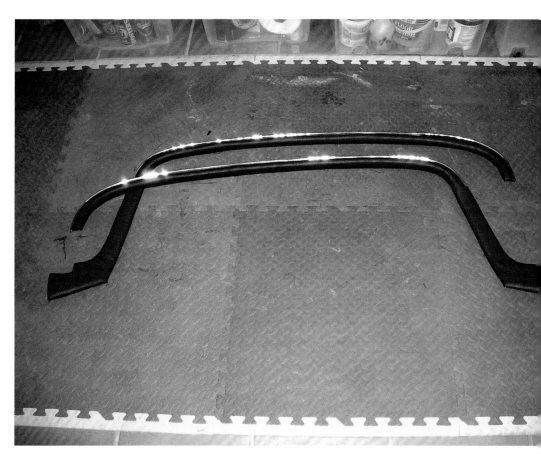

The re-trimmed cant rails with **7.13-2**
chrome edging in place ready to be fitted to the car

The cant rails are held in place **7.13-3**
with clamps as they are screwed to the body

Lessons learnt:

- Trimming and fitting cant rails is a nightmare – a total cant ... rail (apologies, couldn't resist that joke).

7.14 Centre Console Over The Gearbox Tunnel

With the cant rails finally in place (a huge sigh of relief), it was time to trim the centre console over the gearbox tunnel. This was fairly straightforward, but again very time-consuming in order to get right. I covered the sides of the tunnel with vinyl with foam underneath except where it is adjacent to the seats. See Photo 7.14-1. I then trimmed the wooden top of the tunnel with leather. Note that the front of this panel has felt under the leather, not foam. Also note that one fork of the tunnel is wider than the other! See Photo 7.14-2 of the leather glued and waiting to be attached. Cutting the leather to fit the various contours was very stressful as a myriad of cuts are required and, if any one of those cuts had been too deep, the whole piece of very expensive

Connolly hide would have been scrap. In the end, however, I was very pleased with the result. See Photo 7.14-3 which also shows the piping waiting to go on. The piping is then glued to the edge of the top cover, although again it's very difficult to get it so it looks right when assembled. See Photo 7.14-4 of the piping being held in place with masking tape while the glue set.

The next jobs were to trim the central armrest and stowage box, and glue a new rubber seal to the underside of the centre console where the handbrake comes through. The stowage box was fairly straightforward, but the leather-covered armrest wasn't so easy and in the end I took it down to Mick Turley (again!) for him to trim it. I'm glad I did as he was able to make so much better a job of it than I could and it

would always have annoyed me if it wasn't right. See Photo 7.14-5 of my abandoned efforts to fit the leather to the armrest and Photo 7.14-6 of Mick expertly trimming the armrest – also note the wadding in the picture which he used to ensure a perfect result.

I then fitted the gear lever gaiter (pretty straightforward apart from the little chrome/plastic beading around the base of the gaiter that I heated to get to fit but still kinked in a couple of places) and the ashtray (that I'd had chromed – originally it had a black crinkle finish as you can see in the background of Photo 7.14-2) to the centre console. The final job on the console was to fit the leather top to the base. Unfortunately, it wouldn't fit. The top sits in between two low shoulders on the tunnel and, now

7.14-1 *Left: The centre console trimmed in vinyl*

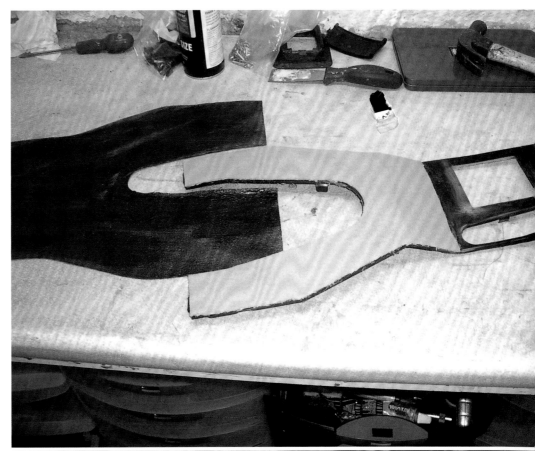

7.14-2 *The leather for the top of the console waiting to be glued on over the felt by the gear lever aperture*

7.14-3 *The leather carefully cut to fit the top of the console and the vinyl piping ready to be glued on*

I'd trimmed the top with leather and piping, it was simply too wide to go in. Eventually, after much persuasion and compressing of trim, it slotted in, but it didn't go down quite as far as I'd have liked. Still, I'm very pleased with the result. See Photo 7.14-7 of the finished tunnel waiting to be fitted to the car.

Lessons learnt:

- If you think you can't do a good job, take it to a specialist (if the part in question can be moved).
- While trimming an E-type, absent-mindedly picking bits of glue off your hands at embarrassing moments becomes a fact of life!

Piping held in place with masking tape while the glue dries **7.14-4**

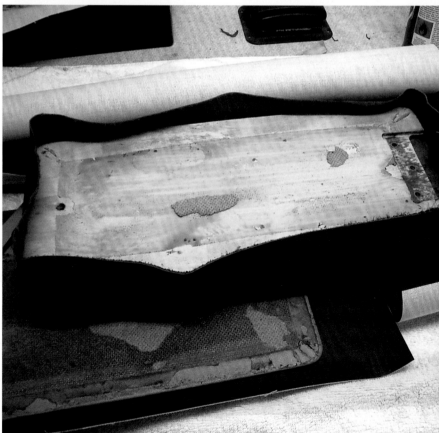

My abandoned efforts at fitting the leather to the centre armrest **7.14-5**

7.14-6 *'Mick makes short work of the job, adding wadding as appropriate to ensure a perfect result*

The finished centre console! **7.14-7**

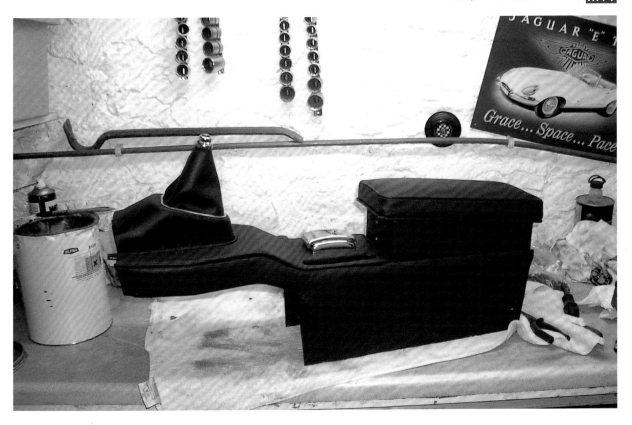

7.15 Upgrading And Refitting The Radio

et me take you through the fitting of the new radio. I wanted to keep the period look of the radio but I also wanted something that I could actually listen to whilst driving rather than the usual white noise with some sort of music in the background that is routinely dispensed by original radios of the period. I therefore opted to have the radio converted/upgraded in several ways: to convert it to an FM radio; to enable an MP3 player to be routed through it; and for it to operate the automatic aerial that I'd already fitted.

Having seen this kind of conversion advertised, I sent my old unit off to *The Vintage Wireless Company* for them to do the work. This basically involved removing the innards of the original radio and replacing them with modern

circuitry. I did feel rather bad about altering such a lovely piece of original equipment but I couldn't see an alternative. I really didn't want to put a modern unit in as I think they look all wrong, but I did want something that worked. In my opinion, this was a good compromise as from the outside it still looks exactly as it did before but with the added benefit of actually working. It was an expensive conversion – nearly £300 (plus the electric aerial) - and the radio is still mono (I could have had it converted to stereo but that was more money still) but worth every penny in my book.

7.15-1 *My converted radio now working on FM with an MP3 player lead. From the outside it looks totally original*

Lessons learnt:

- Original radio, converted original radio or brand new stereo – the choice is yours!
- One man's meat is another man's poison.

7.16 Fitting The Gearbox Tunnel Centre Console

While the radio was away being converted (which took far longer than the three weeks quoted - about three months), I dismantled the old housing with its derisory single speaker. See Photo 7.16-1. I know that Jaguar were trying to economise when they built Series II cars, but I really do think that fitting only one speaker in a two-speaker console was taking things a bit far. Anyway, I decided to cover the console in black vinyl rather than keep with the original black crackle paint finish that I think was first introduced on late Series II cars (another economy?). See Photo 7.16-2. With this accomplished and in an effort to further improve the sound of the radio, I set about finding good quality modern speakers that would actually fit in the console. This proved far harder than anticipated. The problem was that the speakers sit either side of the radio in the console and, due to the limited space available, foul on the radio unless they are exceptionally thin. If you look at Photo 7.16-1 again, you can see how thin the central part of the original speaker is (containing the magnet), enabling it to clear the radio which slides in over the top of it. I think that these speakers were possibly specially made to fit E-types as I'm sure they aren't so good as a result of being so small.

I spent ages trawling the internet in search of very thin speakers, but the thinnest were still too deep. Eventually I bought the thinnest I could find and then removed the plastic trim from the back of the speakers that left just enough clearance for the radio to slide in. See Photo 7.16-3. Having chromed the surrounds for the speaker grilles (it's just another little change that makes such a difference to the look of the interior and suits my 'slightly customised but still original' warped sense of restoration), I fitted one speaker only to realise that the cone was a beige colour and stood out like a sore thumb. See Photo 7.16-4. I therefore simply sprayed the cones black. I'm not sure what this has done to the sound quality, but they certainly look a lot better.

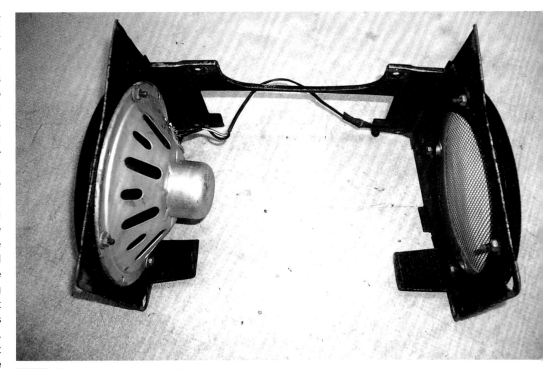

7.16-1 *The original radio and speaker console with only one speaker fitted, as standard*

I covered the console in black vinyl which looks better and isn't as sharp round the edges **7.16-2**

When the radio finally came back from being converted, I fitted a new (slightly different to original) cigarette lighter to the console and screwed on the hard foam surround that Mick Turley had already re-covered for me. It was time to fit the whole radio assembly into the car, under the dashboard. This was a really difficult operation as it's all such a tight fit. I ended up fitting the console at the same time as the central gearbox cover and they just about went back together, but it wasn't easy. The main problem is that you're dealing with your beautifully re-trimmed gearbox cover and you've got to be really careful not to scratch it on the various sharp bits of the radio console (another good reason for trimming the console with vinyl – fewer sharp edges to worry about). The other problem was that the central gearbox tunnel cover is a total nightmare to fit anyway. Trying to insert the gear lever and handbrake lever through seemingly minute apertures at impossible angles is not easy and I ended up sitting on the rear deck of the car 'persuading' the tunnel to slide home with my feet. Trying to then accomplish this at the same time as fitting the radio console doubles the

The thinnest speakers I could **7.16-3**
find were still too thick so I removed the plastic trim from the back and that gave me just enough clearance to fit the radio

With the speakers fitted, the **7.16-4**
cones were very visible so I simply sprayed them matt black – sorted!

problem. Knowing that one slip or 'over exuberant persuasion' (losing patience and using brute force) could ruin the trim you've just spent months creating, triples the problem. See Photo 7.16-5

of the tunnel wedged half in during my attempts to fit it. Finally, with much delicate persuasion, both the gearbox tunnel and the radio console went in. Thank goodness!

Trying to fit the gearbox tunnel **7.16-5**
console and radio console
without damaging the trim
proved really difficult. The only
way I could do it was to fit them
both at the same time

With the console in place I made all the necessary connections for the radio and ran the lead for the MP3 player into the glove box by means of a small hole in the corner of the glove box so it's quite accessible but at the same time out of the way. See Photo 7.16-6. The radio was now in and working well. The old push buttons are still used to change channel but the old Medium Wave buttons are now different FM stations (with the end one switching in the MP3 player) and the old Long Wave button now switches the radio to Medium Wave. I now have a radio that works well (not brilliantly), receives FM and runs an MP3 player. The only downside that I'd forgotten about is that it doesn't automatically re-tune to different frequencies as you drive round the country so, when you're driving long distances, you need to keep re-tuning it. How quickly we become used to such features as automatic re-tuning on modern cars! Anyway, apart from such unnecessary luxuries, I'm really pleased with the result. See Photo 7.16-7.

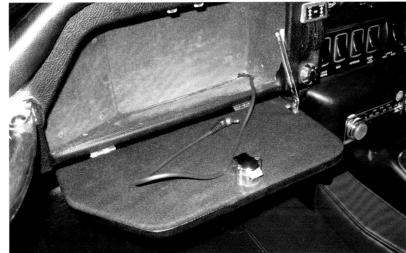

7.16-6 *The lead for the MP3 player*
hidden inside the glovebox

The radio console and centre **7.16-7**
console finally in situ in the car
and looking good

Lessons learnt:

- Series II cars only have one speaker fitted to the console (on the passenger side) so the driver could enjoy the sound of the XK engine without interference - which is all the passenger got!
- E-type speakers are especially thin and finding suitable replacements isn't easy.
- Re-fitting the gearbox tunnel and radio console without damaging them is very difficult.

7.17 Fitting The Rear Hatch

On and on with the interior! I can't tell you how I felt trying to get everything done so the car would finally be on the road, but the jobs just seemed to be never-ending. You just have to keep going and tell yourself that crossing the finish line is the hardest part and not to give up now. Just the rear hatch, the seats, the doors and the boot boards to go. (So only half a year's work then!)

The first thing to be done was the final fitting of the hatch to the body. The hinges had been rather cannibalised by a previous owner and had a strange array of washers and spacers underneath them in an effort to get the hatch to fit properly. The four holes that hold both hinges to the body had been elongated in order to allow the hinges to be moved further down

the bodywork. See Photo 7.17-1. In the photo you can also see the special spacers that should be used under the hinges to try and get a perfect fit.

The main problem with the hatch (as with the doors) is that, when properly fitted, it only clears the bodywork by a fraction of an inch when you open it – that is, if the hinges are in the right place. I had of course trial-fitted the hatch before spraying the car but, as I was now using the proper spacers, everything was slightly different. The hinges can also be adjusted where they bolt to the hatch. Here they are held on by two countersunk screws each. I'm sure that one of the four screws is shorter than the other three to stop it screwing right through the cavity and pushing into the outer frame of the hatch. However, I tried to order

a shorter screw from two different suppliers and they both claimed that all four screws were the same length so now I'm not so sure. In the end, I had to cut one down as it was definitely too long for the available space. Eventually the whole caboodle went together properly.

Another problem I'd been worrying about was that, when the car was on the road prior to the restoration, there were always exhaust fumes in the cabin, coming in from an ill-fitting hatch seal that was impossible to adjust out (the car had been in a rear end crash and not been properly mended). So I knew how important it was to get everything right.

I fitted the rear seal in the groove which was rather more difficult than it sounds. When getting the hatch to

7.17-1 *Left: The rear hatch hinges had been altered to move further down the body. I kept these as they ensured the hatch was an excellent fit. Note: the special spacers to be used under the hinges*

The trimmed down rear hatch seal finally in place at the third attempt **7.17-2**

The trim on the rear hatch. Vinyl was glued to the top section and vinyl-covered hardboard clipped on to the bottom half **7.17-3**

fit properly, prior to painting the car, I found that the whole hatch was ¼ inch too low down the body. I had tried to remedy this but the job was made almost impossible by not being able to open the rear hatch fully. The roof on the rear section of my garage is very low and sitting on a jig the car is quite high. These two factors together meant that I could only open the hatch 45º before it fouled on the concrete roof and working on repositioning the hatch properly was nigh on impossible. (Turning the car round is a four-person job due to the steep slope outside and I didn't want to bother people again to help me out – in retrospect I should have done.) So I'd had to try and get the hatch to fit without being able to open it or hold it open - difficult. I couldn't make the holes in the hinges

any bigger to move the hatch further up the body so I had no alternative but to grind the lower part of the body down by ¼ inch (very difficult) and add ¼ inch to the back edge of the roof with body filler. This had worked and I now had a rear hatch that fitted perfectly.

However, this also meant that the groove for the hatch seal was correct at the sides, rather wide at the bottom, and far too narrow at the top (as half of the original groove was now solid filler). I therefore spent many merry hours whittling away rear hatch seals to try

and get them to fit. I finally succeeded on my third seal. See Photo 7.17-2 of the seal finally fitted. The best thing about this was that you can't really see any of the above alterations in the finished article – you can't tell I've cut the rear seals down to fit.

With the hatch positioning sorted, it was time to fit the trim and rear windscreen to the hatch. The first job was to fit the legendary chrome script 'E-type Jaguar 4.2' to the bottom half of the hatch, a job I'd been looking forward to as this script is so iconic.

Even this proved difficult as the holes that the lugs on the script fitted through were clogged with filler and paint and getting the lugs to fit nicely in the holes without damaging the surrounding paintwork was not easy. The lugs are then held in place with little plastic clips on the inside. I also put some bathroom sealant round the holes on the inside of the hatch to try and prevent water ingress and the resultant rust.

The interior trim went on relatively straightforwardly as you can see in Photo 7.17-3. Note that on Series II (and Series III, I think), there should be a flimsy plastic/glass fibre surround around the top of the hatch. However,

Mick Turley recommended that this be discarded as they never fitted properly in the first place and simply got in the way. Instead he suggested that I should simply fit a piece of vinyl to the top of the hatch, and so this is what I did.

Lessons learnt:

- Don't say to yourself, "I'm going to fit the rear hatch this weekend". Several weeks later, you might just finish it. Rebuilding an E-type takes time.
- Fitting the rear script is great, but make sure it doesn't leak.

7.18 Getting The Heated Rear Screen To Work

My next problem was to try and get the heated rear windscreen to work. For some reason (probably the aforementioned crash), my car was fitted with an earlier heated rear windscreen from a Series I with the tiny filaments running vertically down through the glass. I believe that Series II cars should have a rear windscreen with larger horizontal filaments. (I knew that the previous 'restorers' of my car hadn't replaced the entire rear hatch because, when I dismantled the car, I found the chassis number chalked on the inside of the hatch under the trim. This was apparently standard practice to ensure cars were assembled with the correct panels after they had been disassembled for painting, etc.) The problem with my screen was that the wires coming out of the screen to connect to the wiring loom were virtually non-existent. Despite my best efforts when removing the screen many years ago, the wires had broken off where they exited the glass. I therefore tried to remedy this by fitting new wires. Not easy.

The filaments are **inside** the screen, sandwiched between two laminates (unlike modern cars where the elements are stuck to the inside of the screen). I therefore had to gently dig into the edge of the screen to try and find some wire to solder onto. I was able to solder one wire as it was just

long enough. However, on the other side there was no wire left at all to join onto and the only method of repair I could think of was to Super Glue (yes, Super Glue!) a new wire to what was left of the little metal contact (see Photo 7.18-1) as I didn't know how else to attach it to a piece of glass. I then used my trusty multi meter to ensure I had a circuit (see Photo 7.18-2) and then Araldited the whole thing up. (It's a long time since I last used Araldite

7.18-1 *The only way I could think of reconnecting the wires to the heated rear screen was by using SuperGlue – and it worked!*

- Super Glue is now so omnipotent) Also note a piece of my old beige trim in this photo – how I don't miss it! No matter how many times I tried and how many methods I used to try and clean it, it always looked dirty)

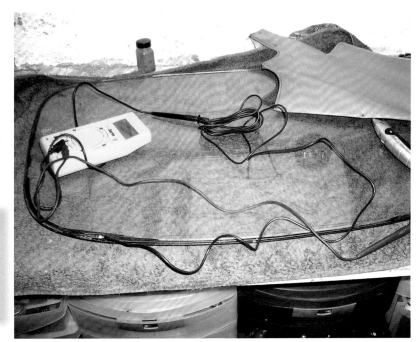

I checked I had a circuit using my **7.18-2** *multi meter before finishing the new connection with Araldite*

Lessons learnt:

- You can mend most things with a bit of determination and ingenuity.
- I've now got two parts of the car held together by Super Glue.

7.19 Fitting The Rear Screen

With everything ready, it was time once again to call upon the services of Messrs. Paul and James to come and fit the rear screen for me. I'm glad I did as, once again, fitting it proved to be a nightmare. How they fitted them originally, I just don't know. The principle is basically the same as for the front windscreen – put the seal round the lip, slide the screen (and the wires) into the bottom lip and then force the top lip into the seal. Finally fit the seal insert and finish it off with chrome trim – easy? No!

The screen simply wouldn't go in. It just wouldn't slide down far enough to allow the top edge to be levered in. However, after much persuasion (physical and verbal – mainly the latter!), it finally went in and all was well. Note that we were using an original screen with an original hatch – and it still wouldn't fit! See Photos 7.19-1, 7.19-2, 7.19-3 and 7.19-4 of various steps in the procedure. In Photo 7.19-4 you can see that the two chrome clips on the chrome finishers were temporarily taped down while the

7.19-1 *Fitting the seal to the hatch and feeding the HRW wires down through it*

Persuading the screen that it really did want to fit inside the seal **7.19-2**

glue, with which they are fitted, sets.

Phew! Finally, time to fit the hatch to the car! Because of all the preparation, this was fairly straightforward – although the hatch was now a lot heavier and harder to lift. See Photo 7.19-5 of the hatch in place on its hinges and the rear stay fitted. The (rather long!) wires for the heated screen have been drawn through the trim and are ready to be connected to the main loom above the wheel arch. The final job was adjusting the catches (on the body and the hatch) for the final time so that it closed properly. I'm really happy with the shut lines and how well the catch works. See Photo 7.19-6 of the finished hatch finally in place.

However, I'm pretty sure that the heated screen isn't working, despite my best efforts. There is a chance it's working as it's difficult to test it without it being misted up – must leave it out one evening in the Autumn, just to see. (3000 miles on and I can tell you that I'm really pleased with the fit of the hatch; it doesn't leak and there are no fumes in the car. I can also very happily report that the heated rear screen actually works! No-one is more surprised or pleased than I am. Thank you Super Glue! Miracles really do still happen)

Using the special beading tool to 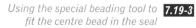 **7.19-3**
fit the centre bead in the seal

The screen and chrome **7.19-4**
surrounds in place at last

Beginning the difficult process **7.19-5**
of fitting the rear hatch to the
car. It's heavy and awkward and
trying to get the perfect fit isn't
at all easy even after having done
this at the bodywork stage

All that hard work finally paid off **7.19-6**
as the rear hatch is an almost
perfect fit

Lessons learnt:

- Get someone else to fit the front and rear screens for you – it's worth every penny.
- It's looking like a car again! (Well, from the back anyway)

7.20 Trimming The Seats – I

Time to re-trim the seats! From Photo 7.20-1 to Photo 7.20-3 in one easy step! The main focus of any E-type interior has to be the seats – they are so noticeable and so beautiful, you can't miss them. My seats, being a late Series II, have perforated leather and the optional head restraints fitted. (They aren't head *rests* as they're way too far back, and even as head restraints I'm not sure how effective they'd be in the case of an accident. I'm sure you'd have done serious damage to your neck before the restraints came into play – but they look the part)

At some point in the car's illustrious history, someone had seen fit to paint the seats a pale cream colour and this is how I'd inherited them. See Photo 7.20-2 from just after I bought the car. At the start of the restoration (way back in 1999), I'd had the rather misguided idea of restoring the original seats rather than replacing them and, in order to do this, I'd stripped the paint off with paint stripper! I have to say that this was spectacularly effective and removed not only the paint but all the original dye as well. The result being what you can see in Photo 7.20-1 – a very sorry looking pair of seats. I'm not sure if there was a way of saving the original seats but by now I'd realised that, in my case, I needed new seats anyway – original seats in an otherwise brand new interior would have looked totally wrong.

7.20-1 *My original seats stripped of vinyl paint and in a really sorry state*

Lessons learnt:

- It's probably not a good idea to attack your seats with paint stripper – but I still don't know of a better method.

The interior as it looked when **7.20-2** I bought the car – covered in cream vinyl paint

My re-trimmed seats – a bit of a **7.20-3** transformation!

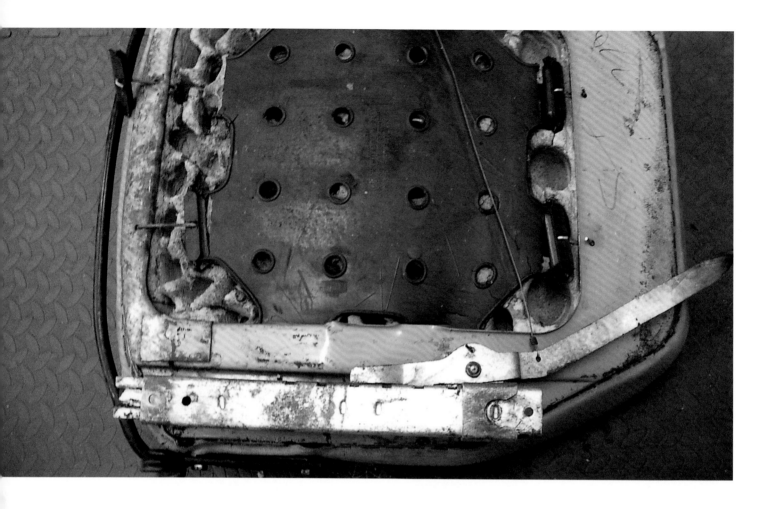

7.21 Dismantling The Old Seats

My first job was to strip the seats down and it soon became clear just how bad they were. Not only was the leather in poor condition but the insides were simply terrible. The diaphragms under each seat had split next to each hook and provided no support whatsoever. The seat foams were horrible. The foam was crumbling and smelly and simply fell apart as I removed the diaphragms. See Photos 7.21-1 and 7.21-2 of the seat cushions being dismantled and the horrors they revealed. No wonder the seats were so uncomfortable before – they were completely gone and provided no support or cushioning whatsoever. (Note that the bit you sit on is called the cushion and the backrest is called the squab) See Photo 7.21-3 showing the original trimmer's signature and

stamp on the leather which can also be seen on the bottom of the seat in Photo 7.21-1. It's nice to see these little glimpses of history and it adds a human aspect to the car – you do somehow feel in touch with those unknown workers on the line who built the car all those years ago.

7.21-1 *The seat diaphragms were split at virtually every point*

Lessons learnt:

- The seat cushion is the bit you sit on; the squab is the back rest.
- I really didn't realise just how bad my original seats were until I took them apart.

7.21-2 *The foam cushions had virtually disintegrated*

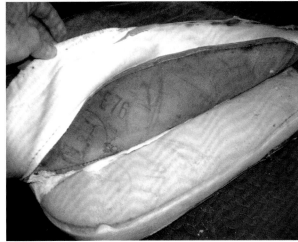

7.21-3 *The original trimmer had signed his (or her) initials on the leather – a little piece of history*

7.22 Trimming The Seat Cushions

Having stripped the seats, I had no hesitation in asking Mick Turley to help me trim them. I knew that I simply wouldn't be able to make a decent job of them by myself and they are so important to get right (and very expensive to get wrong) that it was a straightforward decision. I would never be able to forgive myself if I made a mess of them and I knew he would finish them beautifully. It proved to be a wise decision.

I painted the metal frames on the base of the seat with silver aluminium aerosol to provide a nice, shiny finish. This proved to be a poor decision. This aluminium style paint never really dries

Mick Turley began by fitting new **7.22-1**
diaphragms to the seat bases

properly even weeks, or months, later and for ever after you get covered in silver paint every time you touch it - which you then transfer to everything else – mainly the leather seats! Not a great idea.

Anyway, I set off to Nuneaton full of excitement! The idea was that Mick would help me to trim the seats by showing me how to do one and then I could do the other. The best laid plans of mice and men…

The first thing that Mick did was to fit new diaphragms to the bases (see Photo 7.22-1), using strong pliers, and then fabricated new hardboard pieces that go on the outer corner of each base, see Photo 7.22-2. Also note the air-driven staple gun – an essential tool for the professional trimmer. He then glued the new seat foams (what a contrast to my originals!) to the frames by coating both with glue and then sticking them together when the glue was tacky. See Photos 7.22-3 and 7.22-4. His next job was to prepare the seat covers for assembly by hitting some of the stitched joints with a hammer to make them more supple! See Photo 7.22-5. Do not try this at home!

He then coated the centre section of

Mick then made new hardboard corner pieces for the bottom of each base   **7.22-2**

Coating the new seat cushions with glue ready to attach them to the bases   **7.22-3**

Coating the bases with glue as well   **7.22-4**

International Jaguar XK Club

The XK Club was established in 1997 and has over 1400 members in over 50 countries. What makes this club so different is that it concentrates 100% on XK 120s, 140s and 150s, and their derivatives, the C-types and D-types.

Former Patrons include Ian Appleyard, Rt Hon Alan Clark and Sir Stirling Moss.

At the Club's heart is the XK Gazette, our vibrant 68 page, full-colour, monthly magazine. We have exceptional support from members who contribute from around the world on all manner of topics. There are superb technical and practical articles, event reports, coverage of racing, originality articles, upgrading advice, restoration stories and marketplace updates...

As well as the printed magazine, we also offer a digital edition, free of charge. This is circulated by email, and includes video, search functions, extra photos, live links, and more.

The Club also offers members the chance to participate in a range of XK events worldwide. Activities include regional meetings, informal runs, track days, weekend breaks, dinners and international tours.

International Jaguar XK Club
Tel: +44 (0)1584 781588   Email: info@xkclub.com
www.xkclub.com

Do It Once - Do It Right

BAS *has been trimming E-Types and other Jaguars for 46 years,*
so you can be confident we know what we are doing! We also
manufacture most of the raw materials that trimmers use worldwide, such
as carpet, hardura, vinyl, plastic and rubber parts.

So why not have your car's interior factory fitted by us. Our staff will liaise
with you with stage by stage photos and you can contact the trimming team
anytime for updates and view progress. It is advisable to book your car in at
least 6 months in advance to plan conveniently with your restoration

the cushion and the ribbed section of the seat cover with glue, ready for assembly – do not glue the flat bits on the top of the cushion or the sides. See Photos 7.22-6 and 7.22-7. When the glue had gone off, he then stuck the two together by folding the cover in half and sticking the central ridge in the groove of the cushion - see Photo 7.22-8. Mick took a long time ensuring that they were perfectly in line and, when he was satisfied, he glued them together very firmly as this is a weak point and known to come unglued on occasion. With this accomplished, it was a fairly straightforward job to glue the rest of the ribbed seat cover onto the foam.

Then came the hard part. Using his many years of skill and experience, Mick pulled and tugged the leather on the sides of the cushion to remove all creases and ensure the piping was perfectly in line all the way round. I decided that getting the piping in a perfectly straight line was hard (this also has a lot to do with the quality of the seat covers), and getting the creases out was really hard, but to achieve both was nigh-on impossible! Mick, however, is used to doing the impossible on a regular basis and so

Hammering the edges of the seat covers to ensure a perfect fit!

Gluing the centre section of the cushion

Glueing the ribbed section of the seat covers

he set to work undaunted. Using small pieces of wadding where necessary to ensure a perfect fit he began to fix the leather sides of the seat cover in position. See Photo 7.22-9.

The seat covers are stapled to the bottom of the metal seat base which has a strip of hemp or similar running all round it for that very purpose. Mick began by putting staples in a few key places and then slowly added more and more. Even then he occasionally removed a staple that wasn't in quite the right place as the odd crease appeared. In no time at all, the cushion was trimmed and looking superb. (See Photo 7.22-10) The final job was to trim off the excess leather with a very sharp knife. See Photo 7.22-11. (Mick honed his knife before every use)

Then it was my turn. Having watched Mick and learnt all the techniques, I set to work with renewed confidence. Mick glued the cover to the cushion and then went off for a cup of tea and left me to it. I pulled and stretched the leather and started putting one or two staples in when I was happy it was about right – and then pulled them out again. I kept trying but, as soon as I got the creases

Carefully lining up the seat cover 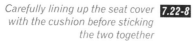 *with the cushion before sticking the two together*

Skilfully stretching the leather *to obtain a perfect fit, adding wadding where necessary and then stapling the leather to the base*

out in one place, they reappeared in another. After about half an hour, Mick returned to see how I was progressing and was clearly taken aback with my complete lack of progress (Photo 7.22-12). I can still remember Mick's slightly quizzical look at me as if to say, "Is this really the bloke who's rebuilt most of his car by himself in a basement?" He then proceeded to 'demonstrate' further and produced a perfect seat cushion in a few minutes. He allowed me to zap a few staples in with the staple gun, just to make me feel better and so I could claim to have helped trim the seats.

So, the cushions were finished but the squabs and head restraints still remained to be done. In the next section, I'll tell you how I managed to re-trim the seat squabs and the head restraints all by myself without any help at all. (Believe that and you'll believe anything!)

In no time at all, Mick produced **7.22-10**
a perfectly trimmed seat cushion

Turley trimmed the excess **7.22-11**
leather with an extremely sharp knife

My attempts at fitting a seat **7.22-12**
cover – the less said the better!

Lessons learnt:

- Aluminium silver paint doesn't dry properly.
- If you know you're really not up to a certain job, it's best to get someone else to do it for you, especially if it's a particularly important one (but don't be afraid to ask to sit in and watch the work being done and learn from them).
- When you start trimming the seats, you know you're nearly there!

7.23 Trimming The Squabs And Head Restraints

With the seat cushions now trimmed, it was on with the seat squabs and the head restraints. If the seat cushions were difficult to trim, the squabs were nigh-on impossible. The squabs are constructed around a metal frame with rubber webbing and a strange sort of matting called *hairlock*. As there's little weight on the squabs compared to the cushions, the insides of both squabs were as good as new, apart from the black plastic guards that cover the head restraint guides. Both of these had broken off and were loose in the back of the old seat. With these mended, Mick started to apply sheets of wadding round the edge of the frames. See Photo 7.23-1.

He continued to glue these in place right round the edges of both frames, cutting a hole for the head restraints.

See Photo 7.23-2. (By this time, we both realised that trimming the squabs was far beyond my capability as a self-confessed trimming dunce and Mick quickly got on with trimming the two squabs himself). With the wadding in place, he then put thin plastic bags over each frame. This enabled the new and tightly-fitting seat covers to be pulled down over the frames quite easily. The plastic bags are then simply pulled out and disposed of. See Photo 7.23-3. Then came the fun part – Mick then teased and stretched and smoothed the covers to shape. Where necessary he added extra wadding and used a pair of pincers to pull the material really tight over the frames. See Photo 7.23-4.

The most difficult job was to take all the ends and cut, trim, shape and staple them in position at the bottom of the squabs. When I'd taken the seats apart a few weeks previously, I'd noted just how complicated the joins were at this point and, despite taking copious photos during the dismantling process, I don't think I'd ever have been able to fabricate the new ones. Needless to say, Mick had both squabs finished and looking absolutely stunning in a matter of minutes with a mesmeric display of stretching, cutting, stapling and trimming.

The final task was to trim the head restraints. To begin with, new foams are inserted in the covers. This was a bit like trying to wrestle with a bag of ferrets (a traditional Yorkshire pastime!) as the slit in the bottom is rather small but, after a bit of argy-bargy *[British slang for a lively or disputatious discussion, or Australian slang for tedious or argumentative. Ed]*,

7.23-1 *Left: Mick started to trim the squabs by covering the edges of the frame with sheets of wadding*

Continuing to cover the squabs with wadding **7.23-2**

Pulling the seat covers down over the seat frames by 'lubricating' them with plastic bags **7.23-3**

Mick used his skill to tension the covers and get a perfect fit – including using a pair of pincers to pull the covers tight **7.23-4**

they went in. See Photo 7.23-5. The metal part of the restraints is then inserted. These are rather strange square lollipop type affairs (see Photo 7.23-6) and they are glued into a ready-made aperture in the foams. The restraints are then finished and shaped by carefully massaging the covers and by the judicious use of wadding pushed into corners and edges where necessary. This is done (as with the seats) by using a metal probe to insert a tuft of wadding and then manipulate it into exactly the right position. See Photo 7.23-7. When everything is right, the loose ends of the cover are pulled tight and stapled to a piece of wood handily secured inside the lollipop frames. See Photo 7.23-6 again where the wood is just visible in the bottom of the square sections.

I finally have the satisfaction of announcing that I did actually trim one of the head restraints all by myself! I think I am justifiably proud of this rather small, but not insignificant, claim to fame.

Speaking as a complete failure as a vehicle trimmer (and anything else vaguely artistic/creative), what may

 *Although it looked impossible, the head restraint foams finally went into the covers*

The metal frame ready to **7.23-6** *be inserted inside the head restraints*

seem as only a minor achievement to many was a really proud moment for me. I had trimmed a head restraint all by myself! (Just in case you missed it the first time)

If you look at Photo 7.23-8, you can see the pair of completed restraints before the plastic finisher was screwed to the undersides of the restraints. Can you tell the difference between mine and Mick's? No! I'm so proud. In fact, I honestly can't remember which is which in the photo (but it's on the driver's side in the car) and you can't tell by looking. (Do you get the impression that I'm pleased with myself?)

Finishing the restraints by **7.23-7** *carefully inserting wadding with a metal probe where necessary*

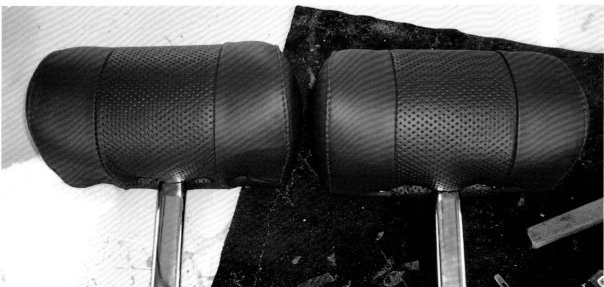

7.23-8 *The completed head restraints – one of them trimmed by me!*

Lessons learnt:

- Re-trimming the seats is definitely a job left to the experts – speaking as a 'non-artistic' person.
- Conquering a job you can't do, like trimming the head restraints, gives you a wonderful sense of achievement!

7.24 Reassembling The Finished Seats

With the seat cushions, squabs and head restraints trimmed, all I had to do was reassemble the component parts. I'd dismantled the reclining mechanisms to repaint them and have some parts chromed or re-chromed as appropriate. As well as re-chroming the levers, I'd decided to chrome the semi-circular cover plates and the long connecting rods, that go round the back of the seats to allow both sides of the seat to recline, just for looks. See Photo 7.24-1 before the cover plates were chromed. To enable me to chrome the connecting rods, I'd had to dismantle them first and it proved to be quite a difficult job reassembling them, but eventually I managed it. I then spent a happy few hours adjusting the mechanisms to try and get them to work a bit more smoothly than

previously and was partially successful. The mechanisms are rather agricultural and, in the end, I decided that, as long as they worked properly (not necessarily smoothly), then this was acceptable.

I then attached the mechanisms to the seat cushions with the appropriate bolts. See Photo 7.24-2. I had to cut holes in the new seat covers for these. This was easily accomplished by hammering the leather round the protruding bolt holes which resulted in the leather cutting itself in nice neat circles. The squabs were next and these were attached with two screws to the sides of the frames. See Photo 7.24-3. The head restraints were then triumphantly inserted into their guides and, with the reclining mechanism covers now chromed, the seats were finished! See Photo 7.24-4.

7.24-1 *The dismantled parts of the seat-reclining mechanisms prior to chroming the hinge covers*

Above Right: Beginning to bolt **7.24-2** *the reclining mechanism to the seat cushions*

7.24-3 *Attaching the squabs with countersunk set screws*

One of the finished seats – **7.24-4**
hurrah!

7.25 Sorting The Seat Runners

Well, when I say finished, there was still the small matter of the seat runners. When the car was on the road previously, the driver's seat wouldn't slide backwards and forwards on its runners. A source of much annoyance: I like things to work and work properly. Not only this but the only time the seat was required to move was when Christine drove the car. This had led to much stress as she fruitlessly attempted to slide the seat forward with limited success and a therefore dangerously 'too far away from the pedals to reach them properly' driving position. It was necessary to get the runners working! (N.B. You can always move a jammed seat backwards, but never forwards!)

Just to digress for a while, one thing I have discovered over the years is that

there are very many, what I term, 'non-mechanical' or 'non-technical' people in the world. I love to use mechanical/technical things and enjoy using them properly, as well as appreciating their design and beauty. On the other hand, there are those who have no natural affinity with mechanical objects at all and spend all their lives battling against them rather than working with them. For instance, many years ago we had a front door that was a nice tight draught-proof shut but required you to pull it towards you a touch before unlocking it in order to ease the tension on the latch. At that time we had a lodger (not a good idea generally) and she just couldn't work out how to open the door easily, no matter how many times I showed her. Instead of trying to work the mechanism properly, she would stand at the door,

thrashing at it with her key and almost breaking the handle off in a vain effort to enter, rapidly losing her temper and blaming, "The silly, stupid door".

I have since discovered that there are many such 'non-mechanical' people in the world. I have therefore learnt that, if you wish to properly test something you've made or repaired, all you need to do is find one of these 'non-mechanicals' and get them to try and use it for you. If they succeed, then you know it's OK. If, after watching them nearly destroy whatever it is they're trying to use, you stand there saying, "All you need to do is just turn it gently to the left before engaging the clip" or similar, you know that either you need to re-do it or never let that person near your car again.

Although, thankfully, Christine doesn't really fall into this category of people, she is not at all mechanically-minded and as, never going near the car again was not an option, I needed to make sure that everything on the car was 'user friendly' for the 'non-mechanicals' amongst us. This included the seat runners, which wouldn't move even for the 'mechanicals' like me.

I therefore spent many long, frustrating hours trying to get the runners working properly. There were two problems associated with this: to begin with, I couldn't work out how to separate the pair of runners belonging to each seat due to the wire link that runs between the two sides. The only way I could see to remove this was by cutting it and, as this wasn't an option, I worked on the two runners still wired together. This was a really difficult and awkward thing to do as the other runner was always in the way – a lot in the way.

Secondly, I found it very hard to work out *why* the runners were sticking. Were they bent, or was the roller jammed or were they too firmly crimped together, or were the sides of the guides fouling on the runners? To be honest, I never really found the definitive answer to this but, after much effort invested in bending, filing, levering and spraying with WD40 the runners finally eased. See Photo 7.25-1 of my efforts to free the runners. Both seats now slide almost as effortlessly as a more modern car. Result!

The final job was to fit the mushroom-headed spigots to the floor of the car ready to slot the runners on. See Photo 7.25-2. Note that the slightly taller of the spigots goes to the front so tilting the front edge of the seat slightly upwards to improve the seating position. With great care, I then fitted the seats in the

car. This wasn't as easy as it sounds as the runners are very sharp in places and the seats large and awkward. It would be very easy to tear the trim on the sills if you aren't careful. Anyway, finally, eventually, the seats were finished and in the car. Job done! Just the doors and boot boards to go!

Lessons learnt:

- Having 'non-mechanical' people around to test different bits can be handy – if rather infuriating!
- Getting the reclining mechanisms and seat runners to work well was a difficult job – but one that had to be done to ensure proper enjoyment of the car.
- Finishing the seats and getting them in the car is a massive moment – and, incredibly, you can actually sit on them and pretend to drive the car. Wow!

7.25-1 *Left: Trying to free the seat runners so they operate with ease*

The mushroom headed spigots **7.25-2** *bolted to the floor ready to take the seat runners*

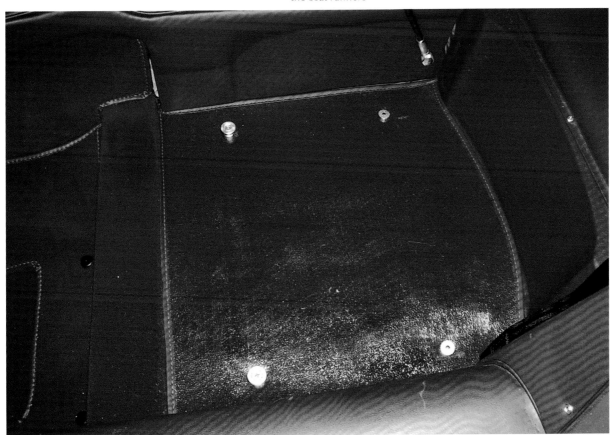

7.26 Door Seals, Locks, Handles And Catches

It was time address the doors. I first fitted the door seals to the bodywork – the 'A' post seal and the 'B' post seal, the rear quarterlight seal and the seal at the top of the sill. See Photo 7.26-1. The seals were very difficult to fit in the retainers, that go above the door and around the quarterlights, especially as I'd screwed the retainers to the bodywork rather than use rivets and the heads of the screws were now in the way of the seals. In places I had to cut a small chunk out of the back of the seal to get them to go in at all. The lower part of the 'A' post seal, the sill seal and the 'B' post seal were glued in place with trim adhesive and went in OK.

Earlier in the restoration, when I had been completing the bodywork of the car, I had spent several days getting the doors to shut perfectly. I thought I had covered all the bases by inserting the

'B' post seal in place to ensure a perfect door shut on the finished car. I was, therefore, rather smugly anticipating that all would be well in this area. What I was not to know was that the door shut on a Coupé depends more on the 'A' post seal than the 'B' post seal. More – much, much more on this later.

Turning to the doors themselves, the first thing to be done was to replace the barrels of the door locks as both had suffered damage over the years from being forced at some time or other and looked unsightly. I was able to buy two new barrels without any problem except that they were slightly different to the originals. The small inscription 'to lock' with an accompanying arrow on the originals was missing from the replacements. See Photo 7.26-2. I must say that I find this the most irksome part of buying replacement parts. Personally

I don't mind if the part is original or not as long as it looks the same, but so many replacement parts look nothing like the originals. This has included parts of the wiring harness, the temperature gauge sender, the clutch master cylinder and the steering rack. I just wish they'd tell you that it doesn't look like the original when you order – many replacement parts are great and look nearly identical to the originals so you only find out if they're different after they've arrived. Annoying.

Anyway, I took the locks apart and fitted the new barrels. See Photo 7.26-3. This was a relatively difficult job as, firstly, the locks are more complicated to dismantle and reassemble than they appear and, secondly, because the new barrels weren't a perfect fit in the locks and needed considerable persuasion to turn freely. One tip here is that if there's

7.26-1 *Left: Fitting the door seals and quarterlight seals to the seal retainers*

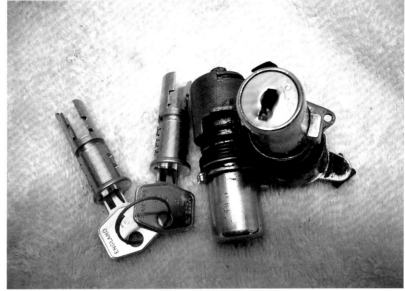

The old and new door lock **7.26-2** *barrels – the new ones without the inscription 'to lock' (with an arrow) engraved on them*

Dismantling the door locks to **7.26-3** *replace the barrels*

The door locks with new barrels **7.26-4** *fitted to the door handles*

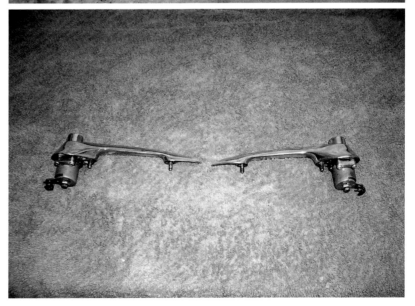

a pair of anything, only work on one at a time so you've always got another to refer to if you can't work out how it all goes back together (as well as taking the usual pictures of the dismantling procedure).

With the barrels finally turning fairly smoothly, I screwed the locks back into the door handles. The door handles are made from an alloy called Mazak which can't be plated but can be polished if they're not badly pitted. Mine were OK so I had them polished. If the locks are working properly, the little bolt at the end of the locks pushes out when unlocked, but not when locked. See Photo 7.26-4.

I then attempted to bolt the handles

The door handles on the car – I'm sure they are fitted upside down! **7.26-5**

The front of the door catches **7.26-6**

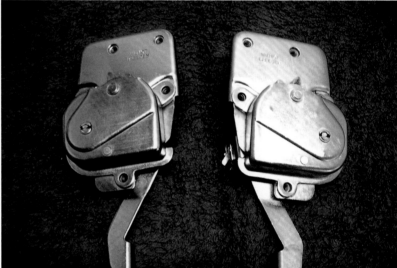

The back of the door catches **7.26-7**

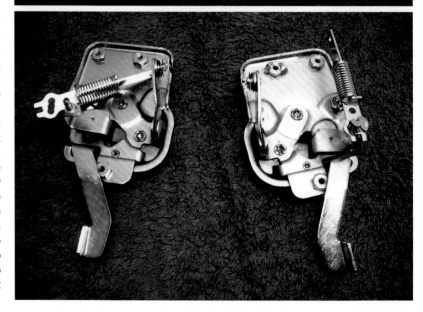

to the doors. This sounds simple, but in fact took me ages as the door handles simply wouldn't fit in the apertures in the door skins. For a while my heart sank as I thought that somehow I had the wrong door skins fitted and I'd have to do some serious bodywork to get them to fit. But then I suddenly saw the light and discovered an amazing fact about E-types that I never realised before ... E-type door handles are fitted upside down! See Photo 7.26-5. Look carefully at the photo (and at your car if you have one) and I'm sure you will agree that the door handles are in fact upside down. I'm not sure why this is, but I'm pretty sure I'm right. That's why I'd not been able to get the handles to fit – I'd been trying to fit the right hand door handle to the left

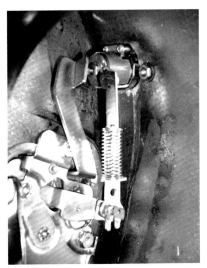

7.26-8 *The door catches on the door. The lever on the top left opens the door and the spring loaded lever on the right locks it, both via the door handle. The half-seen lever on the left opens and unlocks the door from inside the car*

hand door. Anyway, with a great deal of relief (and no small degree of puzzlement – why fit them upside down in the first place? I'm sure they were designed to go the other way up), I bolted the handles to the doors with considerable ease.

The next job was to fit the door catches. I'd had these nickel-plated. I think that Series I cars have catches that are partially chrome-plated, but this is not the case with Series II cars and they definitely benefited from plating. See Photos 7.26-6 and 7.26-7. I fitted them to the doors and tested the catches to check they worked properly. They didn't. The adjustment between the push button on the handle and the lever of the door catch is critical and very hard to achieve. After many attempts at achieving the correct adjustment and failing, I ended up bending the operating arms to give greater clearance and this worked. The door catch now worked properly, as did the door lock. See Photo 7.26-8. (Note the liberal use of rust-proofing wax on the inside of the door) The lever on the left is pushed inwards when the door handle button is depressed and releases the catch, but not when the door is locked when the button won't work. The spring-loaded link on the right of the picture is attached at one end to the door handle inside the door (see Photos 7.26-9 and 7.26-10 of the mechanism connecting the

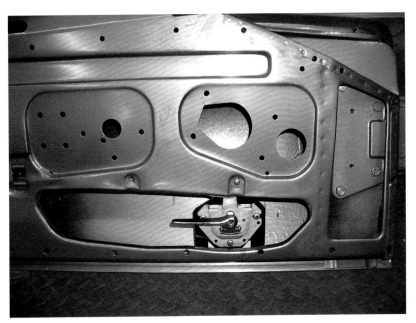

7.26-9 *Top right: The inner door handle operating mechanisms*

One of the inner door handle operating mechanisms in place on the car **7.26-10**

interior door handle to the door catch) and at the other end to the barrel of the lock so enabling the door to be locked from inside the car by having the same effect as turning the key. This spring-loaded link can be adjusted slightly to ensure clean operation, but I had to re-machine one of them to get it to work properly as it simply wasn't long enough, even on full adjustment.

Lessons learnt:

- E-type door handles are fitted upside down (if I'm wrong about this, I'll eat my log book!).
- Some non-original parts closely resemble the originals. Some don't.
- Door locks and catches are fiddly little so-and-so's.

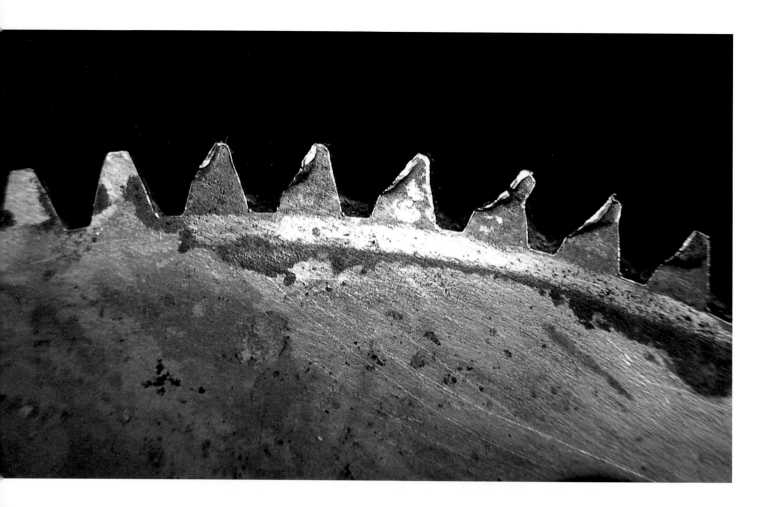

7.27 Fitting The Window Regulator

Next up were the window regulators (winding mechanisms). When the car was on the road before the restoration, the driver's window would slowly slide open by about two inches all of its own accord – very annoying. I checked and discovered that the teeth on the opening mechanism were badly worn and decided that this was probably the cause of the problem. See Photo 7.27-1. I therefore decided to try and mend the teeth, using a combination of adding blobs of weld to the teeth and then grinding them back to shape with an angle grinder. Luckily my efforts in the workshop are a lot better than my work in the trim shop and I'm very pleased with the result. See Photo 7.27-2 of the teeth after reworking. I'm also pleased to report that this seems to have cured

the problem. (However, I now have the problem of a very stiff winding mechanism on the driver's door – yet to be sorted. Yes, even now after 3000 miles, it's still on my 'to do' list. I think the problem is a slightly bent window frame) After thorough cleaning, the mechanisms were ready to be fitted in the doors. See Photo 7.27-3.

With the regulators in place, I fitted the outer rubber weather strip to the top of the door skin. This is one of those small parts that can drive you completely crazy if not fitted properly as it'll keep coming loose. The only way to remedy it is to fully dismantle the door to re-do the fitting. I therefore took a lot of care to fit it securely. I found some large 'U' clips lying around that fitted well, but these weren't the originals and I couldn't find any more,

7.27-1 *The teeth on one of the window regulators showing signs of serious wear*

despite trying various suppliers. They all sold me slightly smaller clips that were only just big enough to grip the bottom edge of the seal. Not having enough large clips, I was forced to use a mixture of clips. See Photo 7.27-4. So far, they seem to have held.

Lessons learnt:

- Ensure that the outer weather strip is held securely in place.

After welding and then grinding down, the teeth look as good as new **7.27-2**

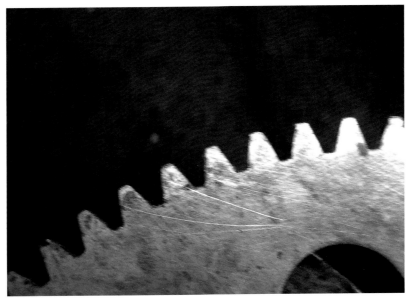

The cleaned and refurbished window regulators ready to be fitted in the doors **7.27-3**

The outer rubber weather strip fitted to the top of the door with 'U' clips – although, in this case, of varying sizes **7.27-4**

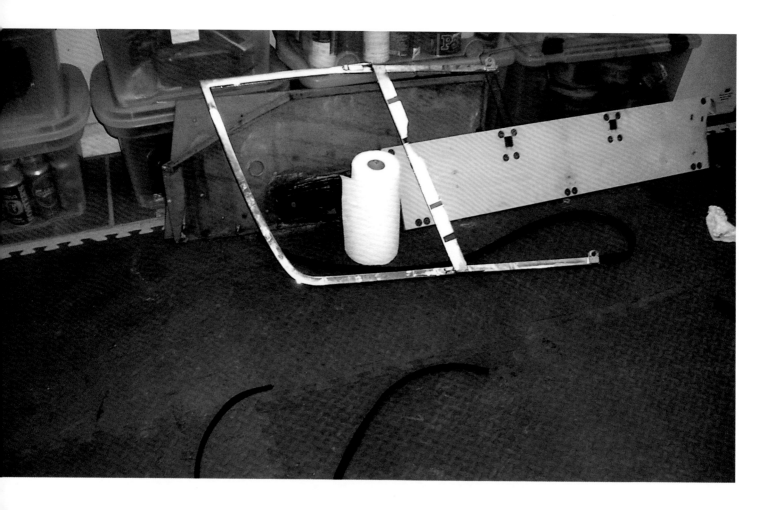

7.28 Door Glass And Frame

The next step was to fit the window glass to the winder mechanism - *before* fitting the chrome window frame. I'd bought some new door glass as I wanted to replace my clear glass with tinted glass and anyway my original (clear) glass was slightly scratched from years of heavy use. I had to take the metal runners off the bottoms of the original window glass and transfer them to the new. That wasn't too hard and I was then able to lift the glass into place and engage the runners on the window-winding mechanism. Without the frame in place, this was fairly straightforward. The windows now went up and down!

The frames then had new seals inserted (see Photo 7.28-1) before being slotted into position in the doors. See Photo 7.28-2. Note how strangely tall and narrow the doors look with the frames fitted and the doors open. It really hits you when you've not seen this for several years. The frames are then held in position with small set screws and a variety of horseshoe (?) shims (See Photo 7.28-3) that come in different sizes. These, in combination with adjustable mountings at the bottom of the frame, allow you to adjust the frame so that the door fits perfectly – allegedly! The new window glass fitted well. I had heard reports that replacement window glass wasn't the right shape or size, but mine were fine.

The doors were now basically complete and all that remained to be done before trimming them was to fit the rear quarterlights and ensure the doors opened and closed easily. You have probably already guessed that that's a whole new story!

Lessons learnt:

- Removing/replacing door glass is quite straightforward when the chrome frame has first been removed.

7.28-1 *Left: Inserting new seals in the runners of the window frame. Note my old door cards in the background - in really poor condition*

The re-chromed door frames **7.28-2** *slotted in position – after the glass has been fitted. (The wires in the background are for my battery conditioner, an essential item for long term storage)*

The screws and 'bar nuts' **7.28-3** *used for holding the frames to the doors and the 'horseshoe' spacers used to try and get a perfect fit*

7.29 Adjusting The Doors To Fit

The doors were now attached to the body shell with the aid of my neighbour Chris who had helped to re-hang them – unless you have access to a proper door stand it is a two-person job removing and refitting the doors: one to hold the door in position and one to remove/replace the four bolts holding the hinges to the 'A' post. The job itself is then very straightforward. Hanging the doors might be straightforward but getting them to shut properly is another matter altogether. I immediately realised that the doors wouldn't shut at all: they became tight a few inches before closing and got progressively tighter, so much so that the doors were nowhere near fastening on the catches. I was annoyed about this as I'd spent ages ensuring a perfect door shut before the body was painted.

Rather than stop and try and identify the cause of the problem and sort it out properly, I elected to use extreme force. I persuaded myself that the seals were new and just needed 'bedding in' (ever heard that one before?) and that, if I could get the doors to close on their catches, the rubber would soon give and allow the doors to close gently. (How easy it is to lure oneself into this warped and clearly suicidal course of action in an effort to justify all manner of unjustifiable bodging)

So, in an effort to get the doors closed, I inadvisedly used my knee to push the doors closed, pushing as I thought, where the seam of the door was and thus not risking denting them. I therefore worked away at the doors, attempting to get them to fasten on their latches by pushing them inwards with my knee. Unfortunately, the seam wasn't where I thought it was and

I made the devastating discovery that I'd made several small knee-size dents in both door skins. I can't really describe how dreadful a feeling this was.

After nearly nine years toil on an otherwise perfect car, I'd put dents in the bodywork and potentially ruined the entire restoration. My next door neighbour Chris tried to cheer me up but I was inconsolable. See Photo 7.29-1 of the driver's door with small dents towards the rear of the door skin (although they might not be too visible in the photo – thankfully!). In desperation, I rang Nick, my bodywork specialist who'd sprayed the car, and asked if there was anything he could do. He duly came straight round and with a variety of strange looking bars and levers he simply pushed most of the dents back out! (After I had removed the windows and door catches from each

7.29-1 *Left: My dented driver's door – what can you say?*

Nick trying his best to get rid of **7.29-2** *the worst of the dents*

The 'A' post seal showing the **7.29-3** *small triangular section at the bottom of the windscreen that caused so many problems*

door to provide easier access) See Photo 7.29-2 of Nick sorting the problem out.

Both doors do still have very slight dents in them as Nick was unable to remove them completely, but they're not really noticeable unless you know they're there. I've had to accept them as some sort of reminder of human frailty – and stupidity. All I can really say in my defence is that I was working with someone else, and that's always a bad idea. I've always found it very difficult to work with someone watching me. I tend to rush and make mistakes and that's what happened this time. Not only this, but I failed to learn from this mistake and potentially even worse damage occurred when Chris and I tried to sort out the doors properly later on! More on this later.

Anyway, having decided to investigate the problem properly, I discovered that it was the 'A' post seals that were the problem, not the 'B' post seals. In particular, I discovered that the strange triangular part of the seal at the bottom of the windscreen pillar had a big effect on how well the door closed. See Photo 7.29-3. The door should squeeze tight against this part of the seal when it is closed but, in my case, the seals were too thick and refused to be squeezed down by the door. I'd already had to carve and sculpt the back of this part of the seal to get it to fit into its locating hole at the bottom of the windscreen. I now had to unglue it and take off some more. I had

to remove the excess thickness from the back of the seal, rather than the front, as otherwise it would look very unsightly.

I eventually ended up removing rubber from all of the seal – from the 'A' post by the leading edge of the door and from all round the windscreen/window aperture in an effort to get the door to close properly. It was an untidy job. I now know what I should have done. Before the car was painted, I should have trial-fitted both the 'B' post **and** 'A' post seals **and**

fitted the chrome window frame to the door, and then checked how well the door closed. Hindsight is a wonderful thing. The doors now closed after a fashion, but I knew that I'd have to try and sort them out properly at a later date. (3000 miles on and they're still not properly sorted. It's a big job to re-do them and, since finishing the restoration, I'm definitely suffering from 'post restoration fatigue' and find it difficult to motivate myself to tackle such tasks)

Lessons learnt:

- Removing and re-fitting the doors is a two-person job.
- If you find it hard to work with someone watching you, don't work with someone watching you.
- Never, never, never use your knee to encourage your door to shut.
- Trial-fit the doors with window frames and **both** door seals in place before the car goes to the paint shop.

7.30 Fitting The Rear Quarterlights

I re-fitted the rear quarterlights without too much difficulty although there are a few points to note:

1. Having changed the door glass to tinted glass, I thought I'd also change the quarterlights to tinted, only to discover that tinted quarterlight glass isn't available anymore (or rather I should say that I couldn't find anyone to supply it). "Oh, dear," I thought, "the car will look silly with tinted door glass and clear quarterlights." But I had no choice and I was forced to refit the original clear quarterlight glass. (Fortunately I can now report that you don't really notice that the door glass is tinted and the quarterlights are clear, even when you know they're different).

2. There's a thin rubber strip that goes round the edge of the glass that enables it to sit snugly in the chrome surround and make a water tight seal, but I couldn't find anyone who even knew what I was talking about let alone supply it. I thought I'd succeeded on more than one occasion but all they ever sent me were the actual quarter light seals for the bodywork. Eventually I found a specialist dealer in seals at Stoneleigh Spares Day (always worth going if you're looking for parts) and he supplied me with a 'U' shaped seal that just about did the job (with a little bit of sealant) See Photo 7.30-1.

3, Fitting the chrome quarterlight hinge stays was OK except I discovered that one of my original hinge stays had been altered to fit the car. My car originally had a new rear wing very poorly fitted and this jutted out somewhat. So the 'restorer' had cut and then re-welded the foot of the hinge stay to make it fit.

As a result, it now no longer fitted the new body shell. Luckily I had a spare stay from somewhere so I had that chromed and it fitted well. See Photo 7.30-2 with my original (modified) stay on the left and the proper one on the right (before it was re-chromed). The hinge stays are screwed to captive nuts in the roof and on top of the wing and special spacers are available to fit at the top and the bottom of the stay to get a good fit. See Photo 7.30-3.

The catches that close the quarterlights have a small wedge-shaped shim under them where they screw through the trim above the wheel arch and into the bodywork, without which they won't fit properly. You have to screw the hinges to the bodywork by drilling two holes and using self-tapping screws – make sure the hinge is in the right place first!

7.30-1 *Left: My quarterlight glass complete with new 'U' shaped seal around the edge before fitting the chrome surround*

My original quarterlight stay on **7.30-2** *the left after re-chroming. I later discovered it was broken and didn't fit, and I used a spare stay instead (on the right)*

The spacers for the top and **7.30-3** *bottom of the quarterlight stay to ensure a perfect fit*

7.31 Trimming The Doors

It was finally time to trim the doors. My first job was to screw a seemingly inconsequential bracket to the aperture at the bottom of the door frame. See Photo 7.31-1. On Series II and III cars, this bracket is in fact an essential item which is used to secure the door cards (see lower down). My second job was to trim the door roll tops. I knew this was a tricky job but set to with determination and confidence after my previous triumph with the head restraint. I glued the requisite thick pieces of foam to the backing plates (see Photo 7.31-2) and then attached the vinyl – or rather tried to attach the vinyl, but with little success; these really are tricky little blighters *[British slang, a persistently annoying person. Ed]*. To cut a long story short, I made two pitiful attempts to cover the door roll tops, each attempt ending with pathetic looking items you'd never

7.31-1 *The very important black bracket in situ which is used later to secure the door cards to the frame*

My initial attempts at **7.31-2** *trimming the door roll tops – unsuccessfully*

The original weather strip **7.31-3** *(bottom) and the replacement item (top) together with one of the special clips for mounting them*

With the roll tops in position, I **7.31-4** *marked the top of the door cards as a guide to where to screw the chrome trims on (through the roll tops)*

consider using - and then took them down to Mick Turley (by this time, I had lost all sense of shame!) who covered them and had them looking wonderful in a trice. Job done!

With the new weather strip (needless to say slightly different to the original) attached to the roll tops with the requisite clips (see Photo 7.31-3 showing the original strip at the bottom and the replacement at the top), I put the roll tops onto the doors – they just hook on at the top. The next job was to screw the chrome trims, that hold the top of the door cards in place, to the door through the roll tops. I therefore trial-fitted the door cards to the doors and used masking tape to mark the position (see Photo 7.31-4)

7.31-5 *The chrome trims now in place. All the holes in the frame are sealed with tape to protect the door cards from moisture*

It's very important to check **7.31-6**
that the drain holes are clear as otherwise water can't escape

and then screwed the trims to the door frame. The final job before fitting the door cards was to seal up the holes in the door frame (see Photo 7.31-5) as E-type doors are actually designed to allow water in – and hopefully out again! This is why it's important to seal the doors on the inside to stop the door cards getting ruined. It's also important to check that the two little drain holes in the bottoms of the doors are clear and not crushed as these allow any water that does get in to escape (out of the bottom of the door and hopefully

The armrests ready to be screwed **7.31-7**
on – with the aid of my patent
'don't let the screws fall back
out of the holes in the armrest'
mechanism

The special long self-tapping **7.31-8**
screw that goes through the trim
and screws into the retaining
bracket behind. The head is
hidden under the chrome beading

Trimming the alloy plates at the **7.31-9**
top front of the doors with vinyl

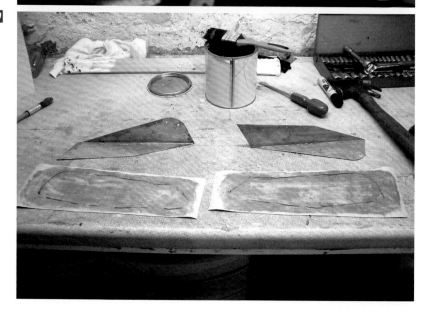

not into the interior). The door sill seal should have two indentations to ensure these drain holes aren't crushed when the door is closed. See Photo 7.31-6 of the front drain hole on the driver's door.

With the new plastic inserts stapled to the door cards with the aid of a staple gun in the trusted hands of Mick Turley (no, no shame at all), I clipped the door card to the door and screwed on the beautifully trimmed armrests (a damned fiddly job but one that was made easier by holding the long mounting screws in place with rubber grommets and large washers, see Photo 7.31-7) and the window winder handle and door handle.

Now for the clever bit: there is a special long self-tapping screw that goes through the plastic insert and screws into the aforementioned bracket above (Photo 7.31-1) and holds the door card firmly in place. The head of the screw is revealed by sliding the lower trim beading backwards. See Photo 7.31-8. The beading is clipped on to the door card in such a way that allows it to slide. I am sure that many plastic inserts have been ruined in the past by owners trying to remove the door card without knowing about this hidden screw, resulting in irreparable damage to the plastic insert.

The final job was to fit the small angled trims to the top front of the door (Photo 7.31-9 and 7.31-10), together with the little chrome escutcheons that operate the courtesy light switches and it was job done. See Photo 7.31-11 of the finished interior and door!

The plates now trimmed ! **7.31-10**

The finished interior! **7.31-11**

Lessons learnt:

- Series II and III door cards are held on with a secret screw under the beading.
- Stuff the economy – I've got an E-type!
- Covering the door roll tops is another of those tricky (i.e. virtually impossible) little trim jobs.
- E-type doors are designed to allow water to run into them – and out again.
- Regularly check that the drain holes on the doors aren't crushed or blocked.

7.32 Trimming The Boot Boards

The final job on the interior was to re-trim the boot boards and the car would be finished! The first thing I discovered was that the stainless steel seal retainers (chrome on Series I cars) were not screwed to the boards but stapled! I mentioned this to Mick Turley and he said that this became common practice on the later cars after some enterprising (lazy?) trimmer had discovered that they could staple through the retainers with their powerful staple guns and finish the job in a fraction of the time it would have taken to screw them down. See Photo 7.32-1 of my old boot boards.

Having stripped off all my old trim, it was relatively straightforward to re-trim the boards (nice and flat with virtually no curves – it's the curves that make trimming such a nightmare). I began with the hinged board behind the seats and used the requisite felt as a backing for the vinyl rather than the usual foam as for the other boards. See Photo 7.32-2. With my newly-acquired staple gun, it was then relatively easy to tack the new vinyl in place along the back edge. See Photo 7.32-3. I subsequently cut holes for the hinged luggage rails and the locking bolts, and then tucked and glued the side edges of the vinyl into a groove specially made for the purpose (see Photo 7.32-4). I then screwed the various pieces of newly re-plated chrome to the board and it was ready for fitting. Inside the car, I fitted a simple strip of vinyl over the lip the hinges go through and screwed the hinges in place by cutting simple slits in the vinyl. The first boot board was now in place. See Photo 7.32-5.

The remaining two boot boards were relatively straightforward to cover using foam, vinyl and my wonderful new electric staple gun, and they were soon in position. The only item of note was that the boards use hidden captive nuts inside them to screw various fittings on and these slightly strange round affairs are called 'Tee nuts'. I mention this as several of mine were rusted solid and needed replacing but, as I didn't know what they were called, it took me quite a time to find a supplier who understood what I was ranting on about. With the boards in place, I began re-fitting the seal retainers. Only re-fit the retainers with the

Left: My old boot boards with the alloy seal retainers stapled on

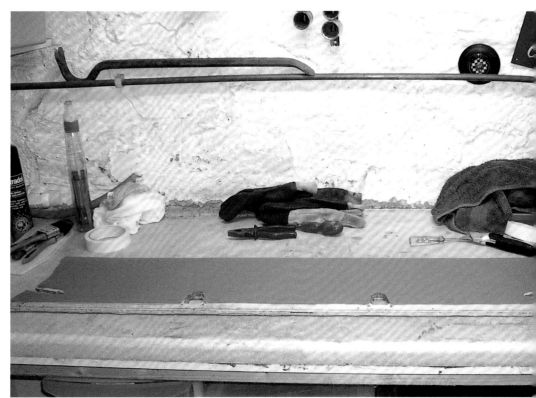

The hinged boot board covered in felt ready for the vinyl

The vinyl on the boot boards is stapled along hidden edges, not glued

7.32-4 The side edge of the vinyl on the hinged boot board is tucked into a special groove cut into the side of the board

7.32-5 The hinged boot board in place after a simple strip of vinyl is glued to the floor to cover the lip for the hinges

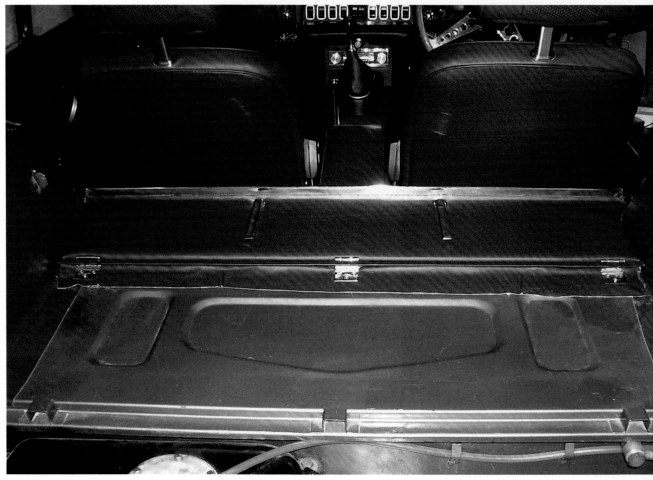

boards in position to ensure they line up with each other. Having learnt that Jaguar stapled the retainers to the boards as standard, I thought I'd do the same (lazy, me?). However, I quickly discovered that my little electric stapler was no match for the stainless steel seal retainers and when I tried to staple them down the staples simply bounced off! I therefore resorted to the proper method of screwing the retainers to the boards with countersunk screws. See Photo 7.32-6.

With the seal retainers in place, it was a relatively simple job to fit the new rubber seals into them, chamfering the ends with a sharp Stanley knife. Job done! See Photo 7.32-7 of the completed boot boards – and therefore the completed interior! – and therefore the completed car! Wow, was I really there? All that remained to be done was to get four new tyres fitted, have all the camber and castor angles checked, get an MOT and I'd be on the road!

Screwing the seal retainers to the boot boards using countersunk screws

The finished interior. Words can't describe my feelings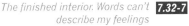

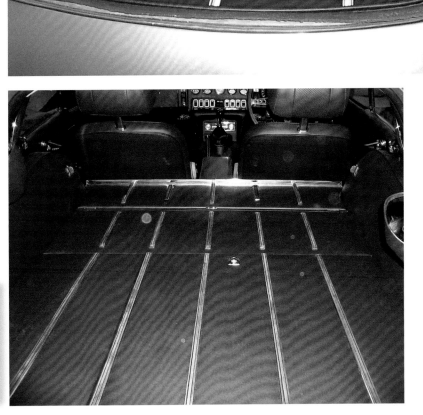

Lessons learnt:

- You can staple your seal retainers to the boot boards, but you'll need a very powerful staple gun!
- Crikey, it's nearly finished!

8.1 It's On The Road!

The E-type was virtually finished - if anything like this can ever be called finished. See Photo 8.1-1 of the car immediately after completion, still with its old tyres on. This picture was taken on my neighbour's drive as we roughly set the tracking prior to the MOT.

It was June and the weather was generally hot and sunny – a good time to be driving the E-type around – and I booked the car in for its MOT at the garage where Nick, who'd sprayed the car for me, works. It was a really momentous day – had I built the car properly and would it pass this first arduous test? Up to this point, I hadn't of course been able to drive the car to check it so I wasn't too sure how it would fare. I had cumpletely rebuilt the car from scratch and, although it

looked good, I really had no idea if it worked at all.

Getting The MOT

I arrived at the testing station with some trepidation as this was the first time I'd exposed the car to scrutiny by some proper mechanics. My worries were soon dispelled, however, as all the mechanics in the garage immediately downed tools and came to admire the car. I was really pleased with the reaction of everyone there as they all thought I'd done a really good job. When it came to the MOT itself, the tester refused to sit in the car to check the brakes/lights/horn, etc., in case he got it dirty! Instead I sat in and worked the controls, as requested. My heart was slightly in my mouth when

we tested the brakes, but I needn't have worried as they passed with flying colours – yes, even the handbrake!

I'd deliberately removed the headlamp rims from the car before the test so the headlamp aim could be easily set as I knew it wouldn't be right. With free access to the adjusting screws, the tester set the headlamp aim in a trice. One thing I was slightly concerned about was the condition of the tyres. I had four very old tyres on the car, two of which were horrible non-original things. All the tyres were due to be replaced after the MOT, but would these four pass for now? The tester looked at my rear off-side tyre in particular with some consternation. He then pointed out to me that the diameter of the tyre was far greater than it should have been and that the

8.1-1 *Left: The car 'finished' and having been driven its first 50 yards onto my neighbour's drive to have the tracking set with his simple tracking setting tool (not shown)*

My finished car in the garage looking stunning - it was all worthwhile! **8.1-2**

centre treads were protruding way above the tread to the sides. Somehow the structure of the tyre had given way inside and the whole tyre had expanded between one and two inches in diameter! Looking at it, I could suddenly see how close it was to the rear sill compared with the other one and, to my horror, we discovered that if you stood well back from the rear of the car the whole car actually tilted to the left as the right hand tyre was so much bigger than the left! Luckily, the garage took pity on me, knowing that

I'd booked to have new tyres fitted the next day – and the car passed!

I now have that most wonderful and glorious of items – a valid MOT certificate with the recorded mileage of 'one'. Now, that's a cool MOT certificate! I'm afraid to say that I fully intended to take some photos of this event but, in all the excitement and stress of getting the car to the garage, I forgot to pack the camera.

Lessons learnt:

- When is a restored car ever finished? Never: there's always something else that needs doing.
- Getting your car through its first MOT is a wonderful experience.

8.2 New Wheels And Tyres

I now had a street legal car, but still not one that was ready to drive around. I'd booked the car in the following day at Longstone Tyres to have the new tyres fitted as they're in Doncaster, not too far away, and they are a specialist supplier and fitter of classic car tyres. I'd decided to have the original Dunlop SP Sport radials fitted as the tread pattern is so unique and wonderful –

At Longstone Tyres I had the spokes checked and two of the wheels failed miserably - only a dull thud from the spokes instead of a nice 'ping' when the wooden handle of a brush was run round them **8.2-1**

8.2-2 *The inside of one of my two good wheels being carefully cleaned to remove any rust or flakes of chrome, etc., that may cause a puncture*

anything else, to me, just looks wrong. The problem with this being the cost – they're about £175.00 each (yes, each!). Multiply that by four and the only way forwards is to go into denial: if anyone ever finds out about the cost, deny it!

There's been quite a fierce debate raging about the advantages/disadvantages of fitting wider wheels and tyres (especially to the earlier cars with narrower wheels), the upshot of which seems to be much as before: you pays your money and you takes your choice. Some people think the cars look better and handle better with wider wheels; some people think they look worse and handle less well. It's very much a matter of personal choice. Series I cars have 5½ inch wheels

and Series IIIs have 6 inch wheels. A couple of other items to note are that earlier cars have 'curly hubs' at the centre of the wheel and later cars have 'flat hubs'. The later wheels were fitted with 'continental' style wheel spinners (Series II onwards) but the earlier eared-spinners will fit. I took the decision to fit eared-spinners right from the start of the restoration as I think they look vastly superior and all mine needed replacing anyway.

So, the next day I took the car to work! Driving through the rush hour in the E-type and parking it in the car park of the Barnsley primary school I was working in that day was the start of a long, hard process of slow deterioration of the car. Even by this time I realised that, with every mile I put on the car, it became less and less perfect – stone chips, mud and dirt, a slowly darkening exhaust manifold colour, creasing leather on the seats, etc., etc., were suddenly unexpected horrors that I had to deal with.

Here was my dilemma - I realised that I had built the car too well! I had

always intended to make it a driver's car and to use it as frequently as possible, but now I had a car in concours condition that I wanted to show off. And every time I drove it, it lost a little of its beauty. I quickly realised that I'd have to get over this and accept that this beautiful object would slowly deteriorate. However, I also realised that as it lost its shiny newness so it would gather patina, age, charm and experience in equal proportion – all those qualities that make a totally original, untouched car so alluring – and that this would compensate. I'm still convincing myself to this day that this is right! It's hard.

After work, I duly drove (slowly – only just running in) to Longstone Tyres. Unfortunately, things didn't go quite as planned. The first thing they did was to check the state of my wire wheels, and they were found wanting. By running a piece of wood round the spokes, they discovered that two of my wheels were in poor condition. The spokes should have given off a nice 'ping' to show that they were still tight and properly tensioned. On two of my wheels, however, all that could be heard was a dull, "thud, thud, thud" from the spokes showing that they were not under tension but loose. (See Photo 8.2-1 of the spokes being checked) This meant that the wheels concerned were in a dangerous condition and had to be replaced. Oh, joy. Add to the total cost of four new tyres, the cost of two brand new chrome wire wheels and you start wishing that maybe you should have accepted all those multiple credit card offers after all.

The only course of action realistically open to me was to have two new tyres fitted to the two good wheels (the spare wheel was actually found to be better than one of the others so they were swapped round) and have the other two new tyres fitted to two new wire wheels. Longstone recommended using wheels supplied by MWS and so I duly did. The ironic thing about this was that the wheels supplied by MWS will actually take tubeless tyres, but I didn't need that option as I was fitting Dunlop SP Sports, a tubed tyre. (See Photo 8.2-2 of one of my old wheels being cleaned with a wire brush to remove any rust before fitting the new rubber liner, inner tube and tyre. Cleaning off the rust and fitting a rubber seat round the wheel is essential to prevent punctures being caused by sharp objects inside the tyre) Anyway, I finally had four good wheels and tyres on the car (and a *very* large hole in my bank balance).

Lessons learnt:

- Your wheels might look nice and shiny, but that doesn't mean that they're in good condition.
- Wheels and tyres are really expensive – but they're worth it as 99.9% of people who see an E-type will say, "Wow! Look at those lovely chrome wire wheels", regardless of the condition of the rest of it.
- Original wheels and tyres? The choice is yours.

8.3 Setting Castor And Camber Angles, And Tracking

All that was required now was to get the camber and castor angles checked and adjusted as necessary, and I'd be able to drive the car properly. I needed to get the castor and camber angles checked as soon as possible for two reasons: firstly, I didn't want to ruin my new (and expensive) tyres by running the car with the wheels at the wrong angle and, secondly, to get a good reading with the tracking, etc., it is best to set these with new tyres on the car.

I therefore arranged for Paul, who'd fitted the front and rear screens, to check and set the castor and camber angles and the tracking as necessary. He and his colleague Andy had access to the proper Jaguar tools for this purpose. I left the car in their capable hands for a weekend, together with my camera, and

The rear link in place, hooked **8.3-1** *round the hub and the 'V' mounting necessary to get an accurate camber reading on the rear wheels*

they assured me they would take great care to ensure that everything was set correctly and within tolerance.

See Photo 8.3-1 of the special ride height adjusting link in position on the rear suspension. Photo 8.3-2 shows the camber checking tool being applied to one of the rear wheels. Photo 8.3-3 shows one of the rear drive shafts removed to enable more shims to be added to achieve the correct camber angle. Photo 8.3-4 shows the front suspension setting link in place next to the shock absorber.

Photo 8.3-5 shows the special gauges for measuring the front camber and castor angles bolted to the wheel hub. I believe that the wheels are sitting on a special turntable to ensure that they are in exactly the right position to facilitate an accurate measurement. Photo 8.3-6 shows Paul checking the tracking.

One simple fault that came to light early on, and shortly after this, was a quite loud knocking sound from the wheels. The knocking sound started to be heard when cornering and slowly got worse. I feared that there was a major problem with the suspension\steering somewhere. Well, to cut a long story short, what appeared at first to be a major problem with either the suspension or the wheel hubs was in fact nothing more than a couple of loose wheels. I

With the rear link in place, Paul **8.3-2**
checks the camber angle with the requisite special Jaguar tool

On one side the camber angle **8.3-3**
was found to be out of tolerance so the drive shaft had to be removed to allow shims to be added, as necessary, between the shaft and the brake disc to achieve the correct reading

The setting link on the front **8.3-4**
of the car between the shock absorber mountings held in place with string to prevent it slipping off

discovered that the two front wheels were a bit loose on their splines as my wonderful new eared-spinners simply hadn't been tightened up properly. Using far more force than I had initially, I fully tightened the spinners and the alarming knocking sound that had been growing steadily worse immediately disappeared never to return. Some problems can turn out to be very straightforward!

N.B. I use a piece of wood and a large lump hammer to tighten and remove eared spinners. There are several proprietary tools on the market for this purpose but they either don't work too well or they can cause damage to the spinners themselves. Nothing beats a good old lump of wood and a good old lump hammer!

At last, I was nearly there! The last couple of jobs to be completed before I could claim that the car really was finished were to have the car tuned and to try and sort out the door seals which had already come loose and needed fettling properly. By this time, I'd already covered about 50 very careful miles and so far everything seemed to be working well, but it was still too soon to know whether everything was really OK. So far, so good! Keep fingers crossed! See Photo 8.3-7 of the completed car on its first outing. Wow!

8.3-5 *The special two-way tool bolted to the front hub to measure camber and castor angles whilst the wheels sit on a calibrated gauge to ensure correct wheel alignment during measurements*

8.3-6 *Paul sets the tracking with a slightly more accurate tool than the one we used on my neighbour's drive!*

8.3-7 *The car's first ever outing to a primary school in Barnsley, en route to Longstone Tyres*

Lessons learnt:

- Setting the castor and camber angles is relatively straightforward when you have the correct tools (and very difficult when you don't).
- Knocking sound from the wheels? Check that your spinners are done-up tightly – really tightly.

8.4 Tuning The Engine

With the car just about on the road, I needed to have the engine tuned. I had done my best setting-up the ignition timing and the triple carbs but my best clearly wasn't good enough and I needed to get someone in who knew what they were doing. The engine was running well but I could tell that it wasn't properly tuned as it was rather lumpy and I couldn't get it to tick over smoothly at the required idling speed. I therefore searched the telephone directory and rang several mobile tuning companies and quizzed them in some detail about their knowledge of triple SU carb set-ups. Needless-to-say, most of them failed the test. There was one chap, however, who clearly knew what he was talking about and so I booked him. He duly arrived and

began by checking the ignition set-up – the timing, dwell angle, points, condenser, spark plugs, coil, etc. He was very thorough and slowly worked his way through the system, using a variety of diagnostic equipment, most notably the ubiquitous oscilloscope which he found difficult to attach from the back of his van due to the E-type's bonnet.

I was annoyed with myself to discover that the ignition timing wasn't set as accurately as I had thought and required some adjustment. The major discovery, however, was that one of my brand new NGK spark plugs wasn't working properly. Looking at the oscilloscope, you could clearly see it misfiring. It would have been extremely hard for me to diagnose this myself and I wouldn't have thought to

8.4-1 *Jim tuned the carbs in exactly the same way as I had done before, but somehow he managed it a lot better!*

suspect such brand new components from a reputable company like NGK.

Having sorted out the ignition side of things he turned his attention to the carbs. With considerable skill and knowledge, he partially dismantled the carbs, cleaned them and set them from scratch. He followed the same procedure as I had done on several occasions previously, but somehow he managed to tune and balance them perfectly. Suddenly, the engine was purring beautifully and ticking over without hesitation or lumpiness. See Photo 8.4-1 of tuning the carbs with an expert touch.

Lessons learnt:

- New spark plugs can be faulty.
- There are still mobile tuners out there who really know how to tune a triple carb set-up.

8.5 Re-Re-Fitting The Door Seals - Disaster!

I then had to turn my attention back to the door seals. The 'A' post seals on both doors were proving troublesome. They seemed to fit OK but, when the doors were opened, the inside frame of the door caught on the inside edge of the seal, peeled them away from their fixing glue and rolled them out of their retainers. This meant that they left a horrible stain where they made contact with the paintwork in front of the doors. See Photos 8.5-1 and 8.5-2 of the dislocated door seals and the stained paintwork. As a result, I had to remove both doors, trim the seals down slightly, re-glue them and then replace the doors.

Removing the doors is a simple operation with two people. With one person holding the door, the other simply undoes the four bolts holding the hinge to the 'A' post and the door lifts away. See Photo 8.5-3 of the four bolts. I also used a marker to go round the hinges so they could be refitted in exactly the same position later on. See Photo 8.5-4. In this picture you can also just about see the old hole in the centre of the 'A' post, drilled when the car was originally built. Apparently they fitted the doors, then drilled a hole through the hinges and 'A' posts to take a self-tapping screw. When the doors were subsequently removed for final fitting, etc., they could be replaced in the right position by means of the screw without a lot of fiddling about.

I tried to ensure that the seals would remain in place this time by securing them tightly in place with clamps while the glue dried. See Photo 8.5-5. It was time to refit the doors and this is

where disaster struck. On refitting the doors, the first thing I always did was to check the clearance at the front of the door as the clearance here is *very* tight. I was really grateful to have the help of my neighbour, Chris, in the process of removing the doors, but this was also the source of the problem. As stated previously, I find it difficult to work when others are around and so it proved this time. Having taken the doors off and replaced them several times, all seemed well. On the final occasion, however, I rushed and forgot

8.5-1 *The passenger side door seal showing where it had rolled out of its channel in the middle, staining the paintwork, and had come adrift from the retainer at the bottom*

to check the clearance at the front of the door before opening it.

Needless-to-say, the door was too tight and the leading edge caught the 'A' post – heavily. I looked on in disbelief as a large flake of paint and associated filler detached itself from the bodywork and fell to the floor exposing bare metal. See Photo 8.5-6. This was a serious blow (understatement of the year!). I quickly took the car back down to Nick who did the paintwork and took the very small amount of mixed paint I had left over. He said he'd see what he could do. To my utter amazement, he was able to repair the paintwork so it's almost completely unnoticeable. Thank heavens for that – I thought the whole thing would be ruined.

On my return I set about trying to get the driver's door to shut more easily. Now that the seal was sorted, the door was still very difficult to close without excessive force. I removed the door trim and set about repositioning the door glass chrome to try and get it further away from the body. To achieve this, I adjusted the brackets in the bottom of the door that hold the chrome in place and have scope to be able to adjust the angle of the door chrome. See Photo 8.5-7. This was partially successful, but I found I had to shave a little off the door seals that went round the top of the doors in order to get the door to shut fully without undue pressure. I was also forced to adjust the hinge very slightly so that the top of the door was further away from the body. This finally cured the problem but the top leading edge of the door is now ever so slightly proud of the bodywork which is annoying.

The driver's side showing the **8.5-2** *loose seal and resultant stain on the 'A' post*

The four bolts (chromed in my **8.5-3** *case – of course!) on the door hinge that need to be unscrewed to remove the door from the car*

Lessons learnt:

- Trial-fit the doors with windows, chrome retainers and all seals in place before spraying the car as you can't adjust them later.
- Always check the clearance at the front of the doors when refitting them – even if someone else is there.
- The door seals are still a source of grief 3000 miles on. Get them right in the first place.

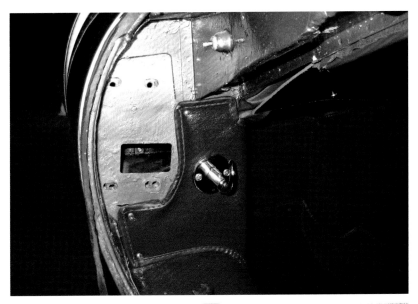

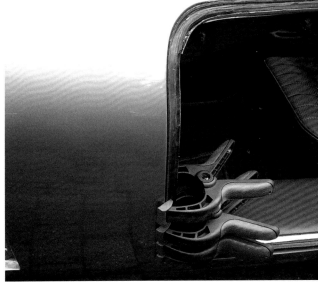

8.5-4 Above left: I drew around the hinge with non-permanent marker pen before removing the door to enable fairly accurate re-fitting

8.5-5 Above right: I held the freshly glued seals in place with clamps while it set

8.5-6 Disaster! I accidentally re-fitted the door too tightly and when I opened it I forgot to check the clearance first and it caught the 'A' post chipping a large flake of paint off, right down to the bare metal. I nearly wept

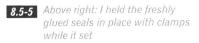

8.5-7 One of the small black metal brackets in the bottoms of the doors that hold the window surround in place. They can be loosened and adjusted slightly to change the angle of frame in relation to the body

8.6 Sorting Out The Hub Bearings

One other problem that became obvious very quickly was that the wheel bearings weren't adjusted properly. Two wheels, one front and one rear, were way too loose. Both wheels rocked alarmingly when off the ground and made a knocking sound when driving – even after fully tightening the eared-spinners. I had rather expected this, especially at the rear where I'd found it almost impossible to measure the shims required and had more-or-less guessed it. I removed the offending rear hub (relatively straightforwardly as the splines were still loose and everything was well greased) and fitted a thicker shim to the back of the bearing. See Photo 8.6-1. I must confess that I guessed the size of the new shim required, but I seem to have got it right,

with just a very little play in the hub when the wheels are off the ground.

As for the front wheel, it was a far simpler task. First, I jacked the car up and removed the wheel using the proprietary tools – lump hammer and block of wood. Next, I simply removed the split pin from the hub and tightened up the central nut a bit more - "Until it's just tight" is what is in the manual, but again I tend to work more by trial and error. If the wheel rocks too much, it's too loose and, if it doesn't rock at all, it's too tight is my rule. It may be wrong but it works for me.

8.6-1 *Despite my best efforts at trying to measure the required end float with a vernier caliper when I rebuilt the hubs, they were very loose and a much thicker one than the 130 thou. shim I'd originally used was required*

Lessons learnt:

- Check all wheel bearings for tolerance soon after rebuilding as they have a habit of 'settling in'.

Getting ready to remove the split **8.6-2** *pin from the castellated nut on the front hub and tighten it up – 'tighten until tight, then back-off one or two flats' is about as accurate as it gets*

8.7 Replacing The Bonnet Gas Strut

The final problem I encountered was with the gas strut holding the bonnet open. This seemingly innocuous part had been in storage for nine years and what I hadn't realised was that it had deteriorated considerably, and was now leaking gas at an alarming rate. The upshot of all this was yet another near disaster (yes, another one!) when I decided to take a picture of the car with the bonnet open. I had half-dimly registered in the deep recesses of my mind that the bonnet wasn't opening quite as easily as before but hadn't really taken it fully on board. I stood back and took my picture. See Photo 8.7-1. A few seconds later, I watched helplessly as a slight gust of wind caught the bonnet and it slammed shut without any restraint from the, by now totally defunct, gas strut whatsoever. Fortunately, the bonnet shut seal on the bulkhead did its job and cushioned the fall so that no damage was done – yet another fortunate escape. I immediately replaced the gas strut and realised just how poor the other one had been. The bonnet now opened totally by itself and required effort to close it rather than to open it.

8.7-1 *I stood back to take a photo of the car with the bonnet up and I then watched helplessly as it came crashing down on the body*

Lessons learnt:

- Gas struts can leak and lose pressure rapidly.

8.8 To Sum It All Up - The Benefit Of Hindsight

Well, I guess it's about time to stop and take stock of the whole restoration project. The car is now on the road and driving well. So the big question is - how well is it going? And was it all worthwhile?

Let's have a look at a few facts and figures and remind ourselves of the entire process. Having bought my E-type in 1997, I quickly realised I'd made a bad misjudgement. If I'd spent more time researching the marque (about which I was fairly ignorant at the time) and then selecting the right car, I probably wouldn't have had to rebuild the car in the first place.

"What, and miss the fun of the restoration?" I hear you say.

Well, yes and no. No matter how good the car is that you buy, there will always be work required on it to a greater or

lesser degree and improving an already good car can be just as satisfying as a complete restoration – but you can't claim the same bragging rights! There are many dodgy cars out there like mine. However, there are also some very good cars at reasonable prices and, with a little more thought and self-restraint, I could have waited and bought one of the latter rather than the former.

The time after the purchase of my car was, therefore, a low point. Having finally bought the car of my dreams, I quickly realised that it was a bad car and that only a full rebuild would be enough to rectify its many faults, and the car of my dreams was now rapidly turning into a nightmare.

Stripping the car down to a rolling shell was pretty straightforward but two problems quickly emerged: how best to

strip the paint from the body shell and how best to store the parts removed from the car. I stripped the paint off with a heat gun and sometimes paint-stripper although this was a difficult process. It had the advantages of being cheap and not damaging the metalwork. However, in retrospect I should have had the body professionally stripped and painted with rust inhibitor. There are several specialist companies offering a variety of 'body shell friendly' methods of paint stripping and these seem to be a very good idea to me.

The second problem was how best to store the parts and where to put them. A stripped car takes up about four times the space of an assembled one so you need a lot of room (consider a bonnet, a body shell, a rear axle, an engine and gearbox, five wheels and tyres, a fuel

8.8-1 *Left: The car back in 1999 just after I'd started the restoration with the paintwork removed and the car down to a rolling chassis – note the '90s toolbox!*

tank, lots and lots of chrome, seats, electrical items, etc., all separate – space is a big problem). Also, in what order do you store them? Do you put all the electrical items together, in which case where does the distributor go – with the engine or with the wiring loom? And the radiator fans and the windscreen wipers, etc., etc. - where do they go? Do you keep the carburettors with the engine or with the fuel pump – or is that with the wiring loom too?

On attempting to reassemble the car years later, trying to find where I'd stored half the parts was a major job in itself. This was exacerbated by having parts stored in various nooks and crannies all round the house, usually in the most inaccessible of places.

My top tip here is to use special storage bags for your smaller parts – obtainable from any supermarket and otherwise known as freezer bags. They are absolutely ideal for storing nuts, bolts and washers, etc., and any small, easily-lost and very hard-to-identify part. I bought vast quantities of small, medium and large self-sealing freezer bags and ... a permanent marker pen. I could then clearly write on the bag what the contents were, add a little oil if necessary to keep the parts in good condition, seal the bag against dirt and moisture, etc., and put them away, safe in the knowledge that the parts couldn't escape from the sealed bag and that I could easily identify them at a later date. I can't tell you how much easier this made things. (Pity I only hit on the idea half way through the restoration!)

The first big hurdle I encountered was moving house with the car down to a rolling shell - see Photo 8.8-1. With this successfully accomplished, I immediately encountered my second and probably biggest problem, and the main obstacle facing all potential restorers – life gets in the way of an E-type rebuild. It may be starting a new job or having children or getting married or getting divorced or becoming ill or any of a thousand scenarios but something is bound to rear its ugly head in the many years such a restoration takes. In my case, it was having to move the entire car in pieces half way through the dismantling process and move into a beautiful but much-neglected Victorian town house that itself demanded (and as I write nine years later still demands) considerable time and money spent on it. Not only that, but it was a house without a proper garage!

Two years passed with not a spanner even waved in the direction of the Jaguar. Two years of the E-type slowly rusting in the very damp 'garage' that was, in fact, a poorly-converted basement, while I did several essential jobs on the house until I could get round to sorting the garage out, knocking a few walls down, damp-proofing it, etc., and making it just big enough to work in. Remember that all this time the body shell was stripped to bare metal and open to all the damp a basement can throw at it (and believe me that's a lot) – and then it even had

to spend a couple of months outside on next door's drive while the garage was altered. (Thanks again to Chris, my very understanding and generous neighbour)

With the garage finally finished and the house habitable, I was able to continue the restoration! But another low point came at this crucial moment when I took a proper look at the rolling shell and saw how much it had deteriorated in the intervening couple of years minus paint and plus damp. It was a very sad sight.

They say that the darkest hour is right before dawn, however, and in this case they were right. Just when the whole restoration seemed destined to be added to the ranks of the small ads: "Unfinished restoration project for sale. All parts necessary to finish included," or similar, a beautifully rebuilt body shell

A virtually completed body shell **8.8-2**
with brand new bonnet and doors – Hurrah! Hole for a Webasto? – Boo!

comes up for sale! A virtually finished body shell complete with new bonnet and doors!

This really kick-started the restoration and we were off! See Photo 8.8-2. The shell just required finishing and the roof replacing to cover the hole where the Webasto sunroof had been. I knew I had to finish the bodywork before I could start on the mechanics of the car and, although there wasn't that much work to be done to prepare the new body shell for painting, it still took several months and an awful lot of hard work before it was ready for the paint shop. See Photo 8.8-3. I didn't enjoy this part of the restoration much at all – very dusty and laborious and seemingly never-ending, but eventually it was done and, soon afterwards, it was transformed by a few layers of paint into the most beautiful body shell I'd ever seen. See Photo 8.8-4.

With the body out of the way at the paint shop, I could start on the mechanics. In my case, I decided to begin with the rear axle unit. I think this was the correct decision in terms of the order of reassembly. I really, really enjoyed rebuilding the rear axle. It was the first time I'd done one and I found the challenge of slowly understanding how everything worked and reassembling it with shiny new parts very satisfying. See Photo 8.8-5.

The engine was next and I also enjoyed this part of the restoration, turning an oily old lump into a beautiful piece of classic engineering was great. Knowing that everything was being completely renewed and done properly was also very rewarding. See Photo 8.8-6. With the engine and gearbox in place, I then tackled the fuel system, the suspension and steering, then the cooling system and the braking system. By this time the car was really taking shape and beautifully-restored (and generally plated or polished) parts were mounted back onto the car and I mainly enjoyed the work. Even then the problem was to just keep going, night after night, and week after week, as it's all too easy to get sidetracked by other events and lose momentum. See Photos 8.8-7 and 8.8-8.

The final work was to re-trim the car with the help of Mick Turley. I quite

8.8-3 *Preparing the body shell for painting – a bit of a low point due to the dust and the mess and the fact that it never seemed to get any better*

The body shell painted and **8.8-4** *looking stunning. Bring it on!*

enjoyed this part of the restoration as it was something very new to me and, as it came together, the finishing line got closer and closer – until finally it was finished! See Photo 8.8-9. Nine years after I started pulling it apart, the car was back on the road and looking wonderful. See Photo 8.8-10 of the finished car on the day of its first MOT.

During the restoration many worries surfaced about how the car would run in practice. Here are a few answers:

Brakes: The brakes are really good. I reconditioned the entire system and fitted 'Greenstuff' pads. The brakes are now excellent, just as good as a modern car's. The handbrake is great! I'm really pleased with how well it works – a success. Hurrah!

Handling: I'm very relieved to say that the handling is now very good (I hesitate to say excellent, but I haven't really pushed it yet). When I bought the car, the handling was lethal. During the rebuild I found the culprit – a very bent lower steering arm on the front suspension. With this replaced and a polybush kit fitted and all new bearings, etc., the handling is transformed. The ride is superb, soft and compliant yet firm and taut – so superior to the go-kart suspension of my MINI Cooper S. This is due in no small part to the Koni Classic shock absorbers.

Engine: Beautiful! It simply purrs along, smooth and quiet, and with so

8.8-5 *At last, a chance to work on the mechanics and transform a big, horrible, oily lump into the legendary Jaguar independent rear suspension unit*

The brilliant XK engine re-built **8.8-6** *and looking superb. What more can you say?*

much torque and power it's a joy to drive around town as much as in the country. I'm really pleased with it. The only downside is a persistent oil leak from one of the cam covers which is currently annoying me greatly. I took so long building the engine and it was the one part of the restoration I felt confident about, and now it leaks! Must sort it out in the winter. (I'm happy to report that it's now sorted. The leak was caused by a poorly fitted end cap on the cam cover) A massive plus, however, is the rear crankshaft oil seal conversion which seems to work really well. No sign of any oil from here – yet!

Gearbox: I had my original 'box reconditioned and they seem to have done a really good job. The changes are smooth and positive, and I really like it. I have to say I'm not sure how much a Series I 4.2 or a Series II would be improved by fitting a 5-speed 'box

as the original's so nice and changing them over is such a big job. Also, I'm not sure what the improvement in fuel consumption would be, if any.

Unfortunately, however, I have to report a major problem with the 'box (that was rebuilt by a professional). In the 3000 miles that I've driven the car, it has twice dumped all (and I mean all) of it's oil all over the road, mainly from the rear seal, but also possibly from the front and no-one seems to know why. This is a major, major headache. The only way to properly investigate the fault would be to remove the engine and gearbox from the car (along with most of my beautiful trim).

Even then, as the problem is so mysterious and intermittent, who's to say that we'll be able to identify the source of the problem. So, I'll then have the choice of putting the existing one back in or replacing it with a new (very

expensive) one. Not only this but the gearbox is now out of warranty. It was, in fact, out of warranty (a year or 5000 miles) before I even started the engine as it was more than a year old by then. I'm just mad about it as it's such a big problem and one not of my own making. Arrrrggghhh!

Bodywork: I'm really, really pleased with the paintwork. Nick, who painted the car, did a great job. It looks absolutely stunning. I'm also very pleased with the panel fit and chrome, etc., and I'm glad I invested so much time getting a really good panel fit. But I'm still not happy with the door seals or the driver's window, which is very stiff. Another couple of jobs for the winter.

Electrics: I'm very happy with the electrics. To my great surprise, they're working perfectly! So far, so good. I'm also very pleased with the halogen headlamp conversion which is very powerful. A definite improvement. My intermittent wiper unit is also very good and highly recommended. My radio conversion to FM is good, but not brilliant – still a lot of interference and constant searching for channels.

Interior: Excellent. It smells as good as it looks! Very comfortable and really finishes the car. The inertia reel seatbelts work well but aren't perfect – they don't run too smoothly through the loops. They're still a vast improvement on the old static ones, though. No leaks and little wind noise. The temperature inside isn't too hot so the special insulation on the gearbox tunnel seems to be doing its job. I'm also pleased to report that it's not too noisy inside either. I neglected to fit any sound deadening under the trim but it doesn't seem to have made too much difference. No squeaks and no rattles, and no smell of exhaust fumes (unlike before the restoration).

And the cost? Well to give you some idea I've added up what I spent on various parts of the restoration. The cost of chrome and nickel plating alone was nearly £2500 and I spent £700

just on stainless steel nuts and bolts. Rebuilding the engine set me back more than £3000 (parts and machining only). The gearbox cost over £700 to get rebuilt and wheels and tyres cost in excess of £1,000 all by themselves. Painting cost £3000 and the rebuilt body shell £6,000 (worth every penny). The interior trim kit was around £2500.

In total, the complete restoration cost me around £31,000. Bear in mind that very little of this was labour as I did as much as I could myself. The total doesn't include the purchase price of the car which was £14,600, nor does it include the cost of essential tools, etc: such equipment as an engine hoist, an engine stand, a compressor, trolley jacks, a mig welder, a mini drill (Dremmel), spanners and socket sets, a bench grinder (with metal polishing wheel), a shed load of special small tools, copious drills, a host of different screws and consumables such as oil, grease, rags, paint, filler, glue and polish, etc., etc., not to mention the costly alterations to the basement to make it suitable for a restoration.

Including the cost of these (without

8.8-8 *The engine bay coming along nicely – bit by bit*

the alterations to the basement), you can add at least £4000 to the total. Consider the above as a percentage of my annual income and you get to a figure which, in no way, shape or form, is to be mentioned within earshot of Christine!

So was it all worth it? Of course it was – every minute and every penny. I've fulfilled a childhood dream to own the most beautiful car in the world and to restore it so that it once again looks and drives like the most beautiful car in the world. It remains an icon of British engineering from the 1960s and one that will endure. I didn't do it to make money (just as well!) but I did it for myself, and every time I drive it I get immense satisfaction. Job done.

And if anyone ever asks you why – just show them an E-type. Now even Christine understands.

Right: A 1969 Series II E-type **8.8-10**
Jaguar Fixed Head Coupé.
Oh, yes!

8.8-9 *Interior trim, the crowning glory*

Lessons learnt this nine years:

- Buy a decent car in the first place and spend your time keeping it nice rather than having to rebuild a heap.
- To complete a restoration you need time, money, space and dedication/commitment/determination/passion/mild insanity.*
- Bodywork finishing is not a great job.
- Be warned, life gets in the way.
- Stick at it and somehow, some way, it will get done.
- Don't do it to make money.
- Restoring the car was good, but driving it is even better!
- If I can do it, so can you.
- Keep the faith.

   *Delete as appropriate

9.1 E-Type Annual Servicing

Servicing an E-type is fairly straightforward, if rather time-consuming and messy. However, if, like me, you enjoy doing the work yourself then there's nothing to worry even the most un-mechanically minded among us.

As with most of us these days, my car is laid-up for the winter and every spring I give it a thorough service and check-over in readiness to enjoy some much-deserved and much-needed trouble-free summer motoring. If you devote a day (or maybe the whole weekend looking at the list!) to making sure everything on the car is in order then there is less chance of mechanical problems developing on the road later on.

Tools required are primarily a grease gun and grease (I use LM high melting point lithium-based grease as a rule),

engine oil, oil filter and a removal tool if required (see separate section on changing the engine oil), some Hypoy 80/90 gear oil for the rear differential and gearbox, six spark plugs (I use NGK BP501ES but it's a matter of personal choice), carburettor dashpot oil, a can of WD40 or similar, a can of Dinitrol or a similar rust inhibitor, a selection of imperial spanners and sockets, a set of feeler gauges, a stroboscopic timing light, a trolley jack (and preferably axle stands for safety), a new air filter element and possibly a new petrol filter element, chrome polish, car wash and car polish, chrome wire wheel cleaner, anti-freeze, battery top-up water, spare bulbs, a tyre gauge and inflator, a rotor arm for the distributor and possibly new points (contact breakers, where still fitted) and brake fluid.

You can carry out much of the work with the car on the ground but, to do a thorough job, you'll need to jack up the car off its wheels. I always jack the car up in two places: under the picture frame at the front of the car and under the differential at the rear of the car. Be aware that when you jack up the rear of the car it can easily roll forwards or backwards as the front wheels are free to turn and, consequently, I always chock the front wheels when raising the rear of the car. To jack the front of the car, place a block of wood under the front engine frame (the picture frame) to avoid damaging it and ensure you place the jack centrally to get a good straight lift. See the section on changing the oil for more details. If you want to rest the car on axle stands for added security, I put them under the

9.1-1 *Left: Grease nipple on the bottom of the rear hubs to lubricate the outer wishbone bearings*

Grease nipples for the inner rear **9.1-2** *wishbones accessed through holes in the bottom plate of the cage. There are four grease nipples here*

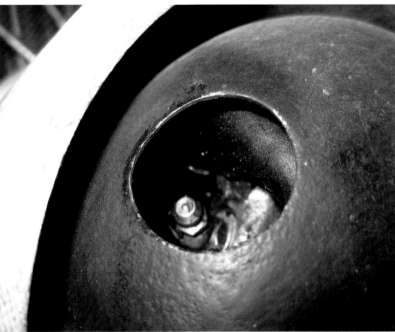

Grease nipple for the UJ at the **9.1-3** *outer ends of the drive shafts accessed through the strange-looking metal shrouds*

central chassis rails at the rear of the car, just in front of the rear bulkhead and under the lower wishbone mountings at the front, at the ends of the picture frame.

The first job to tackle is greasing the various grease points around the car – and there are a lot of them! I usually squeeze two or three shots of grease into a grease nipple and check that there's grease coming out from the edges of the bearing. If there is not, I keep pumping until there is. One

word of warning here is to be sure you haven't missed where the grease is coming out and keep pumping away in the mistaken belief that the bearing requires more grease when in fact it's squirting out from somewhere hidden!

Starting from the rear of the car there are grease nipples underneath each rear hub to lubricate the outer bearings of the wishbone. See Photo 9.1-1. There are then two more grease nipples either side of the car for the

inner bearings of the wishbone. These are accessed through four small holes in the corners of the bottom plate on the rear cage. See Photo 9.1-2.

Next up are the grease nipples on the universal joints (UJs), at either end of the drive shafts (four in total). The two outer ones are accessed through two round holes in the UJ covers. The round holes should be plugged with a small rubber bung which needs to be prised out. If the hole doesn't line up with the grease nipple simply slacken

Grease nipple on the inner end of **9.1-4** *the rear drive shaft*

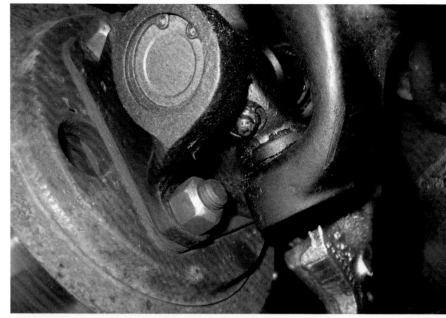

Below: Grease nipple on the rear **9.1-5** *of the prop shaft*

the jubilee clip holding the cover onto the drive shaft enough to allow you to spin it round until the grease nipple is accessible. See Photo 9.1-3. The two inner ones are situated next to the rear brake discs. See Photo 9.1-4.

The final grease nipple at the rear is the one on the UJ at the rear end of the prop shaft where it bolts onto the rear diff. See Photo 9.1-5. (Note that the front UJ on the prop shaft isn't accessible without removing the interior gearbox tunnel, i.e. it isn't accessible!)

Whilst working on the rear of the car, it is advisable to carry out the following work as well:

1. Check the level of fluid in the rear differential. To do this, remove the square filler plug from the rear right hand side of the unit. See Photo 9.1-6. If oil runs out when you stick your finger in it is full, otherwise it may require topping up. However, it is important to note that the level needs checking with the car horizontal – if the rear of the car is jacked up (which it probably is) you'll get a false reading so you'll need to temporarily lower the car back down again to check the level properly. Top up with Hypoy 80/90 if your diff. isn't limited slip or top up with LS 90 if it is limited slip. See Photo 9.1-7. If you're not sure which you have, the general rule is that Series I cars all have limited slip differentials whereas Series IIs often don't. There should be a small alloy tag attached to the

diff and if it is marked 'LS' then you have a limited slip differential. (The tag should also tell you what ratio differential you have)

2. Check for play in the rear suspension by rocking the road wheels. This is problematic as any play found could be the result of several different problems. It could simply be the case that the wheels aren't properly tightened up, or excessive play in the hub

bearings, or worn splines on the wheel hub, or worn UJs on the drive shafts or very worn bearings on the lower wishbone. If excessive play is present or suspected and you're not sure where it's coming from, it may be advisable to have it checked out by a Jaguar specialist (don't forget that the IRS unit was first used on E-types but went on to be used on many Jaguar models for more than 30 years and so many

mechanics are familiar with it)

3. Check for wear in the rear brake pads. As with the front brakes the pads are made with a groove cut in the middle. If the pads are worn beyond the extent of the groove, they need replacing. At the same time, try and assess the condition of the brake pads. Most cars do not have oval inspection plates on the rear bulkhead so it's very difficult to see anything of the brake pads at all. See Photo 9.1-8. (There doesn't appear to be a specific rule as to whether cars have inspection plates or not – mine does not) It's more a question of looking to see if there is anything obviously amiss such as bent operating arms or dislocated pads, etc.

4. Next lubricate the handbrake operating mechanism with either a spray grease or WD40. It's also an opportunity to adjust the mechanism to try and obtain optimum performance. See Photo 9.1-9.

Oil level plug on rear diff and **9.1-6**
breather above

Limited Slip Differential gear oil **9.1-7**

Check the condition of the rear **9.1-8**
brake pads – although it's a bit
easier with the diff on the bench!

5. An important job (especially for those with older petrol tanks that haven't been re-sealed internally) is to clean out the sludge trap at the bottom of the tank. On older cars bits of rust and other foreign bodies can quickly collect in the trap, block the fuel pump intake and lead to fuel starvation issues. It isn't too easy a job to clean it out (you need to drain the tank first through the bolt at the bottom of the trap) but if you have an engine that doesn't run too well, especially at higher speeds, then it's definitely worth doing. With the trap fully removed (it screws onto the fuel tank) you can give it and the gauze filter on the petrol pump (or outlet pipe for Series IIs) which sits inside it a good clean out. Even if the trap is clear at least you know that it's not the source of the problem. See Photo 9.1-10.

6. Check the condition of the exhaust system for signs of leaks and the rubber mountings that hold it in position for signs of splitting or crumbling.

7. Remove the wheels from the car if you've not already done so. I use a large block of wood and a lump hammer to remove and replace wheels as this means you can give the spinners a good whack but not

The handbrake operating mechanism **9.1-9**

Petrol tank sump with drain plug at the bottom. The whole sump unscrews from the petrol tank **9.1-10**

I use a lump hammer and a large block of wood to undo and tighten wheel spinners. This gets the wheels nice and tight and reduces the chance of damaging the bodywork in the process **9.1-11**

worry about hitting the bodywork with the hammer. The wood also obviously saves the spinners from damage. See Photo 9.1-11.

8. At this point you also have access to the grease points for the rear hub bearings. With the small cap prised off, you can push grease into the hub until full. See Photo 9.1-12. But make sure you don't overfill the hub as you may end up with any excess grease coming out later on. See Photo 9.1-13.

9. With the wheels off the car, take the opportunity to give them a really thorough clean with a proprietary cleaner on the inside as well as the outside. I use a good two-stage cleaner for a thorough clean such as the one in Photo 9.1-14 and then clean the wheels regularly with a spray cleaner throughout the summer. Importantly apply a good smear of grease to the splines on the hub before refitting the wheels. Without this, the wheels can actually rust onto the hubs and you have a real problem.

It's now time to turn your attention to the front of the car. There are several grease points here, depending on the model and what replacement parts are fitted. All cars will have a grease nipple for the ball joint on the top wishbone. This is a very important joint to keep lubricated as the ball joint sits in the wishbone and if it wears to excess a

9.1-12 *Rear hubs greasing point*

9.1-13 *Oops! Too much grease*

9.1-14 *Two stage cleaner with brush and gloves*

9.1-15 *Top ball joint with original tie rod ball joint including grease nipple at the top of the picture*

Later model showing tie rod ball **9.1-16** *joint without grease nipple*

new wishbone is required. See Photo 9.1-15. There may also be a grease nipple on the steering tie rod ball joint nearby unless later swivels are fitted that do not require greasing. See Photo 9.1-16.

There may also be a grease nipple for the bottom ball joint although if your bottom ball joints have been changed in the last 10 years they will almost certainly have been replaced with sealed for life units (so much so that I couldn't find an original one to photograph!) See Photo 9.1-17.

If you have an original steering rack, there is a grease nipple in the centre. Replacement racks don't have a grease nipple but should still be greased by pumping grease into the rubber shrouds either side of the rack. See Photos 9.1-18 and 9.1-19. Whilst greasing the rack, you should also check the condition of the two rubber-bonded steering rack mounts as these can start to de-laminate, leaving your steering rack in a dangerous state. At the same time, check that the safety

9.1-17 *Sealed for life bottom ball joint*

bolts (identified by the large washers under the bolt heads) which hold the rack in position in case of sudden mounting failure are in place. See Photo 9.1-20.

There are also two UJs on the steering column, one at the bottom by the steering rack and one at the top, inside the car. These should be checked for wear, but I believe they can't be greased (they are either sealed for life units or if there is a grease nipple you can't get to it – see Photo 9.1-21). So, if there is play in them, they should be replaced.

Original steering rack with grease nipple 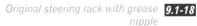 **9.1-18**

Different racks with and without grease nipples **9.1-19**

The steering rack mountings and safety bolt. The safety bolt is pictured at the bottom with a large washer under its head. On some cars two are fitted either side **9.1-20**

Grease nipple on the lower
steering column – inaccessible
without removing the UJ from
the column **9.1-21**

Fluid reservoirs on Series I cars **9.1-22**

Two of the fluid reservoirs on **9.1-23**
Series II cars...

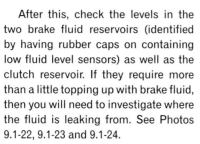

After this, check the levels in the two brake fluid reservoirs (identified by having rubber caps on containing low fluid level sensors) as well as the clutch reservoir. If they require more than a little topping up with brake fluid, then you will need to investigate where the fluid is leaking from. See Photos 9.1-22, 9.1-23 and 9.1-24.

The dustbin style air filter will need replacement (see Photo 9.1-25) and you will also need to check the in-line fuel filter on the right hand bulkhead. If it's a later model, replace the filter if necessary (see Photo 9.1-26). On earlier models, check the gauze filter is clear. (N.B. there are also thimble style gauze filters in the tops of the three carburettor float chambers and if

9.1-24 *...and there's the other one. Check the sensors are working by pushing the domed nipple down on the top of the cap with the ignition on and the handbrake off*

9.1-25 *Original air filter*

fuel starvation is suspected it's worth checking these as well)

Moving on from here, it is time to check the tension on the fan belt. If it needs adjusting, this is done by moving the alternator or dynamo to effect the correct tension. See Photo 9.1-27. It is also worth noting that the jockey wheel on the fan belt fitted to later models has a small hole in the bottom of its groove to allow grease to be sprayed into it using a long nozzle.

The spark plugs can be changed if

Fuel filter fitted to later cars **9.1-26**

The fan belt is adjusted by **9.1-27**
moving the alternator

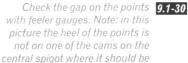

9.1-28 *NGK BP5ES my choice of plug*

Squirt a little light oil down the **9.1-29**
central spigot of the distributor

Check the gap on the points **9.1-30**
*with feeler gauges. Note: in this
picture the heel of the points is
not on one of the cams on the
central spigot where it should be*

required. When to change plugs is a matter of some debate and personal choice. If the car only covers a minimal mileage every year, some owners may wish to change the plugs every year, others may consider this to be overkill and only change them every few years. The standard plug gap is 25 thou. But check the recommended gap as it can vary from plug to plug. See Photo 9.1-28.

The distributor will also require inspection. After removing the cap (or head), detach the rotor arm and spray a little light oil down the central spigot. See Photo 9.1-29. The points will almost certainly need checking and adjusting. To do this, the engine needs to be rotated until the heel of the points sits on top of one the cams on the central spigot so that the points

Check the rotor arm for integrity **9.1-31**
and signs of burning on the
tip. SNG Barratt now supply an
upgraded version of the rotor arm
as this is a known weakness

Header tank on Series I cars **9.1-32**

Radiator expansion tank on **9.1-33**
Series II cars

are fully open. The points' gap needs to be measured using feeler gauges. The gap should be 15 thousands of an inch. See Photo 9.1-30. The condition of the contacts needs checking. Any sign of burning needs to be investigated and is most likely caused by a malfunctioning condensor or overcharging alternator. In this case, replace the points and the condensor and if necessary investigate the cause of the problem. At the same time, check the condition of the rotor arm. These are remanufactured items and are prone to early failure. See Photo 9.1-31. If there are any signs of burning at the tip or the arm coming loose from the Bakelite spigot, then the rotor arm should be replaced. (One spare I always carry with me in the car is a new rotor arm)

After this, check the coolant level in the radiator and/or header tank. On Series I cars the coolant level should be around 1" below the neck of the header tank. See Photo 9.1-32. If topping-up is required, make sure that it is the correct mixture of water and anti-freeze. I use a 50/50 mix. Even in

hot climates it's important to add anti-freeze as it helps prevent corrosion in the cylinder head (and raises the boiling point). With Series II cars, where the expansion tank is mounted on the bulkhead, first check the level of coolant in the radiator which should be fitted with a flat, un-pressurised cap. It should be completely full. After this check the expansion tank (fitted with a pressurised cap) which should be about half full. See Photo 9.1-33. Again top up with a 50/50 mix if necessary. If more than a little topping-up is required, the source of the coolant loss needs to be investigated.

It's then time to check the level of oil in the carburettor dashpots. The level should be around half way up and I always find that the dashpots need topping up with the requisite oil. This oil is important as it serves to dampen the movement of the carburettor slides and produce a smoother throttle response. See Photo 9.1-34.

You should check the levels in your battery unless you have a new 'sealed for life' item fitted and top-up with ionised water so that the plates inside the battery are fully immersed. See Photo 9.1-35. While you're doing this, conduct a visual check of the wiring above and next to the battery and clean the battery terminals if they are showing signs of corrosion. I also coat the battery terminals with a proprietary spray to prevent corrosion. NB Like many people I use a small charger to maintain the battery when the car

9.1-34 *Top: Dash pots require regular topping up*

Don't forget to top up the **9.1-35** *battery but don't overfill it as I did recently causing a major paintwork alert!*

9.1-36 *Battery condition maintainer*

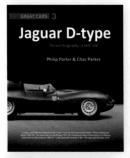
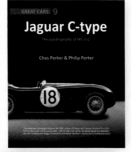
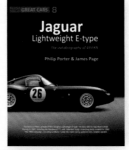
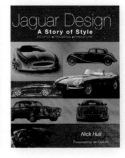
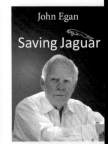

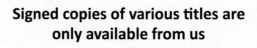

Publishers of the Finest Motoring Books

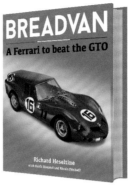

★★★★★

'Get the Breadvan
Great book, great read,
fantastic pictures. Thank you!'
Michael S.

Royal Automobile Club Motoring Book of the Year Finalist

★★★★★

'Beautifully presented book, bursting with details and images, a fantastically detailed archive of this amazing car. Look forward to seeing what other cars will be covered in this wonderful series.' **Paul E.**

★★★★★

'Excellent in every way.'
Roger P.

Many of our books are also produced as superb, hand-bound Special Editions: Limited Editions, Collector's Editions, Unique Editions and Owner's Editions.

★★★★★

'What a superb book on all these lost treasures. The book is like a mental travel find on all of these barnfinds in itself, as if you would find them yourself. fantastic experience. I love it.' **Wolfgang H.**

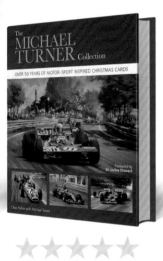

★★★★★

'Excellent
Superb and unique book.
Excellently presented and finished. Service, communication & delivery (& packaging) was also just as good as the book. I can only highly recommended Porter Press and their products. Thanks.' **Andrew B.**

Visit the website for our full range of titles

★★★★★

'Great trip down memory lane. A fitting tribute to the work of renowned and esteemed F1 painter Michael Turner with a great anthology of some of the key moments from the sport over the last few decades!'
Jon H.

Multi Award-winning Title

★★★★★

'Utterly outstanding book of very high quality as usual from Porter Press.' **Philip W.**

Very good book; technically, it is informative of the vehicle's restoration, and photographically it is brilliant, and covers the vehicle's 70 year history.' **Craig L.**

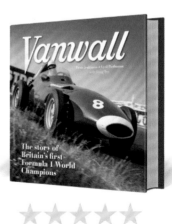

★★★★★

'One of the best books I've seen in along time! Quality A1 and lots of pictures never seen before! Has done the mark Vanwall Justice as first manufacturer champion!' **Craig R.**

isn't in use - highly recommended. See Photo 9.1-36.

The next task is to carry out a full visual inspection of the engine bay for any problems such as oil leaks, fluid leaks or coolant leaks, loose clips, loose nuts and bolts, loose wires, damaged or cracked engine frames, etc. At the same time, use WD40 or similar to lubricate all moving parts such as the carburettor linkages, bonnet bushes and operating springs (early models), not forgetting the bonnet locking catches mounted on the bulkhead that have oil holes in the top of them. See Photo 9.1-37. I always check the condition of all electrical connections, especially those near the radiator, as they get the worst of the weather and spray them with WD40. See Photo 9.1-38. I also try and lubricate all the cables that come through the bulkhead as well as the air flap bearings on the heater box.

Having finished with the engine bay, jack the front of the car off the ground and check the play in the wheel bearings. The wheel should not rock but should turn freely. If it rocks, then the wheel bearing needs tightening.

Oil hole in the centre of the **9.1-37**
bonnet release catch

Exposed connectors for the **9.1-38**
radiator fans close to the
bottom of the nearside picture
frame

To do this, remove the road wheel and then pull out the split pin from the castellated nut in the end of the hub which will allow you to tighten it. See Photo 9.1-39. The manual says the nut should be tightened 'until sticky' and then backed-off one or two flats which is rather vague. I tighten the nut so that the wheel can turn freely but it doesn't rock. While the wheels are off, grease the hub bearings (See Photo 9.1-40) and check the front brake pads and discs for wear. See Photo 9.1-41. Also check for play in the top and bottom wishbone ball joints by rocking the wheel – if it rocks and the bearing's OK, then there's probably play in one of the ball joints. In the case of the top ball joint, this may just require shimming and the bottom ball joint can simply be replaced.

The front wheel bearing **9.1-39**
castellated nut and split pin

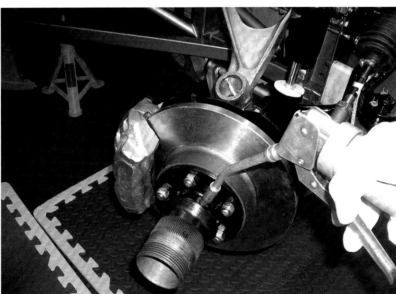

Greasing front hubs **9.1-40**

Front brake pads **9.1-41**

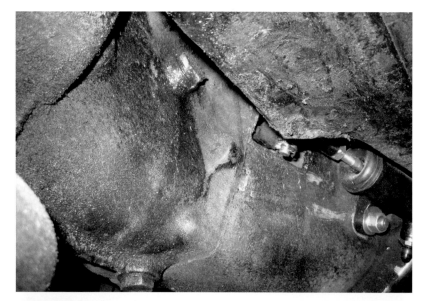

9.1-42 *Gearbox level and drain plugs on an early gearbox*

9.1-43 *Gearbox level plug on a later gearbox*

With the front wheels off the car, give them a thorough clean, as done with the rears, and don't forget to grease the splines on the hubs.

Check the level of the oil in the gearbox by removing the inspection plug. If no oil runs out when you stick your finger in, it requires topping up. Again I use Hypoy 80/90 gear oil, as for the rear diff. See Photos 9.1-42 and 9.1-43.

The final job at the front is to change the oil in the engine.

Now this may surprise some of you but, speaking as one who has completely rebuilt their car from scratch, changing the oil is a job that fills me with dread. It is so simple and yet so difficult at the same time. If you have the correct equipment, this helps tremendously but there are still problems to face, mainly warm oil and lots of it with a tendency to get everywhere.

To begin with, run the engine until warm (not long) so the oil will flow out more easily. Before I rebuilt my engine, I used to use engine flush added to the engine before draining the oil to try and remove unwanted debris from inside the engine, but I'm not so sure how effective it is and, with a newly rebuilt engine, I don't need it anyway.

Secondly, jack the car up at the front to allow access to the bottom of the engine (the sump). The generally accepted way of doing this is to jack the car up on the bottom of the front engine frame (the picture frame) using a trolley jack with a block of wood to prevent damage to the two flanges on the frame (see Photo 9.1-44). This allows both front wheels to be raised simultaneously. I think this is better than just jacking up one side which puts undue stress on the suspension, etc., and doesn't run the risk of damaging the sills or in a worse case scenario putting the jack through the sill (which I once did on my old Mini)! You must ensure that the handbrake is on and that the car is in gear (in case the handbrake fails) and that the jack is free to roll slightly as it will need to do so as the car is raised.

The next job is the easiest and hardest. All you have to do is undo the drain plug from the back end of the

The front of the car jacked up **9.1-44** *by means of a trolley jack under the centre of the picture frame. A block of wood is utilised to prevent damage to the two flanges on the underside of the frame*

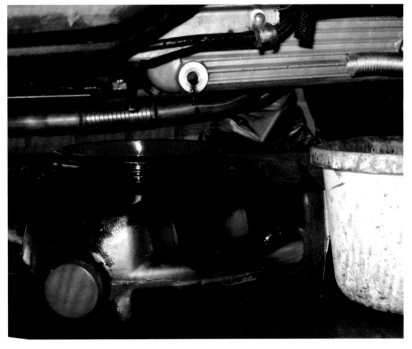

sump and allow the oil to drain into a suitable container. Here you need your first special tool: a suitable receptacle for the old oil. Finding something big enough that will fit under the car is not easy. I therefore use my 'drain easy' oil can rather than just my old washing up bowl for three reasons: firstly, the bowl isn't big enough to hold all the oil and you are left hopelessly watching as it overfills and pours all over the garage floor; secondly, when you drop the sump plug into it (you always do) you have to fish it back out and, thirdly, you later have to decant it into a suitable container to take it to the recycling centre and this process invariably leads to more oil spillage and mess. See Photo 9.1-45.

Even with my 'easy drain' the job is still hard. Why? Because you have to judge the angle at which the oil is going to exit the sump in order for it not to miss the can and pour all over

My 'Easy Drain' oil can and an **9.1-45** *old washing-up bowl used to catch the old engine oil – well, most of it!*

The old and new spin-on oil filters with oil seals, drain plug and socket and oil filter chain wrench 9.1-46

The spin-on oil filter conversion bolted to the engine block 9.1-47

the garage floor. The oil will not drain vertically from the sump but come out almost horizontally at first. The problem, therefore, is where to position the oil can to catch the oil? I always underestimate how fast and how far the oil will emerge sideways and so the oil joyously shoots past my waiting dispenser and pours all over the floor. One or two seconds spent repositioning the oil can equates to about one or two pints of oil on the garage floor and oil all over the outside of the can you will later need to place in the boot of your everyday car to take to the recycling centre. Your arms are now also covered in oil because you have frantically tried to reposition the oil can. Now you can begin to see why I loathe the job so much!

When the oil has finally drained out of the engine (it takes quite a time), you need to remove the oil filter and replace it with a new one. If you have a spin-on oil filter conversion like mine then one virtually essential tool is an oil filter removal tool like the one shown in Photo 9.1-46 which also shows the old and new filters and the sump drain plug. The oil filter is invariably tightened beyond removal with bare hands (no matter how little it was tightened when fitted) and a removal tool is essential. I did once manage to remove an oil filter without such a tool by piercing it with an old screwdriver, using that as a lever to loosen it, but that was a heck of a

messy business. If you have an original oil filter unit, simply unscrew the bolt at the end of the unit and replace the paper filter inside.

Access to the oil filter is gained in two ways. Firstly, from the side by removing the air filter canister (not needed on my car as I don't use the air filter) and from underneath by removing the little 'D' shaped plate from the stone guard below the oil filter by means of the small screw underneath. See Photo 9.1-47 of the engine block with the spin-on oil filter removed. Having removed the filter, it is then replaced by a new item.

When replacing either type of filter you should use a new rubber oil seal around the edge of the canister and this should be slightly smeared with oil before refitting, to ensure a good seal and to make sure it will come off next time and doesn't weld itself to the engine block! Replace the air filter and access plate when the filter's in place - after you've wiped off all the oil that's seeped onto the stone guards, torsion bars and engine frames!

Before refitting the sump plug, check it for metallic particles. The plug is magnetic and any broken bits should migrate to the plug. If there are

9.1-48 *Ensure you have the correct oil for the engine, not just 'off the shelf' oil for modern engines – and plenty of it!*

9.1-49 *My cut-down oil funnel tightly wedged in the oil filler aperture in the left hand cam cover ready to re-fill the engine with clean oil*

any sizeable bits attached to the plug, this isn't good news! In this instance I would keep them and take them to show a specialist who might then be able to gain an idea of which bit of the engine has decided to break up. There will always be some amount of iron filings on the plug to a greater or lesser degree and these should be cleaned off before refitting the plug. You should fit a new copper washer to

the plug to prevent it leaking oil. If you don't and it does leak, the only way to cure it is to drain the oil again. Hence better to replace it now.

The final job is to refill the engine with oil. They are big engines and take a lot of oil (15 pints) so ensure you have enough. I always use Millers (see Photo 9.1-48) as I believe it to be the best available for the XK engine, but I'm sure others will recommend other

oils, probably just as good. Do note, however, that using the correct type of oil in an engine (especially an older one like the XK) is essential. Don't just use any oil as most 'off the shelf' oils available on the high street are suited to modern engines and have very different properties.

At this point I use my next specialist tool: the oil funnel. Again this might sound straightforward but you need to

9.1-50 *Check the wiring under the dash. I also squirt a little WD40 around to keep it all working well*

Oil hole on door catches **9.1-51**

Door lock barrels **9.1-52**

Door hinge with groove in the top for oil **9.1-53**

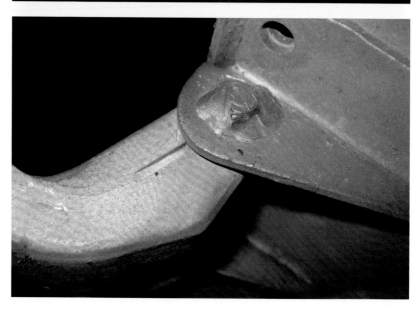

Wiper wheel boxes **9.1-54**

Drain hole under centre of rear **9.1-55**
hatch seal

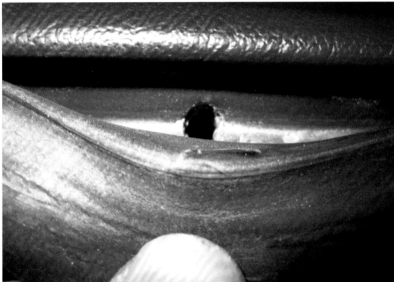

get one to fit. What I've done is to buy one with a flexible spout and cut that down so that it wedges itself nicely inside the cam cover and doesn't fall out or spin round when full of oil (see Photo 9.1-49). Then, very importantly, check that you have refitted the oil filter and the sump plug before refilling with oil! It's so easy to forget and, before you know it, you have (another) pool of oil on the garage floor. You can get away without using a funnel these days as modern oil cans have that wonderful little pull-out spout on them, but it's still easier to use a funnel.

When the engine's been filled with oil, let the car down off the jack, take it out of gear and start it up. This is a 'heart in the mouth' time as you wait

for oil pressure to register on the gauge which can take up to 10 seconds. Leave the car for a minute and then re-check the oil (if it's possible to see new clear oil on a dipstick!) and top up as necessary. Second heart in the mouth job: check for leaks.

Job done! Now all that remains to be done is to remove oil spillages from just about everywhere and everything (white spirit and plenty of it), put your tools away (when also cleaned of oil) and then take the old oil to the recycling centre. Now you know why I hate doing such a seemingly easy and mundane job!

Moving to the inside of the car, I usually open the centre console on the dashboard to check the electrics all

look OK. I then give the compartment a quick spray of WD40 to prevent dry joints, etc. I think a small squirt of WD40 is enough to maintain the condition of the electrics, much the same way as an oily rag in the back of a clock is enough to keep it lubricated. I'm not sure if this is recommended practice but it works for me. See Photo 9.1-50.

Lubricate all the other catches and hinges, etc., around the car as follows:
• Door lock mechanisms on the rear of the doors (as indicated on the top of the locks). Photo 9.1-51.
• Door lock barrels in the door handles (or in the door skin on some models). Photo 9.1-52.
• Rear hatch opening mechanism and

Door drain holes **9.1-56**

hinges.

- Door hinges. Note that most (but not all) door hinges have a small groove on the top to allow oil to run down inside the hinge. Photo 9.1-53
- Petrol flap hinges.
- Radio aerial (if fitted).
- The wiper spindles underneath the windscreen. Photo 9.1-54
- Rear quarterlight catches.
- Up-stand (including sliding bolts).
- Seat reclining mechanism (where fitted).
- Seat runners.
- Armrest hinge on gearbox tunnel.
- Glove box hinge(where fitted).
- Ignition switch.
- Courtesy light operating switches (on the 'A' post just inside the car).

Not only does this ensure correct operation of the item in question, it also serves to prevent rust from gaining a hold inside hinges, etc.

The following checks should then be made:

- Tap the spokes of all (five) wire wheels by running a stick or the handle of a hammer round to check for loose spokes. Good spokes will 'ping' nicely; bad spokes will sound very flat.
- Check tyre pressures and inflate as necessary (again, don't forget the spare wheel – I usually put a few extra pounds in mine as I know it will slowly deflate over the summer months as I don't often get round to checking the pressure on the spare).
- Check that all road wheels are properly tightened on the hubs – use the block of wood and lump hammer again.
- Check that the drain hole underneath the rubber seal in the centre of the bodywork around the rear hatch isn't clogged and drains water freely . Photo 9.1-55
- Check the two drain holes in the bottom of either door aren't blocked or crushed flat so that water can escape. Photo 9.1-56
- Check all electrical equipment is operating properly: headlights, side lights, tail lights, indicators, hazards (where fitted), horn, brake lights, reversing lights (where fitted), number plate lights, windscreen wipers and washers, heater blower, interior lights, lights in all instruments on the dashboard.
- Check the operation of doors and windows.
- Wash the car using proper car cleaner (washing-up liquid, etc., can actually damage your paintwork).
- Polish the paintwork with a good quality polish (in doing this you will protect the paintwork and be able to inspect the condition of the bodywork and notice any blemishes you might otherwise miss).
- Polish all remaining chrome work (not only does it shine but it also

9.1-57 *Series I timing marks*

helps prevent corrosion).
- Wipe all exterior light lenses and, if necessary, remove them and give them a good wash in warm soapy water.

Finally, start the engine and check the following:
- Starter motor – should crank the engine over easily.
- The power of the battery, which should allow the starter motor to crank for some time. All gauges on the dashboard.
- Power steering (where fitted – which should also be checked for fluid level).
- Brake servo operation (put your foot firmly on the brake and start the car, the brake pedal should go down a bit further if the servo is working properly).
- Check for fluid leaks (including petrol).
- Ignition timing. The recommended setting is 9° before top dead centre (BTDC). Assuming the ignition timing has already been set previously, I use a stroboscopic timing light to check the timing and ensure the distributor is working correctly by advancing the

ignition with engine speed. With the engine on tick over and the vacuum advance pipe removed, the timing should read around 9° at tick over and then increase substantially as the revs rise. Don't necessarily worry if your ignition doesn't read 9° as that's the basic setting and certain engines run better on slightly different settings – it can be a case of trial and error. However, if you do suspect that the ignition timing requires adjustment, this is easily achieved by slightly slackening the clamp bolt on the distributor shaft and turning it either way to alter the ignition timing. See Photos 9.1-57 and 9.1-58.
- The engine itself. Listen for knocks, rattles, lumpiness, irregular running, misfiring, etc., etc. Any of these requires further investigation. Unfortunately the list of possible problems and possible causes and possible cures is so long that it cannot be covered here. Suffice to say that, if you can't fix it yourself, now's the time to seek help and check your bank balance.
- Road test. It may all seem to be hunky-dory in the garage but the only

true way to find out if everything's OK is to drive the car and check that all the adjustments, etc., you made have in fact worked. During this test, also check that the thermostat is working satisfactorily by checking the temperature gauge, and likewise the thermostatic switch by ensuring the fan(s) cut in when the engine is hot.

Finished! Now it's time to enjoy the car all summer long, safe in the knowledge that the car's sorted and, as far as possible, problem free. It adds so much to your driving pleasure if you're not constantly worrying about breaking down. Remember: if a job's worth doing, it's worth doing yourself. Also, by servicing the car yourself, you not only get the satisfaction of having done it and done it properly (how many garages will include all of the above in their standard service schedule?) but, if problems do occur later, you've more chance of knowing what the problem is and how to fix it. Now, get in that car and drive, drive, drive!

9.1-58 *Timing marker on my Series II, unusually at the bottom of the sump*

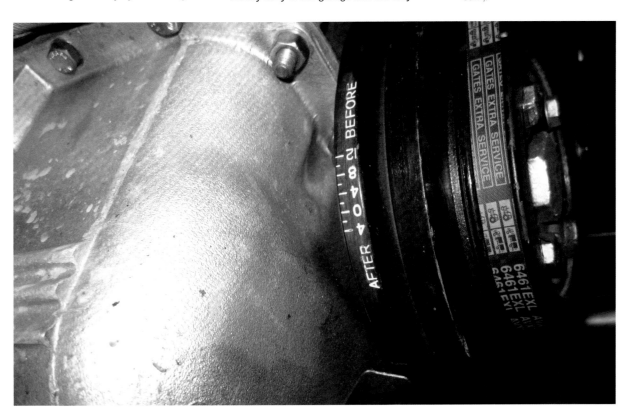

10.1 Tools Required for Working on an E-type

Over the years, and certainly through the course of restoring my car, I have slowly amassed a large collection of tools essential for working on classic cars and E-types in particular. For too long did I sit and look with envious eyes at the garages full of tools of the professionals and serious amateurs. If you're going to rebuild an E-type from scratch you need the tools for the job and bit-by-bit I managed to acquire them. From the humblest screwdriver to the most complicated and expensive power tool, all are as necessary and important as each other.

In no particular order I thought I'd start going through the tools I used to restore my car, evaluating and assessing them as to their usefulness, etc. In these glorious days of the 21st century, we are now safety-conscious and so I guess we'd better start with safety equipment (I think maybe *King Crimson* were right when they wrote *21st Century Schizoid Man*). It may seem pretty obvious but you do need good quality safety gear and enough of it. The last thing you want to do when working on your car is to injure yourself badly and there are plenty of opportunities to do just that. Safety equipment is essential.

First and foremost, goggles. You need proper goggles that fit right over the eyes with elastic round the back. This prevents any bits from falling in your eyes when lying on your side underneath the car. Goggles also need replacing regularly as they get scratched easily and the elastic gives way. Notice in Photo 10.1-2 that I try and keep the goggles in their original packaging in an effort to keep them in good condition. I do use 'pilot' style goggles but only for operations with minimal danger and when I'm standing up. Also, note the yellow-tinted pilot glasses in the picture. These really do make dark areas appear light! I don't know how they do it but they do.

Almost as important as goggles are ear defenders. Not only do you need these to protect your hearing from being damaged by the variety of noisy power tools on offer, but they will also stop foreign bodies going down your ear especially when lying on your side under the car welding. I have heard of people getting stray weld spatter down their ear doing horrendous things to their ear drums. I can vouch for this as it very nearly happened to me once.

10.1-1 *Pliers, mole grips, adjustables, wire strippers and locking wire pliers*

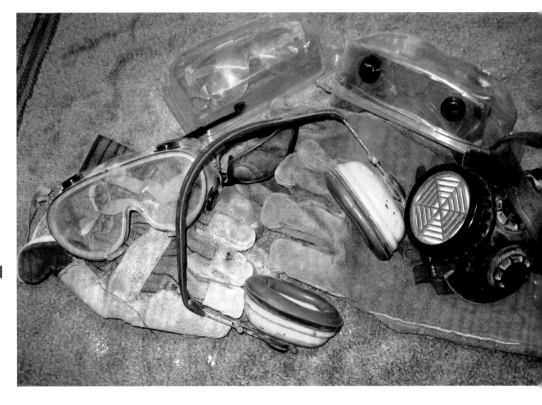

Safety equipment, goggles, **10.1-2** *gloves, mask and ear defenders*

Also, I am partially deaf because when I was a child I donned my father's ex-War Department headphones and plugged the two pins into an electric socket believing I could get music out of it. The resultant explosion destroyed the headphones and permanently damaged my ear drums. I am therefore very conscious of looking after what's left of my hearing. Wear ear defenders.

Gloves are equally important, especially for such as welding, and I profess to having a great range of gloves for different purposes. Essential for welding and angle grinding are good quality gauntlets which are very thick and cover the wrists as well as the hands. These not only provide protection from injury, they also help to reduce vibration when using an angle grinder or drill. One type of gloves in particular that I consider to be essential are latex gloves as used by doctors, etc (not in the photo). I get through boxes of these as they protect your hands from oil and grease, etc. Not only is this fairly essential if you have a day job that requires relatively clean hands, but it protects your hands from all the nastiness that classic cars can throw at you. Many years ago I had problems with the skin on my

hands which was very dry and it was attributed to the green gel cleaner I was using to clean the oil and grease from my hands – taking the natural oil from my skin with it. Now I always wear latex gloves when I work on the car and avoid strong cleaners.

Finally, we come to face masks. These are useful for stopping nuisance problems such as dust from filler, etc., and I also use them when dealing with certain paints and other noxious fumes. For this reason, I now use a professional mask that comes with different filter cartridges which you can change, depending on what you're using the mask for.

Basically, I want to be around for a very long time to enjoy the car that took nearly 10 years of my life to complete, so sensible safety precautions are, therefore, the order of the day. The last word on safety equipment is to actually use it. I keep all my safety gear in a very handy place in the garage to make sure I actually put it on. It's all too easy to start a simple job that rapidly develops into a serious garage session and the safety equipment is forgotten.

OK, on with the tools themselves. Sockets: You can never have enough of them. AF sizes are generally the

order of the day but Whitworth are required at times and metric can be useful to fit corroded nuts, etc., that aren't their original size. As well as ordinary sockets, long sockets are very useful for fitting over the end of bolts, etc. It's infuriating when you've got the right size socket but it won't reach the nut. Wherever possible (as with all tools), try and buy the best. In this case, buy those with hexagonal jaws rather than splined ones as the latter can slip on older nuts and cause even further damage. Also be aware that, if you elect to chrome your nuts (not as painful as it sounds!), then they come back all odd shapes and sizes and so it's good to have a large selection of sockets available as any of them can fit.

At the same time, a variety of extension bars, ratchet drives, universal joints, speed braces, T-bars, etc., to engage the sockets is another prerequisite – the more permutations you can make the better as there are some pretty hard-to-reach nuts and bolts on an E-type. For instance, you can tighten the exhaust manifold nuts next to the engine by using several extension bars coupled together and fed upwards from underneath between

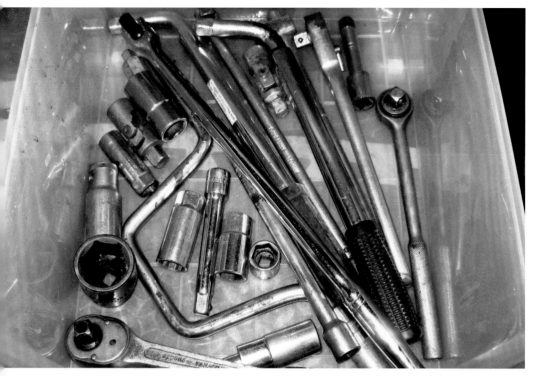

10.1-3 *Socket wrenches and extensions, etc*

me by my father (together with some of the sockets and ratchet drives) - a little rusty now, but still good as he always bought the best he could afford. I have to admit that his motto was always, 'There's nothing more expensive than buying cheap' and he was right – his sockets are still going strong 40 years on. I finally learnt this lesson having thrown away so many virtually useless tools that I thought were a bargain but were just poor quality.

10.1-4 *My dad's old torque wrench, still going strong*

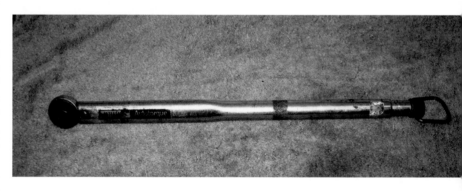

the engine frame and the left hand torsion bar.

Don't forget the mini-socket set. In many cases, this is at least as important as the larger half inch drive set. Mini-sockets are much smaller and can be used in confined spaces and are worth their weight in gold. My set includes AF, Metric and BA sizes, the latter once again being required on some smaller components (such as the windscreen wiper motor cover). One addition I made to my set was a professional ratchet drive which is capable of locking the socket onto the head of the ratchet preventing it from falling off when in use, a real problem with normal sockets. Another consideration when buying ratchets is how far the ratchet has to move round to engage the next tooth. If it's too far then you won't be able to use it in a confined space – that's about 90% of all nuts on an E-type!

While we're on the subject of sockets there's one more essential item – a torque wrench, preferably marked in lbs ft. Never use one of those cheap flexible torque wrenches as they simply aren't accurate enough. Use one with a strong ratchet and an accurate torque setting. Once again the rule is don't buy cheap. My torque wrench is an old one handed down to

Lessons learnt:

- Tools – love 'em and look after 'em and they'll look after you.
- You can never have enough tools.
- Never buy cheap – expensive tools will work better and last longer.
- A beautiful car deserves to be worked on with beautiful tools.
- One day I will have a proper garage with proper tool racks and lots of space! (My next dream)

I will now turn to some more important hand tools:

Spanners.

Possibly the most important tool of all; a set of really good quality spanners is essential. I have bought sets of cheap spanners in the past that I really regretted, especially when I finally bought myself a decent set and realised just how poor my previous ones had been. As with sockets, a set of imperial A/F sizes, Whitworth and metric are useful. Wherever possible, I buy spanners with an open end and a ring on the other. At least two spanners of the same size are required so a nut and bolt can be undone with a spanner on either end especially with popular sizes like 5/16" and ½".

Ratchet spanners are really good, but their main drawback is the thickness of the spanner head. It's amazing how many nuts I can't undo with my ratchet spanners because the spanner head is just that little bit bigger and fouls on something close to the nut. Ensuring the ratchet requires minimum movement to engage the next tooth is another important factor. I must say that I love my professional standard and ratchet spanners – they're so nice to work with! See Photo 10.1-5 of a professional quality ratchet spanner with one of the laughable, cheap ratchet spanners I bought when I couldn't afford decent ones. They're so unwieldy and cumbersome with a huge ratchet that they only fit about three nuts on the whole car.

Screwdrivers.

The more screwdrivers you have of varying sizes the better, in both standard and 'Philips' style. I frequently top-up my screwdriver selection to ensure as wide a variety of widths and lengths and thicknesses as possible. The only thing to remember is that, no matter how many you have, you will always find a screw somewhere that none of your screwdrivers will fit and you'll need to buy more.

Assorted pliers, hammers, hacksaws, mole grips, wire cutters, wire strippers, wire brushes, etc., are also much in demand and you will require a large selection. Adjustable spanners, small and large, are also something of a necessary evil. As a last resort, an adjustable spanner will always fit where all else fails, especially for larger nuts as most spanner sets only include the smaller sizes. Other tools including an oil filter removal tool (if a spin-on oil filter has been fitted) and a ball joint splitter always come in handy. A wooden mallet is very useful – so you can start off gently tapping the offending item with it before switching to the massive lump hammer when the item in question fails to respond to the gentle tapping with the mallet! (Or the head falls off the mallet, which is more often the case) At least you can tell yourself you tried.

Circlip pliers are another essential but, again, good quality ones are a must. My first set of circlip pliers were so poor that the ends of the pliers simply bent when I tried to use them; the circlip remained implacably in place. Also, make sure you have two, one for external and one for internal circlips.

Allen keys are another requirement - again as many different sizes as possible. A swatchbuck holding a selection of allen keys as in Photo 10.1-6 is quite useful but the keys are more awkward to use and you often can't get the same leverage as from an individual key.

An impact driver is another tool that has proved invaluable on more than one occasion, being the only way of freeing nuts or screws that are rusted solid. The square drive accepts sockets, as well as the screw bits it comes with, and this is very useful. Use it with a

good lump hammer and more often than not it will work.

In some ways the most basic and important tools required are the workbench and the bench vice. I constructed a work bench out of an old kitchen worktop as it was very solid and sturdy. I fixed it at just above hip height and this seems to be the correct height for optimum working. I then bought the best vice I could afford – still, relatively, expensive – and bolted it to the bench. I put it to the right of the bench and this has proved OK except that there's a wall at the side of the bench and there were a few times when I could have done with more room. I've never owned up to this before but I did seriously bend the operating bar on my vice, caused by me trying to force the UJs apart on the rear drive shafts after I'd managed to jam them solid during reassembly. The bar was bent by the increasing force of blows delivered by myself with a lump hammer. Numpty *[Fool, buffoon, clown. Believed Scottish vernacular. Ed]*

A very useful tool to have is a half-decent tap and die set. This isn't necessarily used to chase new threads but is really useful for cleaning up old threads, ensuring a good fit between

nut and bolt. In severe cases, it may be that you think the bolt is nicely tightened but it is in fact simply seizing on its thread and is not tight at all.

A set of feeler gauges is essential, although ensure they're Imperial. In the Photo 10.1-7, you can see my feeler gauges which are in fact two sets put together with Imperial on one side and metric on the other. It's so easy to accidentally use the wrong set and get completely the wrong reading that I'd not advise buying a combined set like this. It's also useful to have a set of brushes for cleaning out oilways, etc., in the engine and some small files and sandpaper for cleaning up any parts that are rusty or are damaged. Other small tools that can make all the difference include a magnifying glass for close examination of pieces and a telescopic magnet for retrieving those nuts and washers that invariably fall into the most inaccessible places. I just wish there was a similar tool that works for stainless steel parts too. In the same vein, a telescopic mirror with an angled head is really useful for inspecting parts and areas that you just can't get your head into! Finally, a small flexible torch is so useful. Being able to see into areas that even the smallest

torch or inspection lamp cannot reach is a massive bonus.

There are several general parts that I buy in some quantity as they are invaluable when reassembling an E-type:

Nuts, washers and bolts.

I have three boxes of these: stainless steel, galvanised and the original mild steel ones. Between them, I can usually guarantee to be able to find something suitable. I always try to use stainless steel wherever possible but galvanised ones are occasionally required and these can be plated, if necessary. I always keep any old nuts and bolts removed from the car as a reference and just in case I can't find anything else to fit. Remember, never throw anything away until the replacement is actually fitted to the car – and even then I try to keep as much as I can, just in case.

I also carry a substantial collection of fibre washers, copper washers, 'R' clips, locking washers, stainless steel self tapping screws, stainless washers and cotter pins. A stock of rubber oil seals and grommets, stainless steel jubilee clips, 'p' clips and plastic

Essential lubricants and **10.1-8**
sealants

cable ties are other essentials. When rebuilding my engine bay, I took the decision to use new style zip-up cable ties for the wiring, brake pipes and hoses. I thought they looked neater and are easier to replace than the original Jaguar ones. I think this was the correct decision but there are disadvantages. Firstly, I'm forever cutting myself on the sharp ends left over from trimming down the cables when I work on the engine and secondly the only way to remove them is by cutting them off. I must have had to cut off every tie at least twice and most of them many more times than that as I realised the brake pipe or whatever wasn't in quite the right place.

A good supply of grease, oil, spray lubricants, rust preventative, gasket cement, Super Glue, Threadlock, Copper Ease, etc., etc., is another necessity and they are forever being used. There are two items that I rate above all of these, however - the real secret weapons behind my restoration and more commonly found in the house rather than the garage:

• Kitchen paper towel
• Plastic freezer bags

I have always collected every discarded hand towel, tea cloth, sheet, pillowcase, etc., etc., from the house to use as rags. The problem is that one's need for clean rags exponentially outstrips the supply after only a short while and you are quickly reduced to using oily, greasy rags when you need a nice clean one. Kitchen towel is the answer! It's so much easier to buy huge packs of the stuff and use it and then throw it away. You therefore have a relatively clean garage and you can keep your proper cloths for when

they're really needed. One word of caution though is that they can leave paper fluff behind them so be careful what you use them for.

Plastic freezer bags were a revelation! Suddenly I had a storage system for dismantled parts that was clean, secure, hermetically sealed, totally flexible and could easily be labelled with indelible marker to inform

10.1-9 *Cotter pins, stainless steel self tapping screws, stainless R clips, locking washers and stainless washers*

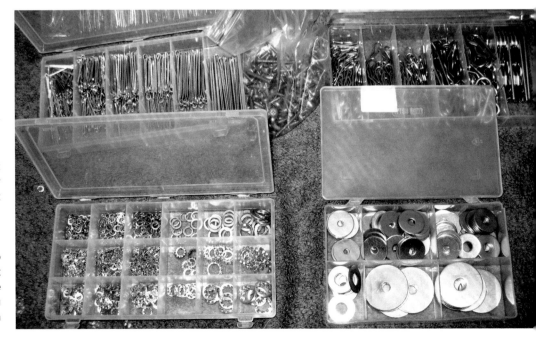

you of the contents (so important!). Up to this point I had used plastic tubs and cardboard boxes, etc., but had soon run out of storage space and plastic boxes, and they were too often left open to the elements and dust, etc. I simply bought three boxes of different size freezer bags and my storage problems were sorted overnight. Fantastic.

Finally we come to look at the real essence of E-type tools:

Power tools, and specialist equipment.

Yeah, Baby! First and foremost is welding equipment. Having looked at the range of equipment on offer and matched them with my skill and knowledge level (very, very low), it was clear that I required a MIG welder. Gas welding seemed way beyond me and arc welding is simply too fierce and spot welders too expensive, and I still don't know what TIG welding is to this day so MIG welding proved the answer. A good welder is worth its weight in gold as is a little practice with it beforehand. There are a variety of settings on a MIG welder, mainly the power setting and gas flow and, although there are recommended settings in the manual, you really need to experiment and get to know the machine properly in order to get the best weld achievable.

Also (although I'm no expert on this so don't just take my word for it) many of the seams on an E-type were originally spot welded. With a MIG welder you can only achieve a linear weld along the edge of a seam which is nowhere near as strong. For this reason, I drilled small holes in the top sheet of metal along some of the flanges and then welded into these holes in an effort to simulate a spot weld, but I'm not sure how effective this is and I didn't use it that much on my body shell as it was virtually finished when I bought it.

10.1-10 *A small air compressor is really useful for checking oil ways, etc - and inflating tyres!*

My engine stand in use during **10.1-11** *the dismantling of the engine - an essential tool*

10.1-12 *Brake bleeding tube*

Angle grinder and assorted grinding/ cutting discs and abrasive brushes.

You really can't do without one of these. You can use them for cutting off rusted bolts, cleaning heavily-rusted parts and even cutting sheet metal. However, these are really mean heavy duty tools and they are so powerful they can ruin your bodywork in an instant if you're not careful. One example that I've never admitted to before was the louvres on my new bonnet. I was worried about the paintwork around the louvres as it didn't look too good and, on my old body shell, the paint had come away from this area in several places. I therefore decided to strip the louvres down to bare metal and used my angle grinder fitted with a heavy duty twisted wire brush to effect this. It worked really well – too well. After a short while, I inspected the louvres only to discover, to my horror, that I had actually ground away the metal itself and the edges of some of the louvres now had shallow curves in them rather than being straight. The wire brush was simply too aggressive. I therefore had to build the edges of the louvres back up again by very delicate use of my welder and then carefully grind them back down to shape - all because I'd underestimated the power of the angle grinder.

Electric drill.

It goes without saying that you need one of these and a copious supply of good quality metal drill bits. I lost count of how many drill bits I went through on the restoration; you simply can't have enough. I also used the drill with a metal 'nibbler' attachment to cut out the roof section of my replacement roof panel to fit the Webasto hole in my new roof. I got through a few bits on the nibbler but it worked well.

Dremel multi-tool.

A really useful little tool. Can get to where your huge drill can't as it's much smaller and more manoeuvrable. It can be fitted with a myriad of different heads that can be used for cutting, polishing, cleaning, drilling, buffing, etc., etc. I also bought the flexible drive attachment which is even more user-friendly and allows even easier access to intricate parts.

I also invested in a bench grinder and metal polisher (well, actually it was a bench grinder that I converted to become a polisher). This was a really useful tool as I was able to polish up many parts to quite a high standard using different brushes and different grades of polishing compound. Although I do have to admit that my best was never as good as the chrome-plating shop who managed to get a shine as bright as chrome on some alloy parts. I did use the grinder occasionally too, but generally on items such as my valve stems which I threw away afterwards anyway.

Engine hoist and engine stand.

Two essential items that you only use very occasionally but without them you'd be stuck. I bought a folding engine crane which meant that storage wasn't too big an issue. I sold mine soon after finishing the restoration for several reasons: I knew that if my engine needed removing again I simply don't have the room in my garage to do it so it's usefulness was at an end; to make room in the garage and to try and make some money as the end of the restoration left me stony broke!

Trolley jacks.

A simple, cheap and effective way of lifting car, engine and back axle off the ground. Absolutely essential. Use them in conjunction with axle stands and/or wheel ramps for safety. Incidentally, I never drive my car on to ramps as once I reversed my Triumph Vitesse on to some, when suddenly one of the wheels span and fired the ramp along the ground towards the front of the car where it wedged itself under the rear floor. It took me ages to lift the car off the ramp (too high for my trolley jack) and it left me with a very bent chassis outrigger and dented floor. I gave my ramps to Chris next door (they were my Dad's – very good quality) at the end of the restoration as they took up too much room.

I finally bought myself a small air compressor after wanting one for many years. It's great to have one now to check all my tyre pressures, but not really essential for a restoration. You will of course require one (a much better/bigger one than mine) if you're going to spray the car yourself but otherwise it's nice to have for blowing out oilways, etc., but not really essential.

Other tools to have include such goodies as a stroboscopic timing light, a compression tester, inspection lamps - both plug in and LED battery ones (the LED ones are more versatile but are omni-diectional – and always in the direction you don't want!), a multi-meter for electrics, a good crimping tool for connectors from a supplier such as Autosparks, a pop-rivet gun and a variety of sizes of pop rivet for the seal channels and headlight trims, etc., a digital vernier caliper (so much superior to the old ruler type ones), a brake-bleeding hose with a non-return valve in the end, a camber and castor angle measuring tool, a decent grease gun, an electric staple gun, Stanley knife, tape measure and a cordless drill/screwdriver, etc., etc.

Wow! That's about it on tools. Almost as much fun as the car itself – but not quite!

Photos by Abigail Humphries

PBH 543H

12 E-type Services

E-Type Services

Below is a list of the companies I used during the restoration of my car. There are many others out there but these are the ones I am familiar with.

Prestige Electro-Plating
Unit 6, Cliff Street Industrial Estate,
Mexborough, South Yorkshire, S64 9HU
Tel: 01709 577004
This is where I had all my parts plated and polished during my restoration. I have always received excellent service and their work is of high quality. Almost impossible to actually find their unit if you choose to visit in person!

Vintage Wireless Company
174, Cross St, Sale, Cheshire, M33 7AQ
Tel: 01619 730438
Website: www.vintagewireless.co.uk
This company will convert old radios to FM and add MP3 compatibility, etc.

Classic Motor Cars Ltd (CMC)
Building 9, Stanmore Business Park, Bridgnorth,
Shropshire, WV15 5HP
Tel: 01746 765804
Website: www.classic-motor-cars.co.uk
Classic car restoration company that provided me with copious amounts of help and advice.

MCT Jaguar Restorations
Nuneaton, Warwickshire
Tel: 02476 371110
Website: www.mctjag.com
Mick and Chris Turley trim E-types to the highest standards, provide top quality trim kits and supply endless patient advice to all their customers.

Series I Spares and Restoration (Ken Verity)
Unit 1, Alma Court, Alma Rd, Rotherham, S60 2HZ
Tel: 01709 838352
Ken is a 'one-man-band' in the old tradition, providing bespoke services to the discerning customer. His knowledge of, and passion for, E-types is endless and he gives freely of his time and advice. Ken supplies a range of parts for E-types, including various stainless steel brackets, etc., often touring the shows with a large selection of those essential small parts.

Frost Restorers Equipment
Albion Park, Warrington Road, Glazebury, WA3 5PG
Tel: 01925 648555
Website: www.frost.co.uk
Very good supplier of tools and equipment essential to the home restorer.

The E-type Club
Hilltop Farm, Knighton-on-Teme, Tenbury Wells, WR15 8LY
Tel: 01584 781588
Website: www.e-typeclub.com
An excellent club that is devoted entirely to E-types. Unlike other clubs, everything is focussed just on this model. Superb magazine, great events, members worldwide, specialist advertising, friendly atmosphere, no committees – a must for every E-type owner and enthusiast.

The Jaguar Enthusiasts' Club
Abbeywood Office Park, Emma Chris Way, Filton, Bristol
BS34 7JU
Tel: 01179 698186
Website: www.jec.org.uk
A large club dedicated to all things Jaguar catering very well for all models from pre-war to present day.

The Jaguar Drivers' Club Limited
3A Driffold, Sutton Coldfield, West Midlands, B73 6HE
Tel: 01582 419332
Website: www.jaguardriver.co.uk
Formed in 1956, the JDC caters to owners of all Jaguars from earliest SS cars to the latest models.

Parts Suppliers

Below is a list of parts suppliers I used during the restoration of my car. There are many other suppliers out there but these are the ones I am familiar with and can therefore pass comment on.

SNG Barratt Group
The Heritage Building, Stourbridge Rd, Bridgnorth, Shropshire, WV15 6AP
Tel: 01746 765432
Website: www.sngbarratt.com
The company I bought most of my parts from. One of the longest established parts suppliers and probably the largest with branches in the UK, USA, France and Holland. Good quality parts. Excellent, rapid despatch and no-hassle returns/ refund policy.

Martin Robey Group
Pool Rd, Camphill Industrial Estate, Nuneaton, Warwickshire, CV10 9AE
Tel: 02476 386903
Website: www.martinrobey.co.uk
Manufacturer of E-type panels. Good quality parts. Nicely non-commercial set-up on the phone. As they say in their advertising: 'The company that put the E-type back on the road'.

RM & J Smith Ltd
PO Box 310, Crewe, CW2 5WD
Tel: 01270 820885
e-mail: rmj@rmjsmith.co.uk
If you can't find a part anywhere else, then Richard Smith will almost certainly have it. He may not be the cheapest but what price that unobtainable part?

Longstone Tyres
Hudsons Yard, Doncaster Rd, Bawtry, Doncaster, DN10 6NX
Tel: 01302 711123
Website: www.longstonetyres.co.uk
A well established enthusiastic and helpful supplier and fitter of tyres for classic cars.

Namrick Ltd
124, Portland Rd, Hove, East Sussex, BN3 5QL
Tel: 01273 779864
Website: www.namrick.co.uk
A really good supplier of stainless steel nuts, bolts, screws, washers and fasteners. Good mail order service. Double check you're ordering the right size bolts, etc., as sizes can be confusing – follow the chart on their website.

Holden Vintage and Classic Ltd
Linton Trading Estate, Bromyard, Herefordshire, HR7 4QT
Tel: 01885 488488
Website: www.holden.co.uk
Good supplier of electrical components, accessories and upgrades for classic car owners – lights, ignition systems, etc.

Rob Beere Racing
Unit 1, Priory Mill, Charter Avenue, Coventry, CV4 8AF
Tel: 02476 473311
Website: www.rob-beere-racing.co.uk
Supplier of engine parts to the Jaguar racing community, some of which can be used in road cars.

Ratsport
Unit 3, White Hart Rd, Plumstead, London, SE18 1DH
Tel: 01825 873551
Website: www.ratsport.co.uk
Supplier of racing and stainless steel parts, etc.

Demon Tweeks
75 Ash Rd South, Wrexham Industrial Estate, Wrexham, North Wales, LL13 9UG
Tel: 01978 664555
Website: www.demon-tweeks.co.uk
A supplier of racing car parts, some of which can be fitted to the E-type.

Agrie Mach Ltd
Wayfarers, Old Domewood, Copthorne, W. Sussex, RH10 3HD
Tel: 01342 713743
Website: www.agriemach.com
Suppliers of specialist heat insulation. I used the self-adhesive mats and I'm really pleased with them.

Publications

Jaguar E-Type 3.8 & 4.2 Owner's Workshop Manual
Publisher: Haynes
ISBN: 978 0 857336 12 5
An essential publication for any restorer

Jaguar 'E' Type Models 3.8 & 4.2 Litre Series I & 2 Service Manual
Publisher: Brooklands Books Ltd, Surrey
ISBN: 978 1 855200 20 3
An essential publication for any restorer

Jaguar World, Jaguar Enthusiast: Jaguar 'E' Type Restoration Series 1 4.2 & Series III V12
Publisher: Kelsey Publishing Ltd, Kent
ISBN: 978 1 873098 52 3
Contains some good information about many aspects of restoration.

SU Carburettors, Haynes Owner's Workshop Manual
Publisher: Haynes Publishing
ISBN: 1 85010 506 5
I was very disappointed with this publication. I thought it would tell me everything I needed to know about E-type SUs and more but, as it covers all SU Carburettors, there's only one chapter on HD8s and there's little more in there than in the general workshop manual.

Jaguar Six Cylinder Engine Overhaul (1948-1986): Including I.R.S. and S.U. Carburettors (Jaguar World)
Publisher: Kelsey Publishing Ltd, Kent
ISBN: 978 1 873098 32 5
Some very good detailed information on rebuilding the XK engine, the independent rear suspension and SU carburettors.

Spare Parts Catalogue for Jaguar 'E' Type Series II Grand Touring Models
Jaguar Cars Ltd. Publication No: IPL 5/2 June 1975
Publisher: Brooklands Books, Surrey
ISBN: 978 1 855201 70 5
This is an invaluable publication for ordering more obscure parts as there's nothing like being able to quote part numbers. Can be hard work finding the part in the first place.

E Type Series I & II Parts and Service Manuals 1961 – 1970 (CD-Rom)
Jaguar part no. JHM 1119.
This is an invaluable publication for ordering more obscure parts as there's nothing like being able to quote part numbers. [Used copies available online. Requires Windows 95 or compatible OS]

The Definitive E-Type Parts Catalogue – SNG Barratt Group (see Parts Suppliers)
Although it's actually a parts catalogue, it also contains a lot of information in an easily accessible user-friendly format

E-type Books

Original Jaguar E-type – Restorer's and Enthusiast's Guide to 3.8, 4.2 & V12s
Malcolm McKay
Publisher: Porter Press International
ISBN: 978 1 907085 93 2

Jaguar E-type – The Definitive History
Philip Porter
Publisher: Porter Press International
ISBN: 978 0 85733 122 9

Jaguar E-type – 3.8 & 4.2 6-cylinder; 5.3 V12
Denis Jenkinson
Publisher: Osprey Publishing Ltd
ISBN: 0 85045 437 9

9600 HP – The Story of the World's Oldest E-type
Philip Porter
Publisher: Porter Press International
ISBN: 978 1 913089 27 6

Jaguar E-type 6 and 12 Cylinder Restoration Guide
Dr Thomas F. Haddock
Publisher: Motorbooks International
ISBN: 0 7603 0396 7

The Jaguar E-Type – A Collector's Guide
Paul Skilleter
Publisher: Motorbooks International
ISBN: 0 947981 15 2

Ultimate E-type – The Competition Cars
Philip Porter
Publisher: Porter Press International
ISBN: 978 1 907085 07 9

The Advantage Of A Parts Catalogue

One particularly useful publication that I only discovered towards the end of my restoration was the E-type parts manual on CD-Rom. These are no longer available new, and also require outdated software to run, but there are alternatives – either as searchable online catalogues or downloadble PDFs. If you can use these or the parts books to source part numbers before ordering, everything is so much simpler – less time spent on the phone to sales people who are trying to work out what part it is you actually want: 'the thingummy on the end of the thermostat whatsit' doesn't go down too well and even when they have ascertained what part it is they then have to find the part number so that by the end of the call you have doubled the cost of the part in phone calls alone.

If you have the correct part number, less time is also spent sending the wrong parts back again, etc., etc., incurring even further expense – and frustration as you can't do anything until the correct part arrives. (Restoring an E-type is expensive and frustrating enough without trying to making it worse!) It's also worth remembering that a lot of parts' suppliers have salesmen who are on commission, so they have a vested interest in supplying you with any part – not necessarily the correct one – and long phone calls don't earn them any money.

Buying Guide

Buying Guide on the E-type Club website
www.e-typeclub.com [Full resource available to members]

I would recommend this to guide you through the many potential pitfalls when buying an E-type. The Club is also happy to give advice and can recommend specialists to check over cars for sale. Furthermore, meeting fellow enthusiasts is a great way to build up your knowledge and sort out the good guys from the bad guys! Take care: the wrong choice of car can ruin the whole experience. Above all, always deal with well-established E-type specialists. They have the experience and genuine knowledge.